DAVID O. McKAY LIBRARY

3 1404 00896 9419

D0764233

FIRES OF FAITH

Frontispiece. The burning of the bones of Martin Bucer and Paul Fagius in Cambridge market-place, Saturday 6 February 1557.

The corpses of the European protestant theologians Martin Bucer and Paul Fagius were burned in Cambridge Marketplace in February 1557, a symbolic purging of the University of its recent heretical past. Cartloads of heretical books were also burned, and Thomas Watson, Bishop of Lincoln, preached a two hour sermon against the dead men's errors. The churches 'polluted' by their burials were reconsecrated, and the Blessed Sacrament solemnly paraded through the streets. The veil in which the Sacrament was carried by Cuthbert Scott, Master of Christ's and Bishop of Chester, had been personally blessed by Pope Paul IV, and was donated by Nicolo Ormanetto, Cardinal Pole's chief legal officer, who oversaw the Legatine Visitation of the Universities. Foxe's print compresses the events of several days into a single vivid image.

FIRES OF FAITH

Catholic England under Mary Tudor

Eamon Duffy

Yale University Press
New Haven and London

Published with assistance from the foundation established in memory of
Oliver Baty Cunningham of the Class of 1917, Yale College.

All rights reserved. This book may not be reproduced in whole or in part, in any
form (beyond that permitted by sections 107 and 108 of the US Copyright Law
and except by reviewers for the public press), without written permission from
the publishers.

Copyright © 2009 Eamon Duffy
reprinted with corrections 2009

Typeset by SNP Best-set Typesetter Ltd., Hong Kong
Printed by TJ International, Padstow

LIBRARY OF CONGRESS CATALOGING-IN-PUBLICATION DATA

Duffy, Eamon.
Fires of faith: Catholic England under Mary Tudor / Eamon Duffy.
p. cm.
Includes bibliographical references (pp. 231–38) and index.
ISBN 978-0-300-15216-6 (alk. paper)
1. Catholic Church—England—History—16th century. 2. England–Church history–History–16th century.
3. Counter-Reformation—England. 4. Mary I, Queen of England, 1516–1558—Religion. 5. Pole, Reginald,
1500–1558. I. Title.

BX1492.D83 2009
274.2'06—DC22
2008049807

In piam memoriam

ANTHONY JOSEPH FRANCIS STOREY
1919–2007

'What will remain of us is love'

Contents

Foreword

This book has been long in the making. In 1992, I published a short account of the restoration of catholicism in the reign of Mary Tudor as chapter 16 of *The Stripping of the Altars*. In it, I offered a much more positive assessment of the religious achievements of Mary's regime than was at that time commonly accepted. I was aware of the need for a fuller treatment, however, especially one that paid proper attention to the most controversial aspect of the reign: the campaign of burnings, during which, in the space of just under four years, 284 protestant men and women were put to death for their beliefs. An invitation to contribute an essay on that terrible episode to the Vatican Symposium on the Inquisition in 1999 determined me on such a larger treatment. But other projects intervened, and the opportunity to tackle these issues only presented itself with the invitation from the Master and Fellows of Trinity College, Cambridge, to deliver the 2007–8 Birkbeck Lectures in Ecclesiastical History. The present book is a much expanded version of the five lectures delivered in Cambridge in the Michaelmas Term 2007. I am very grateful indeed to Trinity College for providing the catalyst for this long-delayed study.

In shaping the book I was anxious not to sacrifice the momentum intrinsic to a course of expository public lectures. This is, therefore, emphatically not a general history of religion in the reign of Mary Tudor. Though the material on the burnings has been greatly expanded in order to confront head on the most controversial but least understood aspect of the reign, I have tried to retain the essential shape and scope of the original talks. So *Fires of Faith* makes no attempt to cover all aspects of the Marian restoration. It has virtually nothing to say about the protestant underground congregations at home, or about the protestant diaspora overseas, though the existence and activities of both groups were a matter of intense concern to the Marian regime. And important aspects of the Marian restoration itself, such as the process of reconstruction in the parishes, the transformation of the universities, the revival of monasticism and the state of the parish clergy, are here touched on lightly, or not at all. I hope that what is here nevertheless provides a coherent 'take' on the intentions, competence and achievement of the Marian church. As will be evident to any reader, I rate highly both the calibre of many of the leaders of the church under Mary, and their actual impact on the religious lives of the people. In view of the horror of the burnings, which I have no wish to palliate or excuse, I am aware that this is still a controversial position. In the last fifteen years or so, a good deal of scholarly work has contributed to the emergence of a more positive assessment of many aspects of Mary's regime. But the burnings remain an obstacle to any such reappraisal. The imposition of religious conformity by lethal force is deeply repellent to modern sensibilities. The religious violence of the mid-Tudor period has particularly disturbing resonances for our times, in which the deadliness of religious hatreds has been repeatedly brought home with terrible immediacy.

Moreover, the Marian martyrdoms loom large in English national mythology. I have ceased to be surprised at the visceral and sometimes violent hostility of even sophisticated and intelligent English people to any attempt at an objective reassessment of the campaign of repression under 'Bloody Mary'. Even in our self-consciously secular times, six-teenth-century stereotypes, consolidated in the triumph of protestantism under Queen Elizabeth, persist in popular culture. The 'Black legend' of catholicism as intrinsically foreign, cruel and obscurantist flourished, and the association of 'popery and tyranny, popery and wooden shoes' became constitutive of English protestant identity in the course of the eighteenth and nineteenth centuries. It has been a long time a-dying: the lurid portrayal of Mary and her court in Shekhar Kapur's enor-mously successful biopic *Elizabeth* is a case in point. But, though histo-rians are as prone as any other men and women to universalise their own values, their job is not that of the moralist or preacher. The histo-rian's task is to explore that other country, the past, and to bring back news of how its people differed from, as well as resembled, ourselves. Confronted by the sanctified savageries of the Tudor age, it would be a hard heart that withheld pity from the victims or felt no indignation against the perpetrators. But indignation at the motives and actions of the long dead is a poor aid to understanding. I have tried to set it aside in dealing with the dauntingly different values of those times.

In preparing this book, I have acquired a multitude of debts: my warmest thanks to the Master and Fellows of Trinity College for the invitation to think and talk about the reign of Mary; to the Cambridge audiences of the original lectures, whose questions, responses and contradictions have stimulated some new thoughts and corrected old ones; to the many colleagues who have supplied information, discussed issues or evidence, debated interpretations or criticised drafts – Dr Simon Ditchfield, the Revd Dr Dermot Fenlon, the Revd Dr David Hoyle, the late lamented Dr Trevor Johnson, Professor Peter Marshall and Dr Richard Rex. Dr Pamela Tudor Craig (Lady Wedgwood) kindly gave me access to unpublished research on the iconography of Mary's reign. As always, Sally Salvesen of Yale University Press has been the best of editors. I owe special thanks to two colleagues in particular. Professor Thomas F. Mayer has devoted a scholarly career to deepening understanding of one of the most significant but least-known Tudor Englishmen, Cardinal Reginald Pole. His great calendar of Pole's correspondence is a major scholarly tool on which I have relied heavily and built highly. He has been unstintingly generous in sharing his expertise, not least in making available to me before publication the invaluable biographical material in volume 4 of his Calendar of the *Correspondence of Reginald Pole*. Though our assessments of Pole's actions and motives do not always exactly coincide, this book would have been infinitely poorer without his fine scholarship. Finally, my largest debt is to Dr Tom Freeman of the British Academy's Foxe project. Dr Freeman's knowledge of the religious history of Tudor England is encyclopaedic, his mastery of that immense cornucopia of fact, legend and unforgettable anecdote, Foxe's *Actes and Monuments*, unrivalled. He has been a support, stimulus and interlocutor at every stage of the preparation of this book, and has read and commented in detail on all the chapters on the burnings. He has saved me from countless lapses of fact and judgement. Those that remain are all my own work.

St Andrew's Day 2008

List of Illustrations

The maps and the statistical chart on p. 129 are based on figures prepared for the British Academy John Foxe Project by Dr Thomas Freeman, during his tenure of a British Academy Research Fellowship: the author gratefully acknowledges permission to use this material.

Abbreviations

APC	J. R. Dasent (ed), *Acts of the Privy Council of England*, New Series, 32 vols (London, 1890–1907)
Calendar of State Papers Spanish	G. A. Bergenroth, Pascual de Gayangos, Martin A. S. Hume and Royall Tyler (eds), *Calendar of Letters, Despatches and State Papers Relating to the Negotiations between England and Spain*, 13 vols (London, 1862–1954)
Calendar of State Papers Venetian	Rawdon Brown, G. C. Bentinck, H. F. Brown and Allen B. Hinds (eds), *Calendar of State Papers and Manuscripts Relating to English Affairs, Existing in the Archives and Collections of Venice*, 14 vols (London, 1864–1908)
CRP	Thomas F. Mayer (ed), *The Correspondence of Reginald Pole*, 4 vols (Aldershot, 2002–8)
Epistolarum	Angelo Maria Querini (ed), *Epistolarum Reginaldi Poli*, 5 vols (Brescia, 1744–57)
Foxe [1563]	John Foxe, *Acts and Monuments: The Variorum Edition*
Foxe [1570]	(hriOnline, Sheffield, 2004), available at
Foxe [1583]	http://www.hrionline.ac.uk/johnfoxe/. Date in square brackets indicates the edition referenced.
ODNB	H. C. G. Matthew and Brian Harrison (eds), *Oxford Dictionary of National Biography* (Oxford, 2004)
RSTC	N. A. Jackson, F. S. Ferguson and K. F. Pantzer (eds), *A Short-Title Catalogue of Books Printed in England, Scotland & Ireland, and of English Books Printed Abroad 1475–1640, first compiled by A. W. Pollard & G. R. Redgrave*, 2nd edn (London, 1976–86)
Strype, *Ecclesiastical Memorials*	John Strype, *Ecclesiastical Memorials, Relating Chiefly to Religion, and the Reformation of it, and the Emergencies of the Church of England, under King Henry VIII, King Edward VI, and Queen Mary I*, 3 vols (Oxford, 1822)
TRP	Paul L. Hughes and James F. Larkin (eds), *Tudor Royal Proclamations*, 3 vols (New Haven, 1964–9)

CHAPTER I

Rolling Back the Revolution

The reign of Mary Tudor has had few friends among historians, and the regime's religious dimension has provided most of the copy for the bad press. Until relatively recently, almost everyone agreed that Mary's church was backward-looking, unimaginative, reactionary, sharing both the Queen's bitter preoccupation with the past and her tragic sterility. Marian catholicism, it was agreed, was strong on repression, weak on persuasion. Its atrocious campaign of burnings was not merely an outrage against human decency but a devastating political blunder, which alienated moderate opinion and helped to inoculate the English nation forever against roman catholicism. Its apologists and polemicists, with the possible single exception of the London artisan Miles Hogarde, were dismissed as unimpressive second-raters, their works tedious and unimaginative, the regime in general fatally unaware of the crucial importance of argument and debate in the battle for hearts and minds, and neglectful of the power of both the pulpit and the printing press in that struggle.

Mary's church was led by Reginald Pole, a man, it was claimed, positively averse to preaching, whose capacity for action had been sapped by disillusionment at the rejection of his theological vision and his understanding of reform at the Council of Trent, an *Inglese Italianato* who had been an exile in Italy for so long that he utterly failed to grasp how deeply the reformation had penetrated the religious life of England. This damning appraisal was most clearly set out in the late Geoffrey Dickens's textbook *The English Reformation*, which appeared first in 1965 and which was to dominate the historiography quite remarkably for the next thirty years. Dickens distilled this overwhelmingly negative picture into the claim that the Marian regime, bedevilled by a 'sterile legalism', had 'failed to discover the Counter-Reformation'.[1]

This verdict – famous, fatuous, but fatally quotable – stuck, and has had an influence apparently directly proportionate to its basic implausibility, and over historians who might have been expected to have known better. It underlies I think, John Bossy's claim that Queen Mary and Cardinal Pole are best regarded not as figures in the sixteenth- and seventeenth-century reconstruction and re-imagining of European catholicism that we call the counter-reformation, but 'as part of the posthumous history of medieval Christendom'.[2] It coloured Rex Pogson's influential Cambridge doctoral study of Pole's legatine mission,[3] and it informed the treatment of religion in David Loades's standard history of the reign, which conceded that the leaders of Mary's church 'were not slack or inept', but nevertheless insisted that they pursued a long-term policy which 'ignored . . . important features of the immediate situation', above all 'the desperate need for spiritual leadership of a high calibre'. Deluded in believing that protestant ideas had established only a superficial hold in England, Loades argued, Cardinal Pole in particular drew back from the strenuous evangelisation that was so urgently needed, and characteristically refused help from the Jesuit order because he 'simply did not want men with the fire of the counter-reformation in their bellies'. He belonged to a nostalgic 'older generation' (Pole was in fact nine years *younger* than the Jesuit founder, St Ignatius), which, like the Queen herself, 'saw the future in terms of the past', at best clinging to the humanist ideals of the 1520s, and an agenda now hopelessly overtaken by the radicalisation of both the catholic and protestant reformations.[4] Professor Loades has since modified some of these positions, and has encouraged efforts to rethink the religious aspects of the reign. His overall assessment of Marian religion remains muted, however, the sound at most of one hand clapping: Mary and her bishops, he believes, did too little, too late.[5]

Over the last twenty years, this negative consensus has been chipped away piecemeal. In 1986, the late Jennifer Loach published an essay offering a positive re-assessment of the Marian establishment's use of the printing press.[6] Susan Brigden's magisterial study of the reformation in London, published in 1989, offered a nuanced study of the impact of the Marian restoration in the capital, which did justice to its effectiveness, despite the presence there of a strong and vociferous protestant minority.[7] In 1992, in the *Stripping of the Altars*, I suggested that the Marian restoration of catholicism had, in fact, displayed high levels of determination and resourcefulness, and that far from being, in another of

Dickens's memorable phrases, 'the prisoner of a sorrowful past', in many instances the key policies of the regime anticipated or directly inspired later counter-reformation developments.[8] And in 1993, in his *English Reformations*, Christopher Haigh offered a similarly upbeat survey of the effectiveness of the Marian regime.[9]

Since then, a number of fresh developments have contributed more indirectly to the continued reappraisal of the reign. First, the establishment (on the initiative of Professor Loades) of the British Academy's Foxe Project has made available annotated online texts of all the Elizabethan editions of our single most important source for the religious history of the period, stimulating a wave of valuable new research, led by the project's own resident guru, Dr Tom Freeman.[10] Secondly, Professor Thomas Mayer, in a stream of essays on Cardinal Pole, a new biography and a monumental calendar of Pole's correspondence, has provided the materials for a radical reassessment of the most important figure in the Marian religious establishment, and thereby encouraged the placing of the Marian episode in its proper European context.[11] The changing historiographical climate has been registered in a series of publications and doctoral theses, themselves signalled in two collections of essays on the religion of the reign, published by Ashgate in 2006.[12]

Yet major barriers to a genuine reassessment of Mary's church remain. The remarkable achievement of the Marian parishes in reconstructing the physical setting for catholic worship is concealed from us by generations of subsequent iconoclasm, first religiously and then aesthetically driven, which destroyed most of the evidence. The material situation that Mary's church inherited was dire. In five years, Edward's regime had bulldozed away centuries of devotional elaboration, and had stripped bare the cathedrals and parish churches of England.[13] The most devastating impact had probably been in music, since the heavy emphasis of reformed protestantism on the intelligibility of the written or spoken word in worship left no place for Latin word-setting and elaborate polyphony. The entire repertoire of sacred music from late antiquity to the recent past, therefore, had been swept aside as redundant in a matter of months. But, after music, it was architecture and its attendant arts – paintings, statuary, stained glass – that suffered most. Virtually all the altars had been pulled down, their consecrated table-slabs or *mensae* often deliberately broken up, or profaned by use as paving, bridge components, walling or hearthstones. With the removal of the altars, the spaces round them – chancels and cathedral choirs – were drastically reordered.

As we shall see, Ridley's radical rearrangements at St Paul's would become almost legendary,[14] but the hammers had been out everywhere – at Worcester, a representative case, Dean Barlow razed the high altar to the ground in August 1552, at the same time removing the medieval choir screens. By the end of that month the organ had gone too.[15] The great crucifixes that had dominated every church in the land had been ritually burned by the Edwardine visitors; every accessible niche had been emptied of its saint; wall and panel paintings were scraped or whitewashed over. Acres of stained glass had been smashed or sold off and, when left in place, as perhaps they mostly were, the faces of sacred persons and the more overtly catholic iconography might be daubed out with paint or whitewash. In the most zealously policed dioceses, such as London, even the brass memorials of the dead, 'superstitious' because of their requests for prayers for the repose of the souls of the departed, had been prised out of the floors and sold for scrap. The vestments, vessels, books and music needed for catholic worship were outlawed, dispersed and (mostly) destroyed. In 1552, Edward's government, desperate for war funds, had turned this religiously inspired repudiation of catholic externals into a fiscal resource, and had carried through the largest government confiscation of local property in English history. County-based royal commissioners had stripped the parish churches of all their remaining valuables, leaving most with little more than a quantity of linen or silk cloth to cover the communion table, a single chalice for communion, a surplice for the priest, and the English books needed for the new services.[16]

I have discussed elsewhere the massive sustained effort required throughout Mary's reign to reverse all this and re-equip the parishes for catholic worship, and I will not repeat myself here.[17] It was a gargantuan task, and inevitably a slow one, hindered by lack of resources, by the scarcity of available craftsmen and specialist workshops, occasionally by the reluctance of communities or individuals to invest in the restoration of a religious system that they inwardly rejected. Perhaps the greatest hindrance was the massive blow that the Edwardine years had delivered to lay confidence in an age-old system of devotional provision and donation, which depended for its momentum on its immemorial and unchallenged character. Yet in churchwardens' accounts, visitation returns, will and probate records, and in the fabric rolls of the great churches, we find abundant evidence that the re-equipping went ahead, gathered momentum and that, by the end of the reign, it was well on the way to reshaping the physical appearance of English worship.[18]

There was of course a great deal of make-do and mend. Impoverished parishes, even when we know them to have been devoutly catholic, might take years to gather the full complement of books, vessels and vestments needed, and even then might have to make do with pewter instead of silver vessels for the Sacrament.[19] Churchwardens' accounts survive for fewer than 140 parishes from Mary's reign, a tiny proportion of the 10,000 or so in the country as a whole. Yet, even in parishes with surviving accounts, a great deal of the work of reconstruction is invisible because it was paid for by individual donations rather than by the parish at large, and so was not recorded in the wardens' accounts.

Cambridge University Library holds a splendid Sarum missal printed in Paris in 1555.[20] Folio-sized, handsomely rubricated and illustrated throughout with high-quality woodcuts, this editon was the most sumptuous liturgical book produced for Marian England. Inscriptions on the title page and before the Canon of the Mass in the Cambridge copy ask for prayers for Richard Perkyn the elder, who presented the book to the Bedfordshire parish of St Peter, Tempsford, on 28 November 1557, just in time for the annual St Andrew's day celebration, commemorating England's return to papal obedience. By that point in the process of restoration, of course, the parish must already have used a mass-book daily for at least three years. Perkyn's gift is therefore an example of devotional elaboration, the provision of an expensive higher-quality item to dignify the parish's worship, designed to elicit the gratitude and prayers of the community for the donor (Plates 12 and 13). There must have been thousands of such gifts of books, vestments and fittings all over England, as local elites or the specially devout contributed to the re-establishment of catholic normalcy. Most such donations, however, like the Tempsford missal, will have been recorded, if at all, only on the object itself. And the overwhelming majority were to perish without trace in the early years of the Elizabethan Settlement. With them disappeared most of the material vestiges of a huge and concerted counter-revolution.

A few *disjecta membra* remain as clues to the likely appearance of English churches, great and small, at the height of the Marian reconstruction. Perhaps the most remarkable of all is to be found in the least expected of places. This is the handsome arcaded wooden canopy that crowns the shrine of St Edward in Westminster Abbey (Plate 10). Dismantled and removed under Edward VI, the shrine was reconstructed by Abbot Feckenham and his monks in 1557, and the royal saint's bones replaced 'with goodly syngyng and senssyng as has been sene, and masse song'.[21] The elegant classical lines of the new covering for the relics themselves say a great deal about the spirit of the great Marian rebuilding as a whole: there is nothing the least backward looking or 'gothicising' about this confident renaissance woodwork. The same is true of the fragments of surviving screenwork from the Marian reconstruction of the choir of Worcester Cathedral, now in Holy Trinity Church, Sutton Coldfield (Plate 11). The east end of the cathedral had been devastated by Dean Barlow in August 1551, as we have seen. In 1556, the cathedral sanctuary was rebuilt and re-equipped for the restored Mass and Offices 'with closure of carved boards round about the choir, double stalls, and high stalls for the canons and petty canons, the lower for the children, and a goodly loft wherein the gospel is read': the Queen herself financed the work. Once again, there was nothing backward-looking about the style of the new sacred enclosure. Nikolaus Pevsner and his team, who knew nothing of its Marian provenance, but only that this woodwork had migrated from Worcester to Holy Trinity in the wake of the Victorian regothicising of the cathedral, were unable to date the panelling stylistically, and speculated that it might be of the mid-seventeenth century.[22]

A somewhat more emphatic renaissance elegance characterises the tomb of Thomas Howard, 3rd Duke of Norfolk, buried in Framlingham parish church in 1554. The magnificent stone tomb chest, with its carved figures of the Apostles standing under scallop-shell canopies, was probably begun at Thetford in the late 1530s, but, with other Howard tombs, was moved to Framlingham in Mary's reign and completed. The completion of this emphatically catholic monument in Mary's reign, in the town where the predominantly catholic gentry of East Anglia had rallied to Mary, is an appropriate symbol of the strength of the regime's appeal to contemporary religious feeling.[23] A more severe renaissance austerity characterises the chantry chapel of Bishop Stephen Gardiner in Winchester Cathedral (Plates 7 and 8), totally devoid of religious iconography apart from the bishop's own cadaver image and the figures of Ecclesia and Synagoga flanking the reredos behind the altar.[24]

The greatest barrier to a positive assessment of the Marian restoration, however, remains the fact of the burning of more than 280 protestant men and women in just under four years, from February 1555 to November 1558. This was the most intense religious persecution of its kind anywhere in sixteenth-century Europe, and it not only constitutes a horrifying moral blot on any regime purporting to be Christian, but has seemed to most historians conclusive evidence of that regime's negativity, short-sightedness and instinct for self-destruction. I do not, of course, contest the horror involved in roasting men and women alive for their religious convictions. But, with some diffidence and discomfort, I do want to argue that the received perception of the campaign of burnings, as manifestly unsuccessful and self-defeating, is quite mistaken.

In sixteenth-century terms, the burnings were inevitable, and, gruesome as it is to speak of the efficiency of mass execution, in practice they were efficiently carried out and tellingly defended. For very good reasons, the regime identified protestantism with sedition. In the interests of political stability, it was convinced that it had to break the back of protestant resistance, and it pressed the device of shameful and painful public execution into service as a powerful tool in that task. Elizabeth, *mutatis mutandis*, would do the same from the 1570s onwards, though her campaign against catholicism was justified in largely political terms. But Mary's regime was also well aware of the potential of such executions to alienate public opinion, and Cardinal Pole and his colleagues took considered and, on the whole, effective steps to justify the campaign to contemporaries. Though it is very unlikely that the protestant minority could ever have been eliminated by force alone, the signs are that the campaign of repression was having the desired effect. By the summer of 1558, the numbers being executed for heresy were tailing off, a trend that has usually been interpreted as a sign of the regime's growing sense of failure and futility. I shall argue that, on the contrary, it reflects the fact that there were fewer defiant activists to execute: the protestant hydra was being decapitated.[25]

In this short book, I do not attempt a narrative survey of religion under Mary Tudor. There are important and still under-explored aspects of the restoration of catholicism that I have time to do little more than mention, such as the restoration of monasticism, or the highly successful reconstruction of the universities (especially of Oxford) as powerhouses of catholicism, a development that, as we shall see in the final chapter, was to have momentous consequences for Elizabethan recusancy and the wider counter-reformation. What I want to tackle here is the overarching issue of the general competence, drive and direction of the regime. What was it attempting to do, how well did it set about doing it, and who was in charge? In the process, I hope to dispose once and for all of some of the misapprehensions that have dogged and distorted the historiography of mid-Tudor catholicism – that it was ineffective, half-hearted, complacent, unimaginative, insular, lacking in leadership, trapped in the preoccupations of the 1520s or 1530s rather than addressing those of the 1550s; in short, that it had failed to discover the counter-reformation. I shall suggest that, on the contrary, as the first protestant nation to return to papal obedience, Marian England was the closest thing in Europe to a laboratory for counter-reformation experimentation.

The eyes of Europe, catholic and protestant, were fixed on the remarkable counter-revolution taking shape after Mary's accession. Pope Julius III struck a special medal to commemorate the religious resurrection of England, and Cardinal Pole and his circle took pains to ensure that every major step in the Marian restoration of catholicism got the maximum European coverage. This publicity campaign began even before Pole's readmission to the kingdom. The scaffold speech of the Duke of Northumberland, confessing his own insincerity and urging the English people to return to the old faith, was being circulated in Europe within days of its delivery, and was rapidly translated and published in French, Dutch, Italian, Spanish and Latin editions, almost certainly at Pole's instigation.[26]

The reform measures devised for England had nothing backward-looking about them. On the contrary, they would be published in 1562 by a reforming ginger-group at Trent, and would provide the inspiration for some of Tridentine catholicism's most distinctive measures and emphases, notably its most important innovation, the creation of seminaries to form a new priesthood. Marian activists would constitute the backbone of Elizabethan recusancy, and some of them would help shape the course of the wider counter-reformation, from the practical reforms of Borromeo's Milan, to the historical and theological underpinning of counter-reformation polemic.[27]

I shall also suggest that the notion that the Marian regime was somehow peripheral to the counter-reformation is not simply mistaken, but positively absurd when applied to the man in charge of the whole enterprise, Cardinal Reginald Pole. Just seven years before his appointment as legate for England, Pole had presided at the opening sessions of the Council of Trent: he had composed the magnificent opening address to the Council, which remains one of the defining documents of the counter-reformation.[28] Throughout the 1540s and 1550s, Pole was the figurehead and spiritual counsellor for some of the best minds and most ardent spirits of the Italian counter-reformation, from Vittoria Colonna and Giovanni Moroni to Marcello Cervini (Papa Marcello), and all that time remained, despite the mounting hostility of his enemy Cardinal Caraffa, in the apt phrase of his biographer and editor, a 'power in Rome'.[29] In the conclave of 1550 that eventually elected Julius III, Pole was offered the papacy by acclamation, and came within one vote of formal election.[30] There is every reason to think that, had he lived through the epidemic of 1558, he would have been a strong contender to succeed Paul IV. In short, Pole had lived for twenty years at the storm centre of the struggle for the soul of the counter-reformation. To suggest that he had somehow failed to notice or chose to ignore it, trapped in an English time warp of the 1520s or 1530s, is preposterous. It was the vision of the church matured in that Italian arena that he brought to bear on the reform and renewal of catholicism in Marian England.

The charge that the Marian regime failed to discover the counter-reformation is, however, a very old one, first advanced by the Elizabethan Jesuit, Robert Parsons. In his book-length memorandum composed in the 1590s, setting out a reform agenda should Elizabeth be succeeded by a catholic, Parsons suggested that Mary's attempt to re-impose catholicism had failed because it was 'hudled' and 'shuffled up with . . . negligence'. It had attended, he thought, only to externals, 'without remedying the Root, the renewing of the Spirit, which should have been the ground of all'. Mary's efforts had been fatally flawed by her church's willingness to settle for half measures, its compromise with apostasy. Married clergy were permitted to return to parish ministry, 'without other satisfaction than only to send their Concubines out of Men's sight, and of some it is thought they did not so much as confess themselves before they said Mass again'. Others 'that had preached against

Catholicks, were admitted presently to preach for them'; ecclesiastical officials 'that had been Visitors and Commissioners against us, were made Commissioners against the Protestants', and, on Elizabeth's accession, 'were Commissioners again of the other side against ours'; and the 'owners' of alienated monastic lands had been allowed to retain them. So 'the matter went as a Stage-play, where Men do change their Persons and Parts, without changing their Minds or Affection'. Who could wonder, therefore 'that the benefit of Religion remained so little a while, or that the second scourge of Heresie hath been so sharp and heavy since, as we have proved'.[31]

This contemporary Jesuit critique may have been a counsel of perfection, but Parsons had undoubtedly put his finger on a real weakness in the Marian settlement. Pole himself lamented the necessity of employing the Henrician episcopate to undo the Henrician schism that they had helped foment. It is hard to see, however, what Pole or anyone else could have been done about this, for the parishes had to be staffed. Parsons's preferred solution – to amalgamate clusters of parishes under the care of itinerant, committed catholic preachers – would have indefinitely postponed the regime's best chance of success, the re-establishment of a regular habit of catholic practice among the population. In the absence of local clergy, such a policy would have handed the initiative to the conventiclers.[32]

How, then, should the revolution have been rolled back? The Marian episcopate as a whole, and Cardinal Pole in particular, were convinced that sincere protestants were an unrepresentative minority, the country at large still, even in 1553, predominantly catholic in sympathy. In this they were certainly correct. There probably were communities in the Stour Valley or (less probably) in the Weald of Kent where protestants outnumbered catholics, but at the start of Mary's reign such places were few and far between.

This perfectly correct numerical perception *might*, initially at least, have misled Pole and his colleagues to underestimate the intensity and depth of evangelical conviction amongst that minority, and the continuing influence of the surviving evangelical clergy over them. The Kentish gospeller John Newman explained the matter to the turncoat bishop of Dover, Richard Thornden. He and his fellow gospellers, he declared, had drunk too deep of the teaching of the Edwardine reformers to renounce it simply on command. For, he told Thornden, their doctrine was not beleued of vs sodainly, but by their continuall preaching: and also by our continuall prayer vnto god that we might neuer be deceiued . . . We wayed that they laboured with Gods word, and we asked the aduise of our frendes: neyther could wee finde that they preached false doctrine. We considered also . . . that the kinges Grace and his Counsell, and the most part of al the whole realme, beleued as they taught, because no man preached the contrary . . . And by their diligent setting forthe of it, by the kinges commaundemente, and the whole consent of the whole Counsell, and by the authoritie of the Parliament, wc cmbrascd it, and rccciued it, as a very infallible trueth taught vnto vs, for the space of vii. yeares.[33]

The bishops would have considered that a doctrine received and endorsed by that 'diligent setting forthe', the consent of the Council and the authority of the Parliament could presumably be reversed using the same backers. And events would show that relatively few people shared Newman's depth of conviction. Committed protestants, we need to remind ourselves again, were everywhere a minority. But any illusions the bishops might have entertained about the likely feebleness of resistance among that minority were quickly dispelled, at any rate in places such as London, Essex and Kent. Pole deplored again and again in his own sermons the hold of reformed ideas among London congregations and more widely,[34] and Bonner's frustrated awareness of the resilience of the protestant underground in his diocese found expression in a characteristically exasperated outburst in June 1555, during the examination of Thomas Haukes: 'yes, yes, there is a brotherhead of you, but I will breake it, I warrant you'.[35]

The eclipse of protestantism would not, therefore, be a pushover. Nevertheless, historians have insufficiently registered the rapidity and extent of the evangelical collapse and the nationwide disarray of the protestant cause in the wake of Mary's accession. Fear and opportunism would have played a role in the apparent changes of heart causing this disarray, but a major element in it was almost certainly the sheer unexpectedness of Mary's political success. The accession of a catholic queen was the signal for a stampede of protestant leaders to escape to the continent – ultimately more than eight hundred exiles, including most of the best brains in the evangelical camp.[36] It was an exodus that the Marian authorities did little to impede, and, indeed, in the early months of the regime, Lord Chancellor Gardiner seems on several occasions to have leaked advance warning of imminent arrests, at any rate of foreign protestants, in the hope that the dissidents concerned would take themselves off and save the state the embarrassment of their presence.[37] But the collapse was hardly less dramatic among those who remained. Mary's astonishing and, as many thought, miraculous defeat of Northumberland's conspiracy, and her rapturous popular reception as queen, seemed to many observers, even to sophisticates such as Cardinal Pole, the unmistakable hand of a directing providence. And this widespread conviction was almost certainly one of the factors that led scores of prominent evangelicals to abandon their reformed opinions and convert to catholicism. Certainly the regime thought this a strong card in the play for hearts and minds.

When the evangelical George Marsh was brought before the Earl of Derby in April 1555 the Earl tried to persuade him to conformity by recalling 'the euill luck of the Dukes of Northumberland and Suffolke with others, because they fauored not the true religion', and the contrasting 'good hap and prosperitie of the Queenes highnes', thereby 'gathering the one to be good and of God, and the other to be wicked and of the deuill, & said that the Duke of Northumberland confessed so playnely'.[38] Marsh was unimpressed, but such arguments undoubtedly prevailed with many. Some of these rapid conversions were both spectacular *and* enduring, the men concerned proving their recovered catholic credentials by taking a leading role in the restoration of the old religion and in the pursuit and conviction of heretics. They included Thomas Harding, friend of Bullinger and chaplain to Lady Jane Grey's father. Harding's much publicised return to catholicism elicited a bitter tirade from Lady Jane as she awaited execution in the Tower, for having become so soon the 'vnshamefast paramour of Antichrist, sometyme my faythfull brother, but now a straunger and Apostata, sometime a stoute Christen souldiour, but now a cowardly runneaway'.[39] Yet Harding was no mere opportunist. Prominent in the examination of London evangelicals and an activist in the restoration of religion in the Salisbury diocese where Pole licensed him to preach, at Elizabeth's accession he remained true to his catholic convictions, fled to Louvain and became the leading catholic controversialist of the 1560s.

There were other equally spectacular changes of heart. Dr Henry Pendleton, an itinerant protestant preacher under Derby's patronage in Edward's reign, encouraged his friend Lawrence Sanders to stand by his convictions at Mary's accession. Pendleton, a corpulent man, vowed that 'I will see the vttermost drop of this grease of mine molten away, and the last gobbet of this flesh consumed to ashes, before I wil forsake God and his truth'. In the event, however, he himself soon conformed, became a notable catholic persuader, preacher and disputant, and, as one of the two authors of Bishop Bonner's book of *Homilies*, was one of the key official voices of the regime.[40] Some of these trophy 'conversions', of course, were indeed dictated primarily by fear, and several leading protestants examined in 1554 and 1555 recanted, only to relapse subsequently, including Bishop John Scory, Bishop William Barlow and the well-known London preacher John Cardmaker.[41]

The impact of these dramatic changes of heart, real or pretended, was by no means confined to London. Professor Ralph Houlbrooke has documented the rapid collapse of the evangelical community in Norwich in the face of the capitulation and recantation of all the leading Norwich evangelicals. Two of these recantations, those of Thomas Rose and Robert Watson, were coerced, and both men subsequently revealed their true opinions by fleeing abroad, but their surrenders were skilfully publicised at the time by the catholic authorities, and certainly helped demoralise the Norwich gospellers.

The recantation of the most prominent Norwich evangelical, John Barret, by contrast, was undoubtedly genuine. Barret, an ex-Carmelite, a preacher and scholar, and a close friend of the ex-Carmelite reformer John Bale, became an active and effective persuader for the catholic cause, and eventually bequeathed his books to Norwich Cathedral library. Bale, appalled, lamented that some deceiving spirit had led his admired friend 'like the vilest of dogs, to return to his own vomit'.[42] Barret's library was characterised by editions of the Greek and Latin Fathers, a range of counter-reformation apologetic works by authors such as John Fisher, Ruard Tapper and Alfonso de Castro, and a notable absence of protestant books. Barret took the Oath of Supremacy again at Elizabeth's succession, but made a fervently catholic will in 1563, which leaves no room for any doubt about the sincerity of his recovered catholic convictions.[43]

Norwich was not an isolated example. In Exeter under Edward, the city's leading evangelical cleric, William Herne, incumbent of the parish of St Petroc, had told his fellow gospeller Alderman Midwinter that he would rather be torn in part by wild horses than ever say Mass again. In December 1553, however, when the Mass became once more the only legal form of worship, Midwinter entered St Petroc's to find Herne robed in Mass vestments and standing ready to celebrate at the altar. He pointed at the priest with his finger 'remembringe as it were his olde protestations that he wolde never singe masse agayne: but parson herne openlye in churche spak alowde onto hym. It is no remedye man, it is no remedye.'[44] One of the leading Sussex conventiclers, Richard Woodman, burned in 1557, was first arrested early in 1554 for standing up in his parish church of Warbleton to berate the curate, who had been a vehement evangelical preacher in Edward's reign, but who now 'turnyng hed to taile, preached cleane contrary to that which he had before taught'.[45]

Throughout 1554 and beyond, devastated evangelical leaders lamented the rapidity and extent of the conformity of the population *and* the clergy to catholicism, and the collapse of resistance even in those communities where reformed beliefs had once appeared to have penetrated deeply. Peter Martyr told Bullinger in April 1554 that 'persons . . . whom you would have considered the most resolute, [are] now wavering and even yielding'.[46] From the safety of his exile in Strasbourg, Thomas Sampson rebuked his former parishioners at All Hallows Bread Street in August 1554, 'inwardly . . . gospellers, and outwardly dissemblers with papistes', for their inconstancy and cowardice: 'O London, London, is this the gospelling fruicte, to be the first that withoute a lawe shouldest bannish trew preaching . . . whyche not in persecution but before persecution cometh dost goe backe'.[47] Another Strasbourg exile, Thomas Becon, deplored 'these perillous and troublesome dayes / wherin we se so many sturte backe and runne awaye from the confession of Gods trueth (whiche whan the weather was calme / they semed constantly to professe)'.[48] And in the bitterness of his imprisonment, Nicholas Ridley came to believe that the Edwardine reformation had never in fact penetrated the hearts even of the nation's elites, much less the common people: he wrote that, of the

> iudges of the lawes, iustices of peace, sergeants, common lawyers, it may be truly sayd of them, as of the most part of the Clergy, of Curates, Vicares, Persons, Prebendaries, Doctors of the law, Archdeacons, Deanes, yea, & I may say, of Bishops also, I feare me, for the more parte. . . . they wer neuer persuaded in their harts but from the teeth forwarde and for the kings sake, in the truth of Gods word, and yet all these did dissemble and bare a copy of a countenaunce as if they had bene sound within.[49]

It has recently been claimed that a leading aspect of the Marian regime was its complacency, a 'naïve assumption that if the government barked loudly enough Protestantism would just "go away"'.[50] In fact, however, the Marian authorities did not leave this general return to conformity to chance or individual initiative, and set about ensuring the conversion of the nation very systematically. In the spring of 1554, Edmund Bonner issued an instruction to lay people in his diocese of London, requiring them to go to confession to their parish priest in Lent, and to make their Easter communion in the newly restored catholic rite. Curates were to note the names of all who failed to do so, and offenders were cited on to the episcopal and archdecanal visitations that got under way in the summer and autumn of 1554.

As a result, 470 men and women were presented, of whom at least half were probably protestants. The overwhelming majority of these conformed, at any rate outwardly, and only three were subsequently burned.[51] And everywhere else in the country, the restoration of the Mass and the outlawing of the Book of Common Prayer after December 1553 signalled a majority return to catholic observance. But the reconciliation with the papacy on 30 November 1554 was the signal for an escalation of the whole process of systematic enforcement, a process given potentially lethal teeth when the heresy laws came back into force at the end of January 1555. In February, with Lent approaching,[52] the bishops set about ensuring that every adult man and woman in the country would be individually reconciled to Rome. As was normal, the bishop of London took the lead here. On 19 February, Bonner issued a new set of instructions, which were then copied by other bishops, spelling out the details. These required every adult parishioner to go to confession to their parish priest to be absolved from schism, and to 'reconcile themselves to the churche', before the first Sunday after Easter (21 April). The laity were warned that

> the sayde tyme being ones past, and they not so reconciled, every one of them shall have process made ageynst hym according to the Canons . . . for which purpose the pastors and curates of every parysche . . . [are] to certify me in writing of every mans and womans name that is not so reconciled.[53]

But Bonner did not rely exclusively on this threat of sanctions. As bishop of London, with its many protestants, he was of course aware that, for many, the return to papal obedience would involve a crisis of conscience. He also recognised that many of the clergy lacked the skills and persuasiveness needed to resolve such doubts. He therefore made special pastoral provision for the anguished but well-intentioned. Since 'diverse pastors and curates in sundry paryshes' might not be able 'to satisfy the myndes and to appeace the consciences of some of theyr parysheners, in cases that shall trouble them', he had authorised his archdeacons to appoint 'certeyne of the beste lerned in everye deanery' to supply that lack. Troubled parishioners with scruples about conformity might choose freely which of these men they consulted 'to be instructed and appeaced in that behalfe'. Those still unconvinced might go to the archdeacons or Bonner's chaplains, or to Bonner himself, 'to be resolved in his sayde scruple'. We have no way of knowing how many people took advantage of these arrangements, or how well they worked, but they reveal a degree of pastoral sensitivity to the issues of conscience posed by the new situation for which Bonner is not usually given credit. Interestingly, other bishops may have been less ready than Bonner was to acknowledge the insufficiency of the parish clergy in handling conscientious scruples. Adapting Bonner's text for use in the Ely diocese, Thomas Thirlby deleted the sentence admitting that some parish clergy 'peraduenture bee not able to satisfye the myndes, and to appease the consciences' of their people, and replaced it with vaguer and less elaborate provisions, to be invoked only 'if any paryshe do lack his curat, for that cause or other reasonable and just cause'.

This process of reconciliation was nowhere, however, a merely routine or cursory business. The bishops seem to have been determined that every adult should make a personal statement of catholic faith before making their Easter communion. The archdiocese of York had been far less deeply penetrated by evangelical ideas than Bonner's London, but here too the instructions for the reconciliation were equally searching, and even more circumstantial. Every curate was instructed to 'examine every his parishioners at the time of Confession, not being Reconciled' on the articles of the catholic faith, enquiring of each of them whether they 'believe undoubtedly' the real presence of Christ in the eucharist, whether they rejected justification by faith alone, and whether they accepted 'that the Apostolicall See of Rome, and our Holy Father the Pope . . . is and ought to be the head of the universall Catholike Church of Christ in earth'.[54] Clergy were also to quiz parishioners about the possession of heretical books, and to order all such books to be surrendered to the bishop for burning. Only after all this, and after an explicit declaration of sorrow for their involvement in schism, might the parishioner be absolved and permitted to receive their Easter communion. Any parishioner who pleaded that they had already been to confession to another priest was to be summoned to confess again to their own curate, so that he could satisfy himself of their orthodoxy.

The same close scrutiny was continued into the Marian visitations of the rest of the reign, especially in protestant hot spots such as the diocese of Canterbury, where Archdeacon Nicholas Harpsfield's eagle eye noted and pursued every sign of deviance, from the refusal of those with good voices to sing in the choir at Mass, to the failure of those who were unable to read to carry rosary beads.[55] A detailed study is needed of this process of enforcement in the dioceses, which must have varied with the competence and commitment of the bishops and diocesan officials. We will return to this issue in a later chapter, but it is clear that, even before the arrival of the Cardinal, and especially thereafter, in the most troubled dioceses the regime maintained and increased the pressure on dissent, deploying a formidable array of energetic and relentless archdeacons, chancellors and court officials, most of them active up to Mary's final months.

It is perhaps no great surprise to find that 'Bloody Mary's' church was rather good at enforcement. Yet it has been widely asserted or assumed that the regime relied too heavily on force, and did not follow through on the evangelical collapse, failing to generate an adequate propaganda machine and especially neglecting preaching. As we shall see in a later chapter, Marian propaganda was in fact both plentiful and formidable. Here and now, however, we need to dispose of the frequently made and largely unquestioned claim that the Marian church undervalued preaching. This is one of the more baffling myths about Marian catholicism, if only because the sources everywhere confute it. Pole's Legatine Synod of 1555 emphasised the fundamental importance of preaching in its fourth decree, which rather remarkably defined the pastoral office itself as consisting 'chiefly . . . in the preaching of God's word' [*potissimum in divini verbi praedicatione consistit*]. The decree demanded that all bishops and archbishops preach in person, and that all clergy with cure of souls 'either personally or through other fit persons

... feed the people committed to them with the wholesome food of preaching, at least on Sundays and feast-days'. This insistence on sustained weekly preaching and catechising in the parishes and dioceses to combat heresy and reform the piety of the people remained a high priority throughout the reign.

The Convocation of 1558 reiterated the episcopal obligation of providing sound preaching as a remedy for 'these dangerous times when heretical wolves have ravaged the flock by false teaching, and many have fallen from the faith', and recommended the recruitment and licensing of diocesan preachers to assist the bishops in this crucial task, with a correspondingly tight control on unauthorised preaching. Pole hammered this message home in the first of his legatine visitation articles for the dioceses, insisting that 'all parson, vicars and curates having the gyfte and talente of preachinge' shall 'frequentlie and diligentlie' preach to the people as the synod instructed, 'opening the scriptures accordinglie'. They were also to use the liturgy as the basis for a re-education in catholicism, teaching 'the right use of the godlie ceremonies of the churche, as they come in course from time to time'. And the legate prescribed that all incumbents and curates 'being no preachers' should, to remedy this lack, 'earnestlie emploie themselves to studie the holie scripture', and make an annual report on their progress to their bishop. Pole was well aware of the extent of the problem, and, discussing preaching in a sermon at St Mary-le-Bow in 1556, told the parishioners that this was a time 'when such holesome fode is nott so plenty as I would wishe'.[56] For the majority of priests unfit to preach, therefore, the synod decreed the composition of an elaborate body of homilies, covering not only the fundamentals of faith and practice, but in particular the issues disputed between catholics and protestants. Pending their publication, Pole himself prescribed the universal use of A profitable and necessarye doctryne and the attached Homilies, issued by Bonner in 1555 for use in the London diocese.[57]

These were serious attempts to institutionalise and improve regular parochial preaching. But the regime became intensely aware of the inroads that evangelical preaching had made under Edward, and correspondingly alive to the need to fight back with special measures. So, contrary to almost everything that has been written about Mary's reign in recent years, a striking feature of the Marian restoration, which positively shouts at one from the sources, was the concerted campaign of preaching that the regime mounted to refute protestant error. In London, star preachers such as John Feckenham, Richard Smith, Henry Cole, William Peryn, Thomas Watson and William Chedsey defended catholic doctrine from many pulpits, but the focus of this campaign was London's major preaching venue, Paul's Cross. As Pole told Bartolomé Carranza in June 1558, care was taken to have a major set-piece sermon at Paul's Cross every Sunday, and multitudes attended.[58] Pole was not exaggerating, for, if the London chroniclers are to be believed, the number of auditors at Paul's Cross frequently ran well into five figures, and the authorities took enormous pains to ensure the highest possible attendance, the Lord Mayor and aldermen in their robes leading the way. Bonner instructed London churchwardens to see to it that, during the Paul's Cross sermons, there should be no 'ryngynge of belles, playinge of Children, cryenge or making lowed noyse, rydynge of horses, or otherwise, so that the Preacher there or his audience was troubled thereby'.[59]

The Paul's Cross sermons were also occasions for set-piece propaganda exercises, such as the public recantation of heretics, the disciplining of married or concubinate clergy and the exposure of protestant conspiracy. In a representative incident in June 1554, Elizabeth Croft, 'the party which played boo pipe in the wall of Aldersgate Strette', recanted at the Cross. Croft was an eighteen-year-old maidservant who had been involved in a notorious hoax, in which an oracular voice issuing from a hole in a wall had praised the Lady Elizabeth and denounced catholicism to a large crowd. She stood at sermon time in a specially constructed scaffold beside the Cross pulpit, and confessed that she had been bribed to mount the hoax by gospellers 'that have the Lorde in [their] mouthes and the devil in [their] hartes'. Croft urged the crowd with tears, 'beware good people beware of these heretyks . . . they wyll undo you all'.[60] Another London pulpit tradition, the Spital sermons, was observed with considerable display, 'of old custom', at Easter 1557, when there were two star controversialists as preachers, Henry Pendleton and Dr John Young, Master of Pembroke College, Cambridge. Twenty-five of the twenty-six London aldermen turned out to hear them, with the children of the Hospital attending uniformed in blue, an array of judges and a crowd estimated at 20,000, 'the wholl cete', as Henry Machyn noted, 'boythe old and yonge, boythe men and women'.[61]

The preaching campaign was not confined to the capital. From March 1555, special preachers were being sent down into heretical hot-spots such as Essex and East Anglia, backed by instructions from the Council and the Queen to local grandees and justices to 'be aiding and assisting' by being present themselves at the sermons and 'us[ing] the preachers reverently'.[62] We have details of one such preaching tour, by the heresy-hunting, former evangelical parson of Great ('Much') Bentley in Essex, Thomas Tye. At the height of the burnings in the summer of 1556, Tye preached a series of Sunday sermons in villages in the Harwich area, and publicly reconciled a group of twelve former gospellers in Harwich itself. Reporting his activities to Bishop Bonner, Tye explained that he had undertaken his tour in the wake of a Paul's Cross sermon by Feckenham directed against sixteen Essex heretics due to be burned the following week.[63] Tye's activities were replicated in other dioceses. George London, a former Benedictine principal of Gloucester College, Oxford, was employed by Pole's collaborator Bishop Richard Pate to preach against heresy in the Worcester diocese, and, in the light of his effectiveness there, Pole subsequently licensed him to preach anywhere in England.[64] Pole showed a similar concern to provide preachers for other dioceses, such as the cluster he licensed for Salisbury in May 1558, which included two notable future counter-reformation activists, both doctors of divinity, Thomas Harding and Thomas Heskins. Harding would be the key catholic polemicist of the 1560s, and Heskins would enter the Flanders province of the Order of Preachers.[65]

Sermons directed not only against heresy but also against particular heretics were an invariable feature of executions themselves, preached from temporary pulpits erected near the pyre, or in the parish church, often with additional sermons on the Sundays before or afterwards. Both the Queen and Cardinal Pole wrote independently to the bishops, insisting on the presence of able preachers at all executions, because, as Pole explained, heretics could harm the ignorant and rude multitude at least as much by their deaths as ever they did alive. In London and elsewhere, condemned heretics were often preached against by name, and might be brought from their prisons into church to hear their errors denounced from the pulpit. The preachers on these occasions frequently drew attention to the extremism and inconsistency of the condemned person's opinions, as when Thomas Pecock, Canon of Norwich, preached against William Wolsey and Robert Pygott at Ely, on the day of their execution in 1555, showing them 'to be cleane out of the faythe, and in many places quite denying the Scripture'.[66] At the burning of a group of seven radical Kentish artisans and their wives at Maidstone in June 1557 the local curate, John Day, was shouted down by the victims as he preached by their pyre. He turned to the people and told them 'Good people, ye ought not in any wyse to pray for these obstinate heretykes, for loke how ye shall se ther bodyes burne here with materiall fyre, so shall ther damnable soules burne in the unquenchable fyre of hell everlastynge'. He preached against them again on the Sunday after the execution. In Elizabeth's reign he was to be denounced for his part in the execution, and would then claim that he could not remember precisely what he had said 'by meanes of the flame of the fyre and the great smoke that the wynde browghte so violently towards me', a vivid evocation of the fraught and gruesome character of many of the executions. But he had almost certainly itemised the heresies of the victims, for, as he later recalled, 'some of them did deny the humanity of Christe and the equalitie of the Trinitie and no man dowbteth but such ar heretykes'.[67] Dean Feckenham preached at Paul's Cross in 1556 against the allegedly sixteen different opinions of sixteen condemned Essex heretics. John White, bishop of Winchester, told a congregation in St Mary Overy in Southwark in May 1557, 'Good people, these men that bee brought before us, being here, deny Christ to be God, and the Holy Ghost to be God.'[68]

Contemporaries were well aware of the range, scale and effectiveness of this preaching campaign. The protestant exile John Olde complained bitterly in November 1555 of the flood of papistical propaganda being poured out by 'the prechours in Englande now promoted and set up in throne by the Queenes highnesse, as wel at Paules Crosse as commonly in open pulpittes'.[69] Bafflingly, however, historians have either ignored, overlooked or denied all this activity, and it has been accepted as an axiom that the Marian church gave 'no special emphasis' to preaching and, by oversight or design, failed to make use of the pulpit in the service of counter-reformation.[70] Like so many other aspects of the historical consensus about the reign, this largely unquestioned assumption is quite simply and demonstrably untrue, and the failure to register it has distorted perceptions of the seriousness and effectiveness of the Marian regime as a whole.

I want now to turn finally, and necessarily sketchily, to the very large question of the realism and effectiveness of the practical programme of the Marian regime as a whole. I will not attempt comprehensiveness here. An exhaustive study of the Marian restoration, for example, would have to pay special attention to the Marian reconstruction of Oxford and Cambridge, since that reconstruction, in which the Cardinal took a close personal interest, has to be judged a major success.[71] (The methods and objectives employed in the reimposition of catholicism in the English universities, incidentally, closely resemble the activities of Peter Canisius in Vienna at more or less the same time, a matter to which I shall return in the final chapter.[72]) So my treatment of the question of the practical programme of the Marian regime will be highly selective.

Professor Thomas Mayer recently published a major re-examination of the business record of Pole's English legation, that is, the restoration of papal jurisdiction as a court of appeal, justice and grace, involving cases ranging from dispensations for irregular marriages, or the regulation of clerical pluralism, to absolution from the sin of schism. In that study, Mayer demonstrated that the volume of business transacted by the Cardinal and his officials was almost *eight* times as much as had previously been calculated. He found 315 appeals to Pole's jurisdiction, in spectacular contrast to the total of 43 proposed in the standard study of the legation carried out a generation earlier. Mayer concluded that, contrary to earlier assessments, Pole's legation must be considered a success, whether measured by bulk – the immediate and sustained demand from English people for the spiritual and legal benefits of the return to Rome – or by the manifest efficiency of the Cardinal and his officials in dealing with that demand. Mayer therefore suggested that the time had finally come to 'abandon the equation between mid-sixteenth-century Catholicism and incompetence'.[73] As we have seen, that presumption of incompetence does indeed saturate almost everything that has been written about the regime. It is one of the central contentions of this book that, on the contrary, the English church under Cardinal Pole had a well-conceived and practical reforming agenda, and set about realising that agenda with notable effectiveness. I have space here to consider just a single exemplary issue, the improvement of the standards of the clergy.

In the magnificent opening address that he wrote for the Council of Trent in 1546, Pole had insisted that the afflictions of the contemporary church sprang from the sins and failures of its clerical rulers. Because the bishops had not been true pastors, but had themselves been ruled by ambition and avarice, heretical teachers had driven out true shepherds, the churches were famished for the word of God and the property of the church, the patrimony of the poor, had been alienated and stolen. So the threefold objectives of the Council – the uprooting of heresies, the reformation of ecclesiastical discipline and morals and the restoration of the peace of the church – must begin with repentance and self-reform.[74]

Pole's analysis of the wider ills of Christendom applied of course with special force to reformation England, all but one of whose bishops had spectacularly failed their flocks, by supinely acquiescing in Henry's usurpation of the spiritual headship of the church, and whose church had subsequently been plundered by crown and aristocracy, depriving it of the financial means of renewal and reform. So Pole looked toward a new kind of bishop – pastoral, theologically informed, loyal to the papacy – and a new kind of clergy – educated, decently paid and so resident, preaching and, once again, loyal to the papacy – and he knew that the reorganisation of the finances of the church of England was the *sine qua non* for the achievement of these objectives. I shall return to finance presently: I pause here to say a word about the renewal of the episcopate and the higher clergy from whom the episcopate were recruited.

Mary inherited or reinstated sixteen bishops who had served her father, her brother or both, and she and Pole made twenty new appointments between 1554 and 1558. The Henrician survivors included key figures in the new regime – Bonner, Gardiner, Thirlby, some venerable figureheads such as Cuthbert Tunstall and one classic timeserver who would doubtless have become a Hindu if required, provided he was allowed to hold on to the See of Llandaff: Anthony Kitchin was the only Marian bishop willing to swallow the Royal Supremacy and serve under Elizabeth as well. But the new appointments have a striking consistency. They represent a quite new kind of Tudor bishop, and reveal a startling clarity of purpose about the kind of bishop Pole wanted.

The twenty new bishops were overwhelmingly recruited from university-trained theologians, with a proven pastoral track record and, in many cases, also a record of loyalty to and suffering for catholic beliefs under Henry and Edward. James Brookes, Master of Balliol, was a powerful preacher and controversialist, who presided at the trials of Latimer, Ridley and Cranmer. John White, Warden of Winchester, was another notable preacher, who had been imprisoned in the Tower under Edward. John Hopton, Mary's former Dominican chaplain, would be a hammer of heresy in East Anglia. Ralph Baynes, a distinguished Hebraist, who had spent most of Edward's reign in exile in Paris, would prove a notable theological hardliner in the heresy trials of Mary's reign. William Glyn was a distinguished theologian, formerly Lady Margaret's Professor of Divinity at Cambridge and President of Queens'. Thomas Watson, Master of St John's, was one of the regime's best preachers and probably the ablest theologian among the Marian bishops. Cuthbert Scott, Master of Christ's, was another eloquent preacher who would lead resistance to the Oath of Supremacy in Elizabeth's first Parliament. A couple of the new bishops – Richard Pate and Thomas Goldwell – had been members of Pole's own household and therefore came with an impeccable record of acquantance with and commitment to catholic reform. Goldwell, indeed, was a member of Caraffa's Theatine order, and therefore emphatically a man identified with the new forces of the counter-reformation. David Pole, one of only two lawyers in the whole bench of twenty, and a first-rate administrator, was probably Pole's kinsman.

This is a remarkable and remarkably homogenous bench. Some of the new bishops, such as James Brookes, were charged with burdensome and time-consuming legatine commissions that kept them out of their dioceses, including the visitation of the universities or the trials of protestant leaders such as Cranmer, Ridley and Latimer. But the group as a whole is characterised by pastoral commitment and energetic action fully in line with later Tridentine norms. Where registers survive, Pole's bishops seem, as a body, to have been resident and active. Glyn, for example, held a series of diocesan synods to propagate and enforce the provisions of the Legatine Synod. Scott at Chester was a regular preacher, threw himself into clerical recruitment and clerical reform, and presided at eight of the nine ordination ceremonies held during his episcopate, an aspect of the remarkable Marian surge in vocations to the priesthood after the disastrous slump of Edward's reign. Pate orchestrated preaching campaigns in Worcester and was himself an active preacher.

Reviewing these appointments in a valuable essay published in 2006, David Loades nevertheless awarded Pole, Mary and their bench of bishops only a *beta* query plus. They were, he thought, a 'mixed bunch', admittedly mostly with respectable credentials, but only a few distinguished by learning and zeal. On the contrary, it seems to me, most *were* distinguished by learning, many by zeal and a surprising number by both. Their dedication can be measured by its cost to them. All but one of the bishops who survived the devastating 'flu of 1558–9[75] refused conformity to the Royal Supremacy and accepted deprivation and, for some of them, a lifetime of imprisonment for their faith. This is a startling contrast with all but one of their predecessors on the early Tudor bench, and it has to be taken as indicating zeal of some kind. Loades comments that it 'took too long to shape an episcopate ripe for the purpose' of catholic reform. In fact, it took considerably less than four years, an astonishingly rapid turnaround, which represented the most dramatic and spectacularly rapid re-engineering of a catholic episcopate anywhere in counter-reformation Europe, and which would remain so for the next two centuries. In the reign of Charles V, only one in five of Spain's bishops was a theologian; by the end of Philip II's reign it was one in two. But the process had taken two generations, and was still nothing like as complete as Pole's creation, two generations earlier, of a bench of bishops consisting almost entirely of theologians and pastors. In France, law graduates still outnumbered theology graduates in the episcopate by three to one in the 1590s, and the gap only began to reduce notably in the 1630s.[76] In that perspective, Marian England was the hare to the rest of Europe's tortoise.

The renewal of the clergy required more than the reform of the bench of bishops: it also required training colleges or seminaries for priests. Pole's Legatine Synod prescribed this in its famous and innovatory eleventh decree.[77] By 1558, the establishment of four such diocesan schools had been inaugurated or adapted from existing institutions, at York, Lincoln, Wells and Durham, and Bishop Day of Chichester left £20 towards the establishment of a similar establishment there 'according to the decree of the synod'. The declaration of the canons of York that, in founding their school, they intended to 'put to flight the rapacious wolves, that is devilish men, ill-understanding the Catholic faith, from the sheepfolds of the sheep entrusted to them', strikes an authentically counter-reformation note. Once again, moreover, the speed of this response compares very favourably indeed with the snail's pace of implementation of the Council's decree on seminaries across the rest of post-Tridentine Europe.[78]

But the key to all clerical renewal was money, and it is in his focus on money that Pole most clearly displayed the practicality and determination of his reforming vision. The English church had been financially pulverised by the reformation. The dissolution of the monasteries not only involved the massive secularisation of all monastic property, but transferred the revenue from benefices formerly impropriated to the monasteries into the hands of the new lay owners. The crown itself systematically impoverished the church by the imposition of First Fruits and Tenths as a charge on every benefice. Under Edward, the further plunder of episcopal lands became chronic. The diocese of Exeter lost two-thirds of its episcopal lands; the diocese of Durham was divided and plundered. The protestant reformers themselves repeatedly lamented the catastrophic consequences of this plunder, and deplored the diversion of funds intended for God's work.

Pole saw that his ideal of an educated resident preaching pastoral clergy could not be achieved without financial reconstruction and recovery: the sins of simony and pluralism, which Trent would also address, could not be reformed until benefices provided priests with an adequate living. He therefore made the recovery of ecclesiastical property one of his highest priorities, and his determined refusal simply to write off the lands and revenues lost under Henry and Edward delayed his admission to the kingdom for a year. When, eventually, he bowed to political reality and agreed that the possessors of church lands would not be legally obliged to return them as the price for the restoration of papal jurisdiction, he absolutely refused to concede that they were not *morally* obliged to make restitution. That obligation was to remain a feature of his preaching, and that of his collaborators.[79] This financial preoccupation has been taken as another sign of Pole's ploddingly mistaken priorities, in Rex Pogson's words, an indication 'that he aimed at a restoration of traditional Roman order . . . rather than a vigorous, new-style Counter-Reformation campaign of preaching'.[80] In fact, Pole rightly saw that the one depended on the other. Without preachers, no preaching; without revenues, no preachers. Hugh Glasier, Canon of St Paul's, preaching at Paul's Cross in 1555, told his audience

> I my selfe have a poore lyvinge within twelfe miles of this citee, and rownde about me there are to the number of xv or xx parishes, and amongst them all there be not past foure or five prestes that do recyve one tithe sheif, for all be impropried (as they call them). . . . And some

of these parishes bee without a priest a quarter of a year together . . .
For the farmers be so devout men, that the passe not muche, if there
were no masse sayde in the churche, tyll our ladye had a new sonne.
They carry the tithes away, the poore people unfed, the multitude
untaughte, and the churches unserved . . . there be not in half a shyre
scarce two hable men to shewe their faces in the pulpit. And I praye you
howe can heresies by these good meanes be rooted out, how can
sedition be ceased and extinguished amongst the people? They having
no better pastours and teachers then thei have. Which thing God
graunte be looked upon and amended shortly.[81]

Pole was determined to amend it, and his relentless insistence that the
plunder of the church was a sacrilege that must be reversed bore fruit
in Mary and Philip's agreements to return the crown's share of the loot
of reformation. Mary duly surrendered to Pole the crown's rights to
First Fruits and Tenths, Pole in return agreeing to take on the obligation
to pay monastic and chantry pensions as a first charge on the recovered
revenue. A meticulous and exhaustive Exchequer report was drawn up
for Pole so that he had an accurate account of the pensions and annuities
outstanding, and, at the Legatine Synod, he charged the bishops with
collecting the First Fruits and Tenths, and paying the pensions in their
dioceses. He also ordered episcopal visitations to survey in detail the
financial state of every benefice in their diocese, so that the recovered
income could be directed where it was most needed. Pole's intention
was that the surplus after pensions had been paid should be used to
supplement the income of the poorest incumbents, and the sum
available would of course have grown as pension-holders died off.

The gathering of the necessary information proved a complex and
time-consuming task, but Pole thought it indispensable, and twice
postponed the planned reassembly of the Legatine Synod until the
returns had been completed. In the meantime, he alleviated the worst
hardship by remitting First Fruits and Tenths altogether on livings worth
twenty marks or less, and appointed a central committee of audit for
episcopal incomes. By April 1558, armed with the findings of that
committee, he was in a position to take more positive action. He
dispensed with half of all First Fruits and Tenths due, on top of the
remissions for poor livings made earlier, and he ordered all dioceses with
a surplus after the payment of pensions to assist those dioceses with a
deficit. He himself specified both the destination and the amounts of the

levies to be paid: Canterbury, Coventry, Gloucester, Lincoln, London, Oxford, Rochester, Winchester and Worcester were beneficiaries of this arrangement; Salisbury, Norwich, Exeter, Peterborough, Hereford, Chichester and St David's, losers.[82]

Pole's plans for the centralisation and redistribution of diocesan revenues in order to augment impoverished livings and thereby to raise clerical standards were imaginative, practical and drastic. The redistribution of revenues, and his pressure on the bishops to provide him with the information on which he based it, was almost certainly the reason for the series of complaints from an anonymous bishop to Rome reported by Mary's ambassador there in December 1557: clearly his reform measures were beginning to bite.[83] But these measures were also exactly what was required to bring some sort of order and equity into the lottery of English parochial funding, and no pastoral measures so ambitious or so practical would be attempted again until the eighteenth century, perhaps not until the establishment of the Church Commissioners in the nineteenth century.

Pole's drive to recover from crown and eventually aristocracy the alienated revenues of the church, therefore, take us to the heart of his plans for a renewed English catholicism, his vision of counter-reformation. Pole's practical programme has often been described, sometimes commented on, rarely, I think, fully understood. But his underlying vision of the church is even less familiar, and the extent to which the Marian restoration was shaped by Pole's distinctive interpretation of the causes and the course of the English reformation has hardly been grasped at all. So it is to that distinctive vision, to Pole's ideas and their impact in England, that we turn in chapter two.

CHAPTER 2

Cardinal Pole

Reginald Pole is the invisible man of the Marian restoration. First as legate, *a latere* representing three successive popes, and then as archbishop of Canterbury, when his legatine authority was withdrawn by his old enemy Giampietro Caraffa, Pope Paul IV, he presided for four years over the restoration of catholicism in England. Yet the nature and extent of his role in shaping the religious history of those four years is still elusive. The cardinal legate remains for most historians of the reign a shadowy and non-integrated figure, eclipsed in practical leadership by Gardiner, or Bonner or the Spaniards, even by Mary herself. It is hardly an exaggeration to say that the established narratives of the reign would not look very different if Pole were to be edited out of them altogether.

This invisibility is not new. Despite his obvious personal prominence on both the domestic and the European counter-reformation scenes, many of his contemporaries did not know what to make of him. An unstoppable word-spinner on paper, and a charming and eloquent conversationalist among friends, he could appear forbiddingly austere, taciturn, even secretive, in public. Given his deep involvement in Italian catholic reforming circles, and his adherence to a radically Pauline understanding of grace, which his enemies, including and especially Caraffa, persisted in interpreting as crypto-Lutheran, it has been suggested that there was an element of self-fashioning and self-preservation in this taciturnity.[1] It confused observers, as on this reading it was perhaps meant to, and it has gone on doing so. However that may be, there is no doubt that he has been consistently underestimated.

The Spanish Ambassador in London, Count Feria, thought that Pole was sleepwalking through his task of restoring catholicism to England. He was a 'dead man', whose listlessness was stirred to ardour only by news from Italy, and who was radically deficient in the zeal necessary for the reconversion of England.'The Cardinal', Feria wrote,'is a good man, but very lukewarm: and I do not believe the lukewarm go to Paradise, even if they are called moderates.'[2] From a different perspective, another contemporary, the martyrologist John Foxe, also thought Pole half-hearted and ineffectual.Though a papist, wrote Foxe, he was 'none of the bloudy and cruel sort of papiste', but steered away from punitive action against protestants.[3] Hence, in contrast to his polemic against the supposedly vengeful savagery of Gardiner and Bonner, Foxe largely absolved Pole from responsibility for the most notorious aspect of the regime, the campaign of burnings. That has been an influential exculpation, which has softened historical judgement about Pole ever since, but it carried of course the clear implication that the Cardinal was not *in charge* of one of the most controversial but consistent of the regime's policies.

The immediate occasion of Feria's outpouring against Pole was the Cardinal's apparent stonewalling of St Ignatius's offer of Jesuit assistance in the reconversion of England.[4] Pole's alleged refusal of Jesuit help has been seen by historians as evidence of his aversion to the more adventurous aspects of the counter-reformation, a fatal lack of imagination that would have doomed the Marian restoration even if death had not brought it to an abrupt end.This is the perspective that informed Rex Pogson's influential study of Pole's legatine mission, which was suffused by an insistence on Pole's supposed lack of imagination. The Cardinal was a 'negative personality', 'unfit for the solution of English problems or the cooperation of English colleagues'.[5] He 'possessed valuable gifts for leadership of a Church in peaceful times', but 'nothing more': he recoiled from the extraordinary measures which the reign of Mary demanded. He 'expected a quiet return to harmony' when what he was faced with was 'a fight to the death'. Above all, Pogson insisted, the Cardinal distrusted preaching:'Right to the end of the mission he took the line that preaching was useless for the time being, for people were corrupted by the schism and so listened with avarice in their hearts and were untouched by God's Word.' In this, Pole could not be excused simply as a man of his times. Others saw what had to be done, even if he did not, and so he 'differed crucially' from advisers as various as St Ignatius, Queen Mary, King Philip and Pope Julius III, on the 'urgency to be attached to the organisation of vigorous widespread preaching'.[6]

These suggestions are representative of a perspective on Pole that, over the years, has hardened into an orthodoxy. So, according to the standard history of the reign, Pole and his colleagues 'were not slack or inept, but they were committed to a long-term policy which ignored certain important features of the immediate situation', above all 'the desperate need for spiritual leadership of a high calibre'. Pole 'simply did not want men with the fire of the counter-reformation in their bellies'. The Cardinal was thus 'unenthusiastic about preaching', 'seldom preached himself' and, when he did, 'his main theme was exhortation to gratitude and obedience'.[7] Even Christopher Haigh, whose *English Reformations* made a robust case for the broad effectiveness of Pole's efforts, nevertheless conceded that 'Pole regarded energetic evangelism as unnecessary and inappropriate'.[8] This supposed lack of imagination and dynamism is generally attributed to Pole's disillusionment with the outcome of the catholic reform movement in Italy, the defeat at Trent of the faith-centred soteriology current in Pole's Italian circle and the consequent cloud of suspicion under which he and his friends laboured. On this account, Pole distrusted 'preaching campaigns' because, in Diarmaid MacCulloch's words, he associated them 'with brilliant former associates like Peter Martyr or Bernard Ochino, who had betrayed the Church by turning Protestant'.[9]

Let us pause for a moment to examine the linchpin of all this theorising, Pole's alleged refusal of St Ignatius's offer of help in the reconversion of England. There are basically just two observations to make about this: St Ignatius did not say what people think he said, and Pole's lack of interest in what St Ignatius had to offer almost certainly sprang not from timidity about the counter-reformation, but from an imaginative counter-reformation project of his own, with which St Ignatius's offer would have interfered. For the fact is that Pole seems to have been hatching plans for an English seminary in Rome, which would have made Ignatius's help redundant, perhaps even an embarrassment, at any rate in the short term. Discussion of Pole's 'snub' to the Jesuit offer of help is often unhelpfully vague about just what it was Ignatius suggested.[10] Though the saint seems to have seen in the reconciliation of England to the papacy the potential for a new mission to Northern Europe, there were hardly any English-speaking Jesuits in the mid-1550s.

The immediate help that Ignatius offered Pole was necessarily therefore rather limited: not a troop of Jesuit preachers but, quite specifically, an invitation for Pole to send two or three hand-picked young men to study either in the *Germanicum* in Rome, or else in the *Collegio Romano,* both, of course, Jesuit run. Once imbued there with a proper Roman spirit, they could return and assist in the reconversion of their native land.[11] But a memorial addressed to Pope Gregory XIII in the early 1570s, almost certainly from one of Pole's closest collaborators, Nicolo Ormanetto, reveals that Pole had definite ideas of his own in this direction, which were incompatible with Ignatius's offer.

Ever since Henry's break with Rome, the English pilgrim hostel in Via Monserrato had been a largely wasted resource, its revenues diverted to the support of superannuated clerical sinecurists. Pole was specially interested in the hostel, which was under his jurisdiction, both because it was the only English institution in Rome, and because it symbolised one of his favourite apologetic themes, the loyalty of the English to the papacy from Saxon times, manifested in generations of pilgrimage to Rome. Ormanetto told the pope that Pole had planned to convert the hostel into a school or seminary for elite ordinands, to be educated in *Romanitas* ('per assuefarsi alla religione et alla lingua di questa santa Citta') alongside young laymen selected from good families who had remained faithful during the schism. Such a school would revive and consolidate the ancient catholic loyalties of the English ruling classes, and would provide a pool of educated and gentlemanly priests from whom a distinguished and loyal catholic episcopate could be recruited. Characteristically, Pole, always conscious of his own Plantagenet blood, told Ormanetto that the supine acceptance of the royal supremacy by the Henrician episcopate was due in part to the low breeding of Henry's bishops. Recruited from plebeian career clergy, they were despised by the aristocracy and lacked the courage to resist the evil desires of their royal master, and stand by the papacy. An English seminary in Rome would rectify all that.[12]

Ormanetto's memorandum is a late witness, for it was written fourteen years after the end of the Marian project. But it undoubtedly reports Pole's wishes for the hostel in Via Monserrato accurately, and catches unmistakeably Pole's voice, his characteristic attitudes and even his phrasing. Given these plans for the foundation of what would in due course emerge as the Venerable English College, it seems obvious enough why the Cardinal did not accept Ignatius's offer of places for students in the German College, which was couched in much the same terms. Pole wanted an English national seminary in Rome, training elite diocesan priests, not places in an international school recruiting Jesuits, who might end up, whatever Ignatius's intentions, working in Prague or Vienna, as the first English Jesuits did in fact do. It is also clear why such a thoroughly counter-reformation institution would not in fact emerge for another generation. The shaky finances and tangled legal status of the hostel would have needed careful unravelling and a substantial injection of capital. Meanwhile, Pole's bitterest enemy was elected pope in 1555, and Caraffa's mounting paranoid hostility over the next two years meant that complex projects of this kind would have to wait not only for the restoration of normality in England but for the pope's death, an event providence saw fit to delay until it was too late. But it was Pope Paul IV, not lack of either imagination or counter-reformation zeal, who prevented Pole from creating an English seminary in Rome.

I want to suggest, therefore, that the current negative historical consensus about Pole, his objectives and his actual achievement, is profoundly mistaken. From the moment of his arrival in England, indeed even before his arrival, Pole, though by no means the only activator, was the single most influential figure in the Marian restoration: put briefly, he was in charge. He had long brooded on the return of England to the unity of the church, and told one correspondent that, in refusing the papacy, he had been moved in part by a sense that God might intend to restore his beloved country to the household of holy mother church through him: 'Quid si Dominus meus velit dilectum meum introduci in domum genitricis suae per me'.[13] In matters of religion, no sustained course of action, not even the burnings, was pursued without his consent and approval. His influence and effectiveness are evident in the practical programme adopted by the Marian regime, in the terms in which that programme was justified, and in the choice of the personnel who carried the programme out.[14]

The gulf that historians have discerned between the young and eager Italian reformer and the allegedly weary, disillusioned and passive English legate, therefore, is an optical illusion. Pole's profoundly Trinitarian piety, with its strong emphases not only on the centrality of Christ but also on the universal agency of the Holy Spirit in the church, prevented him from ever identifying *reformatio* with mere human effort and activism, as the extraordinary tranquility of his response to news of the suspension of the Council of Trent in 1552 revealed.[15] But he had not, in fact, been frightened into inactivity by the rejection of his understanding of justification at Trent. By 1553, he had long since reconciled himself to the Council's teaching on justification, but there is no radical discontinuity between the ideals and methods of the Italian and the English Pole. He was a remarkably consistent, even *persistent* thinker. To read through Pole's letters, sermons and speeches during the Marian restoration, indeed, is to be struck by the almost intimidating consistency, passion and, despite the distractions of his entanglements in Marian policy and European diplomacy, singleness of religious focus to be found there.

In response to the executions of John Fisher and Thomas More, Pole had formulated in the mid-1530s a strikingly original analysis of the English reformation, spelled out in his *Pro Ecclesiasticae Unitatis Defensione* (normally referred to as *De Unitate*), the ferocious and self-consciously prophetic open letter to Henry VIII, written in 1536 and published in 1539.[16] That unblinking analysis of the motives for and consequences of Henry's schism, and the high ecclesiology and exalted understanding of the papacy that Pole evolved as he wrote it, informed his thinking to the end of his life.[17] Pole was at work on a new edition of the *De Unitate* in the very year that the call came to return to England and undo Henry's schism.[18] Updated to take account of the apparently miraculous character of Mary's accession and her early months of rule, the analysis he had set down there provided the theoretical underpinning of all his actions and utterances as legate and archbishop. It also provided the ideological basis for crucial aspects of the Marian regime's powerful official polemic. Reworked and extended by Elizabethan catholic writers who included some of his close collaborators, notably by his right hand man in Marian Canterbury, Nicholas Harpsfield, it would go on shaping both English and European counter-reformation thinking into the seventeenth century and beyond.

The Marian restoration, therefore, did not lack 'spiritual leadership of a high calibre': in Pole himself it possessed one of the formative figures of the European counter-reformation. But the counter-reformation was never a single energy or type of activity. Generalised head-shaking over the allegedly pedestrian character of the actual reforms implemented by Pole, and his alleged failures of imagination, have blinded historians to the fact that the central thrust of catholic reform after Trent consisted *precisely* in apparently pedestrian institutional reformation. In particular, these centred on efforts for the reform, training and adequate funding of the parish clergy, coupled with the nurturing of the laity in a regular sacramental piety, and therefore corresponded precisely to Pole's plans for England. In what follows, I want to focus on Pole's distinctive intellectual leadership of the Marian enterprise, and to suggest an originality, depth and imaginative power to his thought that has been drastically underestimated, with a consequent distortion of our understanding of the driving forces of the regime. I have space to focus on only two issues: the nature and extent of Pole's distinctive *intellectual* leadership of the Marian restoration; and the myth of his hostility to preaching, and hence to the more dynamic and charismatic aspects of catholic reform.

Any assessment of Pole's intellectual legacy must begin with the only book by him published in his lifetime, *De Unitate*. It was triggered by two contrasting stimuli – a demand from Thomas Cromwell that Pole satisfy the king who paid his pension by writing a treatise on the Supremacy, and his horror at news of the executions of Thomas More and John Fisher. *De Unitate* is, among other things, a powerful theological defence of papal primacy in the church, the heart of which is a nuanced exegesis of three Gospel passages in which Christ sets out Peter's distinctive vocation.[19] The most sustained and the most ardently papalist defence of papal authority by any English writer of the sixteenth century, the book also addresses unflinchingly Henry's personal sin in abandoning the unity of the church and, in the Royal Supremacy, usurping the place of Peter's successor. In this, Pole insisted, Henry was driven both by the contemptible obsession of an ageing man with 'the love of a harlot', Anne Boleyn, and by avarice for the goods of the church.[20] The inevitable consequence was progressive moral degeneration, for the divorce from Catherine was simultaneously a divorce from the bride of Christ, the church, and hence from all grace and virtue.

The King, and because of the King the whole country, had been cut off from God, as happened to all who separated themselves from the communion of the church: 'heaven is closed to you . . . Through these years since you lapsed into this impiety, no heavenly shower [of grace] has poured into your soul'.[21] Henry had thus become a scourge to his own people: usurping the highest office in the world, that of Christ's vicar, he had overturned all order, despoiling his subjects not only spiritually but materially, scorning the nobility, plundering the clergy, bringing the very succession into question by disinheriting his daughter Mary and adopting a 'Turkish domination' by placing himself above the ancient laws of England.[22]

There was a strong providentialist element to Pole's argument. He was not greatly interested in legal or constitutional theories of papal sovereignty, and focused instead on the providential role of the papacy in England's history. From the beginning, he argued, God had shown special favour to England, always through the papacy. England had first received Christianity from Pope Eleutherius, who sent missionaries at the request of the second-century British King Lucius.[23] When Britain had been overrun by Saxon paganism, the faith was restored by Pope Gregory the Great. Ever since, the English people had been ardently attached to the popes, their fathers in the faith, and they had prospered in proportion to their filial devotedness. But even now, when England under her apostate king had repudiated her spiritual father, God remembered his special love for England. He had raised up to himself witnesses to the unity of the church and the authority of the pope, martyrs whose blood both accused and pleaded for the nation that had fallen away from Christ and his vicar. The blood of the Henrician martyrs, above all the blood of Thomas More and John Fisher, was God's special grace to England, and to London. It was the privilege of martyrdom, granted to no other country afflicted by religious division. These two men, the paragons of their age, were special legates from God to England, their credential letters written in blood: 'They have accomplished their embassy; they have reported; they have brought back the most certain opinion of Christ.' Indeed, if there had been any theological doubt about the centrality of papal authority to the unity of the church, as Henry's stooge theologians pretended, the deaths of More and Fisher had removed it. God 'has sent us books against your deceitful wisdom . . . we have these writings from the finger of God, the very holy martyrs of God . . . a certain book written not with ink but with blood'.[24]

We need to note these theological and historical convictions – the indispensability of communion with the pope for membership of the church and access to grace, the providential role of the papacy in English history, the culpability of Henry VIII in precipitating the schism and all the ills that flowed from it, and the unique witness of More and Fisher as interpreters of God's will and martyrs for the unity of the church. They constituted a fundamental rejection of the whole Henrician settlement, whose apologists of course maintained that More and Fisher were traitors who had died for a superstition. For Pole, they would remain not merely the touchstones of true religion but, during his legation, the determinants of policy.[25] As a result, Pole's distinctive, and even idiosyncratic thinking about these matters was to have a profound effect on the shape of the Marian settlement. I have room here to tease out only one aspect of this influence, but it is a crucial one: his role in determining the regime's official attitude to Henry VIII.

The natural instinct of the Marian regime, to begin with at any rate, was almost certainly to emphasise continuity with the reign of 'good King Harry', in order to facilitate the dismantling of the Edwardine reformation. For the conservative majority, the worst aspect of Edward's reign had been the assault on the Mass and the stripping away of an immemorial sacramental and ceremonial order. That order had been essentially intact at Henry's death, and its deconstruction under a child king was easily presented as the work of a self-serving faction, intent on plundering the churches. So the western rebels in 1549 had called for a moratorium on religious change and the retention of all things as they had been in King Henry's time. This reading of the reformation had been enormously strengthened by Northumberland's scaffold speech, in which he acknowledged that his own zeal for reform had been a sham, motivated by ambition and greed. The fault line between the good old days of true religion and those of chaos and destruction, therefore, might very naturally and effectively have been drawn by Mary's councillors with the accession of her brother. Mary herself implied as much in the first days of August 1553, when she informed the Council of her decision to have a requiem Mass celebrated for Edward, claiming that, in doing so, she was 'bound to the late King Henry's will' and that 'Religion . . . had been changed in England since her father's death and during her brother's minority, because the late Protector would have it so.'[26] The Imperial ambassador was convinced that this was as far as Mary could safely go, restoring the Mass and other ceremonies 'to the condition they were in at the time of the late King Henry's death', but doing nothing as yet to restore papal obedience.[27]

To begin with, this was Pole's anxious perception as well. It was clear that Mary would restore catholicism, but he feared that reasons of state might lead her to settle, at least in the short term, for a Henrician version of catholicism without the pope. However, reasons of state, he believed, had been the poison that murdered catholic England. As Pole told Vicenzo Parpaglia, he had high hopes of Mary because of her sufferings for the faith under Edward, and because the whole reason for the schism had been to divorce Katherine of Aragon and bastardise her daughter. And yet, Mary had consented to the schism, however reluctantly, and she had not protested publicly at the execution of More and Fisher. Could she therefore be relied on to grasp that obedience to the pope must be the foundation stone of any restoration of religion?[28]

On 13 August 1553, he wrote to Mary herself to ensure that she did. Her accession was the miraculous work of God, he told her. She had come to her throne unaided by any human agency, not even that of the pope or the Emperor Charles V, so that she might learn to rely on the God whose providence rendered mere human prudence and calculation powerless. The root cause of all the evils endured by Mary herself, and by England, was the rejection of papal obedience. The ancient enemy of mankind, the devil, had persuaded her father into schism by 'impure counsel', and from that wicked seed a poisoned fruit had sprung, which had corrupted the whole kingdom and obliterated all trace of true religion and even common justice. God had lovingly schooled her in adversity, planting the seed of grace in her heart, which must now bring forth quite different fruit, rooted in obedience to the Holy See. As legate, Pole's task would be to guide her into the true meaning and necessity of that obedience. Henry had abandoned it because the pope, defending Mary's succession, would not accede to his base desires. Despite all the years that had passed since then, during which the evil of schism had eaten deep into the souls of the people, there could be no better time than now, when God had displayed his mighty providence on Mary's behalf, for Pole's legation from Christ's vicar. It was a call to obedience on which depended her own happiness and consolation, and that of the whole nation. He awaited her response.[29]

Pole never receded from this passionate if politically naive conviction that the restoration of papal obedience should be the first step in the Marian reconstruction of religion. Over the next year, he would bombard not only Mary but also the Emperor with letters and embassies hammering relentlessly away at that point. To delay a measure essential to the salvation of so many souls, and for which the best and most learned men of the kingdom had shed their blood, was a mortal sin that would cause irreparable damage.[30] The blood of More and Fisher declared more

clearly than any book her only course of action.[31] There must be no
dissimulation: for Mary to acquiesce in the continuation of the schism,
even temporarily, was to endorse it. Northumberland had been a catholic
in his heart, but, on his own admission, he had concealed what was in his
mind 'to mayntayn his state and for ambition': Mary would be no better
if she did not openly and immediately declare her obedience to the
pope.[32] The lessons of history were unmistakeable: every people that had
fallen away from papal obedience had been plunged into ruin. The
Byzantine Empire had repudiated the pope, and had immediately
succumbed to Turkish rule: Hungary, Bohemia, Germany, all were
steeped in misery for the same cause.[33] When Mary's first Parliament
recognised the validity of Henry's marriage to Katherine of Aragon and
revoked the Edwardine religious legislation without restoring
communion with the papacy, Pole brushed aside Mary's suggestion that
he should look on the bright side and see this as '*auspitium et initium
laudabile, et quasi viaticum ad obedientiam ecclesiae recognoscendum*' [an
auspicious and praiseworthy beginning, and a step on the way towards
recognising the obedience of the church].[34] He urged Mary to repair
the omission unilaterally by proclamation: fortunately for the stability of
her regime, she ignored his advice.

Pole's disgust with all this temporising was heightened by outrage at
the terms in which Mary had informed him of the legislation of her first
Parliament. Religion, she wrote, had been restored to the state in which
it had been at the time of the death of King Henry, '*piisimae recordationis,
patris nostri*' [our father, of most blessed memory].[35] How could she speak
in this way, he asked her, about a king 'knowen of all men the onely
author of the hole schisme'? To speak well of Henry, however
conventionally, would be to appear to condone his acts. Pole knew, he
told her, that she did not in fact approve of Henry's 'impietie in this act
of schisme', and had only written unguardedly out of 'pietie naturall' for
a parent. In an almost untranslatable pun, he told her, however, that if
she had Henry for a father, she could have neither '*partem aut patrem*'
[neither part nor parent] in Heaven. Had she not read Christ's own
precept that those who did not hate father and mother for the sake of
the Gospel were not worthy of eternal life?

> Whiche if it be to be understande of those fathers that be infidels, and
> lett not their children to come to the fayth, muche more is it to be
> understand of those that being incorporate within the body of the

churche, wherein is taught the trew fayth, doeth pluck them out thereof.

If Henry was 'of blessed memory', then More and Fisher had died in vain. Mary's mother was indeed of blessed memory, but her father 'had no such grace'. On her fidelity to Christ, therefore, Mary must never again use such language about Henry, whether in public or in private, 'so that yff yow wyll not speak yll of him, let hym alone, speake no good off him'.[36] Mary did not follow Pole's advice about the pace of the reintroduction of papal obedience. But she took to heart his extraordinarily blunt condemnation of her father, and the official acts of her reign were framed accordingly. Her Injunctions for Religion, issued on 4 March 1554, necessarily alluded several times to the restoration of the religious *status quo* as it had been 'in the latter time of King Henry VIII', but with a notable absence of even the most conventionally laudatory adjective that might appear to honour Henry's memory.[37]

In urging the necessity of reunion with Rome on Mary, Pole was in fact pushing at an open door. In her very first audience with him, the Queen had told Simon Renard, the Imperial ambassador, that she intended to restore religion 'even to the Pope's authority'.[38] Her only hesitations were about timing and political practicalities. Matters were rather different among her councillors. Nicholas Ridley recounted a supper-table debate about the sacrament of the altar during his imprisonment in the Tower of London, in the course of which the dean of St Paul's, John Feckenham, had declared that 'forty yeares agoe . . . all were of one opinion' about the Mass. When Ridley replied that this proved nothing, since 'forty yeares agoe all held that the Bishop of Rome was supreme head of the vniversall Church', Feckenham, himself a papalist, replied, 'What then?' But Sir John Bourne, Mary's Secretary of State, cut in dismissively, 'Tush, it was not counted an article of our fayth.'[39]

How long and how far Mary's chief councillor, Bishop Stephen Gardiner, shared this lay indifference to papal authority is not clear. Though he was the author of the Henrician regime's standard apology against papal obedience, a fact which was to prove an acute embarrassment to him in Mary's reign,[40] he had probably hoped during Henry's last years for some sort of rapprochement with the papacy. Yet, during his imprisonment under Edward, he had repeatedly appealed to the Henrician settlement as a bulwark against further change – in particular, to the mature statement of Henrician theology, the *King's Book* (which he had helped draft), with its strong denunciations of papal usurpation, as 'a true, resolute doctrine, passed by mature delyberacion, confyrmed by acceptacion and use'.[41] But there was probably an element of *argumentum ad hominem* about this praise for the *King's Book* and Henry's other measures. Gardiner's imprisonment had given him ample time to reflect on the consequences of the schism. He had seen enough of the escalating radicalism of the reformation under Cranmer and his colleagues to dispel any lingering illusions he might have had about the long-term ability of the Henrician settlement to resist the advance of a more thoroughgoing and consistent protestantism. According to Thomas Mountayne, during his interrogation in October 1553 Gardiner had demanded, 'Tel me, I praye the, what good workes was ther done, other yn kynge Harry's days, or yn kyng Edward's dayes?', which does not suggest any very high estimation of the state of religion under the old king.[42]

Probably, therefore, Gardiner himself would have concluded independently that a return to papal obedience was desirable. But there is no doubt that he was slow to advocate it openly, and that he came to this conclusion after the Queen had done so. He himself insisted that, in this matter, 'the Queen went before him, and it was her own motion'.[43] As late as mid-March 1554, he was telling the Imperial ambassador that there could be no move towards reunion with Rome until the question of ecclesiastical property had been settled by Parliament.[44] By 12 April, however, he had changed his tune, and was causing unease in the Council by pressing urgently for legislation 'concerning religion and the Pope's authority'. During a trial in the Star Chamber the same month, he held forth on the providential character of the Queen's accession:

> how myraculously almighty God had brought the Queenes Maiesty to the Crowne, the whole Realme in a maner being against her, & that he had brought this to passe for this singular intent and purpose, that this Realme being ouerwhelmed with heresies, shee might reduce againe the same vnto the true Catholicke faith.[45]

Though Gardiner did not explicitly mention the pope on that occasion, there is no mistaking the echo of Pole's voice in this utterance. And, in fact, it appears that Gardiner was actually paraphrasing part of a letter that he had received just days before from the Cardinal. On 22 March, Pole had sent Gardiner a characteristically uncompromising broadside, reminding him of his schismatic past, under the guise of congratulating him on his penitence for having followed Henry into schism, 'with marks of true repentance for the frailty which did lead you to that'. Gardiner should be doubly grateful, Pole told him, that, having succumbed to fear and ambition, and so fallen into schism, he had not fallen even further and become a heretic, as schismatics almost always did. His preservation to defend the truth in a time of heresy was a mark of God's special favour to him and to England. An even greater one, Pole reminded him, was the fortitude of those who had never fallen, but had shed their blood rather than abandon the unity of the church. There was a sting in this reminder, for Pole must have known that Gardiner had composed the Henrician regime's official defence of the execution of Fisher.[46] The infinite mercy of God, he concluded, had given a further pledge of the return of England to papal obedience in the person 'of that good saint the Queen, fair as the moon, whom God hath not suffered to be tainted with any spot, either of schism or heresy' so that, through her, the truth might be 'diffused and communicated' to the whole kingdom.[47] To concentrate Gardiner's mind on the way forward, Pole sent him a copy of his unpublished treatise on the papal office, *De Summo Pontifice*, begun during the conclave of 1550 in which he himself had come within a single vote of being pope.[48]

It can hardly be a coincidence that Gardiner began to agitate for a speedy return to papal obedience within days of the receipt of this letter, or that his words should so closely echo those of Pole's paragraph on the Queen. His conversion did not entirely cloud his political judgement, however, and he angered Pole by advising a prudent reserve in broaching the question of papal authority in any approach that he might make to Parliament. Papal authority was an issue on which Pole did not pull punches.[49] Pole had already drafted an immense and unflinching address to Parliament, rubbing in the nation's complicity in Henry's sin, rebuking the delay in reunion with Rome 'for more suretye to kepe your spoyle', insisting on the need for trust in him and in the Holy See over the question of church lands, and emphasising that 'The retourne must be free and liberall, if yow will have God liberall with yow'. Pole sent this 'discorso' to England with Thomas Goldwell in December 1553, but, although it has been suggested that rumours of its contents may have heightened the anxieties of holders of monastic lands and so actually delayed reunion with Rome, the letter itself appears never to have been used: Gardiner was certainly unaware of its existence in March 1554.[50]

But both Queen and Chancellor had taken aboard Pole's insistence on Henry's responsibility for the evils of the schism, and their shared aversion to any celebration of Henry's memory manifested itself in the course of Philip and Mary's marriage procession through London on 18 August 1554. Richard Grafton, the evangelical printer whose presses had been closed down at Mary's accession, had devised and painted the pageants that decorated the Conduit in Gracechurch Street. One of these depicted Henry VIII, in armour, handing a bible, labelled '*Verbum Dei*', to Edward VI – a subject deliberately evoking the title pages of Coverdale's Bible and the Great Bible, both of which Grafton had helped publish, and an unmistakeable gesture of defiance towards the new order. Enraged, Gardiner summoned Grafton, denouncing him as a traitor and a villain, 'saying to hym that he should rather have put the book into the Queenes hand . . . for that she had reformed the church and religion, with other things according to the pure and sincere word of God in deede'. When Grafton pleaded innocence and protested that Gardiner need only have sent him a command to change the pageant, Gardiner told him that 'it was the Queenes will and commaundement that he should send for him'. Henry's bible in the pageant was duly painted out, and replaced with a pair of gloves. Grafton's provocative gesture would probably have irked the regime anyway, as it was meant to do, but the Queen's personal involvement and the vehemence of Gardiner's reaction almost certainly reflect Pole's consciousness-raising insistence on the need to establish a sharp boundary between Mary's regime and that of her father.[51]

Pole himself got his first public opportunity to spell out in person his own reading of the English reformation in his remarkable speech to Parliament on 28 November 1554, when he was at last able to absolve the members of both houses, and to reconcile England to the Holy See. The address, only sketchily used by historians, was one of the major programmatic utterances of the reign, gathering up many of the themes that Pole had explored in *De Unitate*, now updated in the light of the intervening twenty years of reformation.[52] Thanking Parliament for reversing his attainder and so ending his exile, Pole wove what he had to say around the fact that he had come to put an end to the far worse state of exile in which England had languished for two decades, 'you being cutt of from the Churche through your owne wilfull defection and schismaticall revolting from the unitie of the same'. He painted an idealised picture of the peace and tranquillity of the country in Henry's early years, the king himself 'beatified and adorned . . . with all giftes of nature bodily, [and] . . . excellent virtues of the mynde', and the people living under him 'in Libertie and fredome of conscience, and perfecte suertie of bodie and goodes, and in most assured expectation of indifferente iustice'. But Henry's breach with Rome had ended all that. Carnal council and avarice, starting with the robbery of the church, had plunged England into nightmare:

> For . . . what man in these last yeres might safely use his conscience or bee free to live as his herte would serve him upright towardes God, when all religion was overturned and changed from the antient institution of the Church, all holy rites and observances neglected and held for superstition and abomination.

Civic justice too, had foundered utterly: 'Neither was any man so sure of his goodes and possessions, but he stood continually in abjecte daunger and hazard of his life too', and 'the beste sorte, and the moste innocente' had most to fear.[53] All this, Pole claimed, was a repudiation of England's special place in history, for under King Lucius in the second century England had been the first kingdom 'by the public consent of king and people to accept the faith'. Ever since, England had been cherished by the popes, and in return had given 'singular obedience . . . unto their father in faith the Pope of Rome'.[54] They had exported this obedience: it was English missionaries who had brought the Christian faith and fidelity to the Holy See to the other nations of northern Europe. But Henry's 'fleshly wille full of a carnal concupiscence' had forced his people into an utterly un-English schism, from which all the evils of the last generation had flowed. Special grace had been mocked by a special fall. As England had first received the Gospel with the universal consent of king and people under Lucius, now under Henry the consent of the people in Parliament had implicated all in guilt. And yet,

> I will and maie truly excuse you and saie, that this deliberacion came first of one alone, and afterward of a few, which by renouncing of that obedience thought to have the waie more open and free, yea and also more safe for the following and accomplishing of their carnall appetites, and for none other purpose.

The moral earthquake and darkness that had descended on the realm when its rulers, with the people's consent, had crucified papal authority was the same darkness that had descended on all other nations that had crucified Christ again in his vicar – the Christian peoples of Greece and Asia, who had also abandoned papal obedience, now groaned under Turkish tyranny.[55] But England had been spared: though he had scourged the nation with these plagues, God in his miraculous providence had preserved that 'desolate Ladie' Mary, in purity and innocence, to restore her people. At her intercession, Pole himself had come as legate with power to cast their sins into the sea, and so restore them to life. This tender and fatherly mercy of God towards the nation that had rebelled so ungratefully against him would be intelligible only to those 'well instructed in the mercie of God showed in the great mediator his sonne Jesus Christe our Lorde'. The deaths of the Henrician martyrs had been a sign of God's special favour, their bodies a barrier to prevent their countrymen abandoning the church entirely. As the blood of Christ's death had turned to life for mankind, 'so the bloud of those his servauntes whom ye giltlesse putte to death, hath been a meane to bring you to this mercie . . . that ye might bee such as thei were in faith and constancie, and in participation of Goddes grace'.

Not all the preaching of the early English missionaries, nor all the books ever written 'have geven so muche light of truth and of true catholike doctrine, as God hath wrytten to you and to all the worlde in their blood'.[56] This was a unique 'honour, pre-eminence and dignitie', for, in an age in which 'the Catholike feith having been and yet still being persecuted in diverse countreyes and naciouns, yet have wee not before heard of any that in these late yeres have dyed for the unitee of the Churche, whiche is the maintenaunce of the true feith and religion'. So now, in this hour of grace, the English were called on to be a beacon to the rest of reformation Europe. By acknowledging wholeheartedly God's infinite mercy in their return to the church, they would show themselves 'a similitude of suche persones as in the primitive church were called to this grace, in so great aboundance of the gifte of Goddes spirite, that your notable example in this behalfe might bee, as it were, a second foundacion of his moste glorious catholike Churche, to other nations'.[57]

Behind Pole's address to Parliament lay twenty years of reflection on the roots of schism, on the providential action of God in history and on the spiritual and pastoral (as opposed to the merely juridical) role of the papacy, now brought to bear on what he saw as England's moment of truth. In summoning England back to unity, he deliberately set her reconciliation in the wider context of a divided Christendom, to which this act of restoration, the first of its kind in Europe, would be a sign of hope. No one else in Marian England had reflected so deeply on such matters and none of his collaborators, with the possible exception of Nicholas Harpsfield, shared this breadth or depth of vision. Nevertheless, with one notable exception – his insistence on the providential role of More and Fisher, to which the regime at large proved resistant until his own circle took the matter in hand – the themes of Pole's St Andrew's day speech to Parliament passed almost at once into the mainstream of Marian polemic. It is not hard to see why. The conservative theological case in Edwardine England had been shackled to the Henrician settlement, an attempt to formulate a catholicism without the pope, whose only anchor was the formidable personality of the old king. Men such as Gardiner, Tunstall and Bonner had invested all their moral credibility in the defence of a system that had been simply pushed aside by the more thoroughgoing and ruthless protestantism of Edward's reign. Pole's long-pondered analysis of the English reformation, indeed of the whole sweep of English religious history, provided a rationale for theological renewal that was stark, clear and uncompromising, and that endorsed the conservative instincts of the majority of the population, while shaking itself free of the intellectual and moral compromises of Henry's church.

The appeal of this synthesis was immediate. Pole's distinctive take on the papal history of England, from Pope Eleutherius's mission to King Lucius, through Gregory the Great and the *Romanitas* of the Saxon kings, provided the framework for George Marshall's metrical potted history of catholic England and its recovery from schism, published by the Queen's printer less than three weeks after Pole's address, in December 1554, complete with the marginal note 'Poli', leaving no doubt as to Marshall's source.[58]

> Lyke to this scysme in this Realme neuer was
> With so great destruction to sone now alas
> Fiftene hundred yeares past we in writing find
> Synce Lucy was Kyng of Englande by kynde
> Whyche sent to the Pope called Eleutherius

That he woulde send or els sone come
This Realme to conuerte to holy Christendome
Which sent Damian with his fellow Forganus
Then was this Realme to Christ conuerted
Which we agayne hath falsely subuerted.

Marshall's use of Pole (presumably the *De Unitate*) was perhaps marginal in more ways than one, but the Cardinal's synthesis was deployed to much greater effect by Archdeacon John Harpsfield, one of the regime's star theologians and preachers. Harpsfield was the author of the crucial sermons on the primacy in the book of *Homilies* issued by Bishop Bonner in 1555. These, along with Bonner's own *A Profitable and Necessarye Doctryne*, would serve as the regime's official body of pulpit teaching pending the completion of the *Homilies* commissioned by the Legatine Synod. Pole's influence is visible throughout the Marian *Homilies*,[59] but it is clearest in the second homily on the Supremacy, where Harpsfield simply paraphrases Pole in describing the evils that have always befallen nations who have abandoned the papacy: 'looke but on those countries, and those persons, that now be in captivitie under the great Turke'. And Harpsfield goes on, once again in terms drawn directly from Pole, to summarise the history of papal favour to England, from the time when 'from that see came the fayth into this land . . . in the daies of King Lucius', down to the calamities of the recent past when 'temporall princes dyd take upon them that office, which is spirituall', the consequences of which 'you have felt the smart thereof in dede, and to this day are not quyte of God's plage for the same'.[60] Bonner's pastoral letter in February 1555 to the people of his diocese followed Pole in tracing the 'plagues' that had flowed directly from Henry's break with Rome – 'such slaunder to the realme, such malice and disagreement among our selues, the inhabitants thereof, such treasons, tumultes, and insurrections agaynst our prince, such blasphemy and dishonour vnto God, as no mans tong or pen is able to expresse'.[61]

The extent to which these opinions permeated the thought of the Marian establishment as a whole, and not merely that of the clergy, can be gauged from the New Year's gift presented to the Queen in January 1556 by that aged court conservative Henry Parker, Lord Morley. This took the form of a manuscript treatise on the miracles of the

Sacrament.[62] Morley's work was, in fact, a celebration of Mary's own role in restoring catholicism. Once again, there is an obligatory reference to the conversion and baptism of King Lucius by Pope Eleutherius, and the whole of the first half of his treatise is devoted to an extended elaboration of Pole's providentialist analysis of the dire consequences of the abandonment of papal obedience on the churches of Africa, Greece, Bohemia and Germany, all of which, having 'forsaken the head of the Church of Rome, the popes holynes, fyll . . . to innumerable of erronyous opynyons', and succumbed to temporal as well as spiritual disaster as a consequence.[63] There was a particular piquancy about the ardently papalist tone of Morley's gift. In the late 1530s, he had sought to ingratiate himself with Henry VIII and to extricate himself from association with Pole's relatives and the lethal political fall-out from the so-called Exeter conspiracy, by composing an anti-papal treatise against 'the detestable ydolatrye of this wicked monster of Rome'. Now, under the Cardinal's guidance, loyalty to 'the holy father, Pope of Rome' became the mark of dynastic allegiance as well as religious orthodoxy.[64]

By January 1556, therefore, Pole's voice had become the official voice of the Marian regime, both in print and in private. But his influence was also felt in less formal ways, above all in the rapid emergence from 1554 of an open polemic against Henry VIII. Until Pole's arrival, the regime's writers and preachers had targeted the enactments of Edward's reign rather than those of Henry. Gardiner's protégé, the civil lawyer Thomas Martin (who would lead the prosecution at Cranmer's trial), published a powerful attack on clerical marriage in May 1554. This was a programmatic text, designed to accompany and to justify the deprivations of married clergy that were taking place all over England that spring.

Early in his work, Martin suggested that the lechery of heretical priests was rooted in the lechery of their schismatic king, identifying Henry's desire for a divorce as the motive for the appointment of heretical bishops. Martin did not name Henry, however, instead relating a rather convoluted anecdote in which the Greek Emperor Michael Paleologus appointed a heretical bishop of Constantinople, who had then renounced communion with the pope in order to allow the Emperor to make an incestuous marriage. Martin added that 'I woulde the lyke hadde never been practised synce els where.'[65] The hint was of course both broad and transparent,[66] but its crablike obliquity reflects the nervousness of the regime in the summer of 1554 about open repudiation of the Henrician legacy. As late as September 1554, Gardiner was still confining his public denunciations to the evils of Edward's reign only.[67] After Pole's arrival, however, the gloves were off, and the Marian episcopate now routinely described the heresies and disorders of Edward's reign as the inevitable outcome of Henry's schism and spoke of Henry himself as a tyrant.

Gardiner led the way. When Rowland Taylor reproached him in January 1555 with breach of his oath to 'that blessed King Henry of famous memory', Gardiner brushed the accusation aside: 'Tush, tush, that was Herodes othe . . . I haue done well in breaking it: and (I thanke God) I am come home agayne to our mother to the Catholicke Churche of Rome.'[68] In August 1555, Roger Coo, a defiant gospeller on trial before Bishop Hopton, compared his own stand to Shadrach, Meshach and Abednego's defiance of the wicked King Nebuchadnezzar: 'Then the B. told hym, that these 22. yeares wee haue bene gouerned with such kings.'[69] When, during the examination of Thomas Haukes in the spring of 1555, William Chedsey, archdeacon of Middlesex, asked 'How say ye to the Bishop of Rome', he received the predictable reply, 'From him and all his detestable enormities, Good Lorde deliver us', upon which Chedsey retorted, 'Ma[r]ry so may wee say, from king Henry the eighth, and all his detestable enormities, goode Lorde deliver us.'[70] By the end of 1555, such sentiments had become the commonplaces of Marian polemic. During his last examination, John Philpott could denounce his judges not merely as idolaters but 'also traytors: for in your Pulpits you rayle vpon good kings as king Henry, and king Edward his sonne, which haue stand agaynst the vsurped power of the Bishop of Rome'.[71]

By the end of the reign, the full range of Pole's powerful interpretation of the English reformation would be translated, point by point, into racy polemic in Nicholas Harpsfield's juicily rancorous *Treatise on the Pretended Divorce*. There Harpsfield unsparingly portrayed Henry as Pole and his circle saw him, a ruined angel of grace and intelligence deformed by schism 'into a quite contrary monstrous shape', a Solomon transformed into an Ahab. To underline the biblical comparison, Harpsfield told how Henry's corrupted blood, dripping from his split coffin, had been licked from the floor like Ahab's by stray dogs, a token of the damnation of that lost soul, surrounded by time-serving heretical priests as Ahab had been surrounded by the priests of Baal, and leading thousands to hell in his wake.[72]

I turn now to my second issue: the myth that Pole, and therefore Pole's church, was suspicious of preaching and consequently reluctant or slow to provide it. In the first chapter, I argued that preaching was, in fact, one of the regime's most important priorities, insisted on not only by the Legatine Synod, but also and more directly in Pole's legatine visitations of the dioceses, and in the visitations carried out by his fellow bishops. As I argued then, from the very start of the reign, the regime grasped the crucial importance of set-piece controversial sermons in the major public pulpits, above all at Paul's Cross in London, and put their best efforts into staffing them. But they were also aware of the vital role of ordinary parish preaching and, confronted with the same drastic shortage of suitably qualified clergy with which the Edwardine reformers had wrestled, they sought to meet the short-term need in the same way, by the comprehensive provision of printed sermon material, and by enforcing its use.[73]

My concern here, however, is with Pole's personal attitude to preaching, and with his own record as a preacher. As I indicated at the start of this chapter, it has become an orthodoxy that the Cardinal was 'unenthusiastic about preaching', 'seldom preached himself', distrusted 'preaching campaigns' and thought that preaching in general was best left on the back burner, until the more important matter of discipline had been properly established.[74] I have shown elsewhere that these widespread views rest on a straightforward mistranslation of a crucial letter from Pole to his friend and former collaborator, Archbishop Bartolomé Carranza, in June 1558, in which Pole had discussed the provision of preaching in London and his own record as pastor and preacher. He has been taken to have said there that 'it was better to check [hinder] preaching' until 'the discipline of the church has been fully restored'.[75] In fact, Pole described to Carranza in some detail the major preaching campaign being carried on in London, and stressed his own active commitment to preaching. He complained, however, that, despite the abundance of preaching in the capital, London remained an unregenerate city in which heresy was rife. This he thought was because, in the capital in particular, preaching was more often treated as a shallow entertainment than as a call to true penitence and amendment of life, which Londoners desperately needed. In such circumstances, preaching might harden hearts rather than break them, and so might do more harm than good.

> From ample daily experience I learn how corrupt and diseased is the state of that body [the city of London], [and] I find that wherever the word most abounds, men least profit from it, when it is misused: we see this to be nowhere more so than in London. Of course I don't on that account deny the necessity of preaching the word, but I do say that the word can be more of a hindrance than a help, unless it is proceeded or at the same time accompanied by the establishment of church discipline, because carnal men turn [preaching] into an empty ear-tickling entertainment, rather than a health-giving discipline and food for the soul.[76]

But Pole emphatically did not denigrate the importance of the preaching of the word of God, without which, he insisted, there could be no reformation, '*quamquam hoc sine verbo recte fieri non potest*'. Certainly, there is no doubt that Pole himself took his own personal obligation to preach deadly seriously. Common sense is needed in assessing what that entailed. Sixteenth-century archbishops of Canterbury were not parish priests: they were great officers of state as well as church administrators, and they did not preach as a matter of course, Sunday by Sunday. But Pole's record on this score is, as Professor Thomas Mayer has pointed out, markedly better than that of his protestant successor, Matthew Parker.[77] Pole assured Carranza that he had preached '*saepius*' [often] in his diocese. He evidently had in mind short sermons in pastoral contexts such as visitations, when he perhaps preached extemporaneously or from sketchy notes: at any rate none such has survived. But texts of three major set-piece sermons, two preached in London and one in Canterbury, do survive – a sermon commemorating the reconciliation with Rome for St Andrew's day 1556, preached in his diocese;[78] another St Andrew's day sermon preached at court in 1557 in the presence of the judiciary and the Lord Mayor and aldermen of London;[79] and a sermon preached at St Mary Arches on 25 March 1556, when he received the pallium and assumed office as archbishop of Canterbury.[80]

We also have texts for three other full-scale vernacular sermons – one addressed to the clergy in charge of the campaign against heresy in

Canterbury diocese;[81] and two homilies written as sequels to the St Mary Arches pallium sermon, and intended for publication with it, rather than for preaching in person.[82] When Pole told Carranza about this proposed book of sermons in June 1558, he mentioned that he was having his text vetted by theologians prior to publication, and one set of detailed comments by an anonymous theological adviser survives among Pole's papers.[83] It all indicates the importance that the Cardinal attached to this sermon collection, designed, as he explained, 'to feede and instructe' those who 'for ignoraunce of the truthe be fallen in diverse diseases of the mynde', and for whom, 'Nott being possible to speak with so manye bye mouthe, I have putt in writing that I wold speake if I were present for their instruction.'[84]

Pole's English sermons merit a separate study of their own. Written over a two-year period from March 1556, they form a sustained set of variations on a series of key reformation themes. These include the authority of the church, the relation between scripture and tradition, the presence of Christ in the eucharist, the meaning of the peace of God and who may receive it, and, in the last of the surviving sermons intended for printing, a remarkable, and, in Paul IV's church, theologically risky exploration of the relation of human vocation and human work to the one meritorious work of God, the cross of Christ. Pole also reflects in several of the sermons on the relation between his own teaching authority as archbishop, that of his predecessor, Thomas Cranmer, and the religious meaning of the succession of archbishops of Canterbury.[85]

Of particular interest in our context, however, are Pole's remarks on the related questions of preaching and scripture reading, themes that recur throughout the sermons. He had not intended to preach at the pallium ceremony, he told the congregation of St Mary Arches on 25 March 1556, but the rector and parishioners had sent a written petition pressing him to do so. He expressed himself 'well pleased . . . that yow ask this spirituall foode of me, that am your spirituall father, in such a time as this, when such holesome fode is nott so plenty as I would wishe'. He would never decline such a request, lest it be said, in the words of the Lamentations of Jeremiah, that 'the children (*Parvuli*) begged for bread, and there was none to break it for them'.[86] But Pole was intensely conscious of his audience. By this point, he had taken the measure of London and its disputatious gospellers, and, in the demand for a sermon, he suspected more than mere readiness to hear the truth. They had to understand that there was only one right way to receive the word of God, and that was precisely as the *Parvuli* [children] of Lamentations:

> with that simplicitie off mynde . . . which is for your need, and nott as menye be wont to do now a dayes. . . . for no necessitie theye fynde but rather for curiositie to see whatt bread their newe pastours bring with them, some also to tempt their Curates, making them selfes iudges of their sayings, redye to reprove them when thei maye take any occasion thereof by any cavilation.

These were 'great abuses', which God never failed to punish, hardening their hearts so they could not benefit even from the truth, or sending the scourge of false preachers, 'the bredd of lyfe tourning to them that receive it nott worthily to theyr poison and death. . . . which be all some ponnyshment of god, lightynge apon them which do nott with symplicitie of hart desyer the foode of his worde'.[87] Nevertheless, 'trusting better of yow and enterpretateng your demaunde in best parte', he would preach. It being the feast of the Annunciation, Pole took the Virgin Mary's response to the angel's message as a paradigm for the devout hearing of God's word. The Virgin was 'troubled' by the Angel's words, and so they must not take 'godes meaning' lightly, 'but let it penetrate your hart, and move your hart, altering the same with the effect of feare at the furst hearyng'. Negligent hearing brought 'great hurt': great hurt might also come, however, 'sometyme of the contrary, for to(o) much diligence out of tyme and place and to(o) moche thynkeng thereof'. There had never been an age more preoccupied with preaching the word of God, 'nor more diligent studie putt to com to the understanding therof', never more 'professors' of the word of God. Yet there had never been more heresies and 'never more licentious disorder in the lyffes of Christen men then is at this tyme'. God forbid, Pole insisted, that 'the disiyer of the knowledge of those thenges which be written in Scripture . . . should be repressed or reproved', but God forbid also that this desire be indulged without proper restraint and direction. And, therefore,

> of those that by the ordinaunce of Christ and the Church have by theyre office authoritie and bonde to teache and preache scripture, there must be a moderation found, that nother the desyer of

knowledge of those things that be written in scripture be reproved nor utterly repressed, but rather nourished and encouraged, and yet not permitted to everyone that hath this desyer to feade hym selfe as hym lyste and his owne wytt leadeth hym,

for that 'is the most perilouse state that the wyll and wytt of men can putt ytt self unto'.[88] They must put aside the arid curiosity and opinionated views that were the mark of the age. Like the Blessed Virgin Mary, they must submit their minds and wills humbly to the voice of Christ, expressed in the words of lawful preachers, but even more in the prompting of the Spirit in their hearts and consciences.

This lett the poore man do, what so ever worke he hath, lett every man, woman and childe do of what degree or state so ever he be, for to the hole mankynde the promise is made and the grace offred, all may praye for the perfourming of goddes graciouse offer unto them, and with the mynde of a faythfull handmayde . . . everye one in his conscience where the spirit of Chryst doith continually speak and commaunde hym to do according to his vocation *donec formiter in eo Christus* [till Christ be formed in him].

Doing this, they would be surer of the grace of God 'than by any reading or heareng of outward preachours'. Both the voice of conscience and the voice of the preacher were good, 'but to come to the latter, the furst must have furst place'.[89]

Pole went on to develop these ideas further in the sermons he prepared for publication over the next two years, insisting that the desire for preaching and bible-reading that he recognised 'to be universallie in the people through the realme' was entirely laudable, 'and such as if it were nott in the people, I shulde wyshe itt were, and by all meanes ought to procure, nott fyndinge it, to styre up the same'. On the importance of preaching the doctrine of Christ, 'herein is no controversie att all, in thys both the catholike and the heretike wyll agree'. But 'of whom this doctrine should be learned . . . here nowe begynneth the great controversie and dissentions in religion'.[90] If such eagerness for the word was to bear its proper fruit, the people must hear only orthodox preachers, duly commissioned by the church, and, even more, they must pray for a deep interior conversion of heart and mind in response to the spirit of God in their consciences, without which all external preaching was barren. This applied as much to hearing or reading scripture as to sermons. To read the scripture was good, 'and I saye it wyll do yow marvellouse good taken in tyme and place'. But, to the merely curious mind, scripture remained 'a deade voice written with inke and penne in a book'. It would only become a book of life for them when read 'with that convenient preparation of mynde and humilitie it ought to be', and interpreted aright by the church: 'as you take the boke off your mothers hande so also take the interpretation of the same off your mother . . . and not of your self'. True doctrine 'must be received and not invented'.[91]

At the root of all Pole's thought about the value and place of preaching and of the Bible lay his doctrine of the church as the only house of God, the one location of grace. The truth could be heard only in the church, and, important as learning was, not all the scriptural and patristic learning in the world would avail us to salvation if we did not receive the truth in the heart of the church.[92] He returned repeatedly to a text from Deuteronomy, read in Lauds every Saturday morning: 'Ask your father, and he will show you, your elders, and they will tell you.'[93] The church provided an unbroken chain of witness, the truth handed on from father to son without interruption. The claim of the protestants to have the ancient fathers of the church on their side was false, for they could not trace the doctrines they preached back through their own fathers and grandfathers to those remote times. The chain of witness was broken. To claim to have discovered new Christian truth, not by receiving it from the church, but by reading the Bible, as the protestants did, was to attempt to invent oneself, to 'make their own hedd by reading their master and father, which is a great absurditie'.[94] The church was the ladder that the patriarch Jacob dreamed about in the book of Genesis, the house of God, the gate of Heaven, on which the angels of God ascended and descended. Step by step, from Pole himself through Archbishop Warham and Cardinal Morton and so on back through the great teaching archbishops of the Middle Ages such as Lanfranc, to Augustine of Canterbury and beyond him to Pope Gregory and so to St Peter and at last to Christ, there was an unbroken ladder of teaching, witness to the saving truth of Christ, the same truth that Pole proclaimed and the protestants denied.[95] In that ladder of witness, there had been only one rotten rung, one false teacher: Pole's predecessor, Thomas Cranmer,

> beyng butt one broken steppe amongst so meny sounde and good, and such a one that you being upon itt, not onlye yow founde no

resting place . . . but wythall travayle there yow took a sorier faulle then iff you had faullen from heaven to earth and from thence to hell, as ye dyd.[96]

Unlike his reading of the history of Henry's reign, Pole's views on preaching, bible-reading and the nature of tradition were too personal to be entirely representative. On major issues of faith, of course, his views coincided with and, as we have seen, in some cases set the tone for the mainstream of Marian apologetic. His distinctive insistence on the transmission of catholic truth from father to father, for example, offered a powerful theological rationale for the more visceral emphasis in Marian polemic, and, in the examination of heretics on the reliability of old-time religion, for the powerful question 'Do you think your father and mother are in hell'?[97] But the views set out in these sermons also bore the mark of the Cardinal's own intellectual journey, of his complex and enigmatic personality, and of his own overriding and abiding preoccupation with the unity of the church. The anonymous and dryly cautious theologian whose comments Pole sought on his sermons clearly had some reservations about the Cardinal's distinctive theology. He was ruffled by some of the Cardinal's less literal and more adventurous uses of scripture, and displayed his unease at crucial points in Pole's argument: 'Yt wolde be more at large declared that men can not by theire owne wytte, understande scripture'; 'Yt were goode some proofe were sette that scripture ys noisome to such as be not *parvuli.*'[98] The point to emphasise here, however, is that whatever reservations Pole himself had about the value of preaching were related specifically to *heretical* preaching. They were certainly not rooted in a timid suspicion of the charismatic and imaginative in the church's life, in fact rather the opposite.

Pole was convinced that protestant insistence on the overriding priority of scripture and of preaching, however admirable in theory, had in reality given birth not only to fatal error, but also to an arid and rancorous intellectualism that left hearts hardened and withered, and the community of believers divided and confused. The antidote was not the suppression of preaching, but the provision of catholic preaching. The reform of the universities, the in-service training of the existing priesthood and the foundation of seminaries were all designed to ensure this. Once again, the Cardinal's theological take on preaching was not a barrier, but an incentive, to educational and spiritual revival.

CHAPTER 3

Contesting the Reformation:
Plain and Godly Treatises

Could Mary Tudor's church persuade as well as punish? By and large historians have thought that the answer to that question was no, or, if yes, then yes only with heavy qualification.[1] A general consensus that the regime's record in print was poor was challenged by Jennifer Loach nearly twenty years ago. She managed to dent but did not dislodge the older view, which is perhaps sufficiently summed up in the title of an article published in 1981 by Professor J.W. Martin: 'The Marian Regime's Failure to Understand the Importance of Printing'.[2]

This consensus is all the more puzzling because, whatever else may be the case, the Marian regime was certainly fully alive to the dangerous potential of protestant books, and exercised a tight control over the domestic press. Historians of the book no longer see the establishment of the Stationers' Company in 1557 as motivated primarily by a desire to tighten censorship,[3] but there is no doubt that the regime tried hard to prevent protestant books circulating. Mary's first proclamation on religion, on 18 August 1553, complained of the damage done out of 'evil zeal for lucre and covetousness of vile gain' by printers who disseminate 'false fond books, ballads, rhymes and other lewd treatises in the English tongue concerning doctrine in matters now in question and controversy touching the high points and mysteries of Christian religion': the proclamation forbade the printing or selling of any such material.[4] The suppression of 'corrupt and naughty opinions, unlawful books, ballads and other pernicious and hurtful devices' was a priority in the Royal Injunctions of March 1554.[5]

A separate proclamation in June 1555 inaugurated a crackdown on heretical and seditious books and the illicit book trade. It included a lengthy index of prohibited books, ranging from the Edwardine Books of Common Prayer to works by both foreign and native authors, from Oecolampadius and Calvin to Bale, Cranmer and even Hall's *Chronicles*. Justices of the peace, mayors, sheriffs and other officers were given extensive powers of search, entry and confiscation in the houses of suspects. Successive heresy commissions in 1556 and 1557 included special clauses against heretical writings, and some of the regime's ablest legal enforcers were given responsibility for hunting down such books and those who were importing them. In June 1558, another proclamation extended martial law to the search for heretical books, authorising the summary execution of anyone caught in possession, a ferocious measure that seems never to have been enforced and that may indicate panic over the scale and persistence of the illicit book trade, but that certainly does not suggest any complacency about the power of print. Given all this huff and puff, the actual number of prosecutions was surprisingly small, and the punishments meted out comparatively light. It is abundantly clear, nevertheless, that the regime thought it all *mattered*.[6]

And there was certainly a measurable impact on the press. Very few English printers actually left the country under Mary, but key protestant printers, such as Richard Grafton and Edward Whitchurch, were put out of business and their presses were handed over to reliable catholics.[7] Grafton's press, which had produced among much else the Books of Common Prayer, went to the catholic zealot Robert Caly, 'Papist Robin', who acted as an informer and pursuivant against protestants, as well as printing some of the most important catholic books of Mary's reign. Whitchurch's bible-printing shop went to John Wayland, who printed the Marian regime's official Book of Hours, and that powerful and uncompromising defence of the burnings, the *Plaine and Godlye Treatise concernynge the Masse*.[8] The number of printers at work remained roughly the same, but the number of publishers shrank because tighter controls discouraged speculative publishing ventures funded by non-stationers. Marian book production, though slightly more prolific year by year compared with that of Edward's last three years, overall represented less than half the quantity of print issuing from the press in Edward's reign as a whole. The most prolific Marian year, 1555, saw 132 books printed in England, but that was dwarfed by the Edwardine boom years – 1548 when 232 books were produced, and 1550, which saw 205, a reflection of the explosion of radical religious activity in Edward's first years.[9]

Control of the press is one thing. But why have Mary's propagandists been thought to have neglected or, at any rate, to have been bad at the *positive* use of the press? The reasons offered include judgements about both quantity and quality, and neither measure is at all straightforward.

Let us take the purely arithmetical first. Edward Baskerville, who compiled the standard bibliography of religious polemic in Mary's reign, calculated that 114 works by protestant writers survive from the period 1553 to 1558, against 93 by catholics. If reprints and reissues are excluded, the figures shift further against the regime, with 103 protestant works against just 72 catholic ones. Given that protestant books were produced either on clandestine presses in England, or, more often, in continental Europe, with all the problems attendant on smuggling them in, while catholics could print and sell books freely, this might seem to suggest a dramatic underperformance or lack of interest on the part of the regime.

But the count is problematic on several scores. Although Jennifer Loach underestimated the numerical superiority of Edwardine books generally, she rightly pointed out that Baskerville's bibliography was misleading in excluding devotional and liturgical works. In fact, although Baskerville almost wholly ignored catholic devotional and liturgical works, he did include protestant ones, such as Bradford's *Treatise on Prayer*, Bale's *Meditation in Two Prayers* and the Genevan *Form of Prayers*, on the grounds, I suppose, that sixteenth-century protestant prayers were often rather argumentative.[10] Since by far the largest single category of printed books produced for Marian England was the Latin books needed for the restored liturgy, this omission dramatically skewed perceptions of catholic use of the printing presses. Those presses were, as a matter of fact, working night and day for the regime, but what kept them busy most of the time was the urgent need for multiple editions of the Missal (five editions),[11] Processional (eight editions),[12] Manual (six editions),[13] and Breviary (eight editions)[14] for the clergy, and of the primer for the laity (thirty-four editions).[15]

In any case, a mere count of books is seriously misleading. Baskerville counted every title as one book, no matter how small or large its print run or likely readership. Bonner's *A Profitable and Necessarye Doctryne*, with its attached *Homilies* for the London diocese, for example, went through at least ten printings. In 1556, Cardinal Pole ordered it to be read aloud from pulpits every week in every parish in every diocese in his province. The wardens of remote Morebath on the Devon/Somerset border bought a copy, and their priest, Sir Christopher Trychay, a dutiful man, presumably read them out to his congregation of 150.[16] There were approximately 10,000 parishes in England, most of them bigger than Morebath. There were thirteen homilies, so that you could read through them, one homily a week, four times in the year. A great many parishes obviously did as Morebath did, hence the ten printings, the largest for any book of the period. But, even if more than half the parishes in England never got round to buying the homilies, and allowing for the fact that people often do not listen very attentively to what is said to them in church, the potential impact of a text read out from so many pulpits to so many people several times a year is not to be dismissed lightly. Yet, on Baskerville's arithmetic, the *Profitable and Necessarye Doctryne* counts as a single book, on a par with ephemeral pamphlets with a likely print run of just a few hundred. Mere arithmetic here obfuscates rather than illuminates the realities.

There is another problematic dimension to mere arithmetic. The number of protestant book titles has generally been taken as a sign of the superior grip of the propaganda machine, an indication that mid-Tudor protestantism was modernising, mid-Tudor catholicism reactionary. But we need to register that, after 1553, protestants were *obliged* to concentrate their propaganda effort on the press, because they had no other platform. England's 10,000 pulpits were closed to them, and they could reach an audience beyond the small and beleaguered circle of the protestant underground only through the dangerous hit-and-miss method of the distribution of *samizdat* literature. Hence there was a fevered aspect to much protestant book production between 1553 and 1558, which has not really been registered in all this counting. I calculate that 24 out of Baskerville's 103 protestant titles (just under 25%), should, in fact, be classified as a literature of crisis, publications aimed primarily at an existing protestant readership, and designed as sometimes frantic attempts to hold the line in the face of evangelical collapse, to staunch the haemorrhage of those conforming to the restored religion: a sign, therefore, of the precariousness as much as of the strength of the protestant minority.[17]

Something needs to be said about the distribution of Marian propagandist literature through the reign. It was heavily concentrated in the first three years: ten titles in 1553, including what was perhaps the most devastating of all Marian propagandist successes, the Duke of Northumberland's scaffold speech;[18] twenty-six in 1554; peaking in 1555 with thirty-two items, and halving in 1556 to fifteen items, though these included some of the regime's most effective apologetic, including Hogarde's *Displaying of the Protestants* and Proctor's *Way Home to Christ and Truth.*[19] In 1557, there were just six catholic publications, which included Rastell's magnificent edition of the *English Workes* of Thomas More[20] (bafflingly, excluded from Baskerville's count altogether), and only five in 1558. Clearly, by 1556 the regime thought that the arguments had been sufficiently aired, and was putting its efforts into the reform and renewal of institutions and the pursuit of heretics. The legatine and episcopal visitations of the province of Canterbury were in full swing, as were the visitations of the universities, the bishops were gathering information for Pole's financial reforms and the campaign against the conventicles was at its height (seventy-five burnings in 1555, eighty-five in 1556, eighty in 1557). But the reduction in catholic polemical writing, while certainly reflecting shifting priorities, may also have been the consequence of deflected energies in the calamitous condition of England in those years – atrocious weather, crop failure, mounting mortality from epidemic disease and, from 1557, a war with France for which the church was paying. It is worth noting that book production in general plunged in those years (132 titles in 1555, only 70 in 1558), while specifically protestant books, from presses mostly located in Europe and not England, also tailed off dramatically in 1557 and 1558 (a drop from twenty-eight items in 1556 to twelve in 1557 and eleven in 1558).

So much for quantity. What about quality? Here the historians have let themselves go. The Marian catholic polemicists were, according to A. G. Dickens, 'at best a group of devoted mediocrities',[21] and their apologetic efforts, according to David Loades, were 'tedious' and lacked 'the cutting wit and humour which their opponents sometimes displayed'.[22] *De gustibus non est disputandum.* Tediousness is, to some extent, in the eye of the beholder, and it is true that the Marian catholics had no writer who rose, or descended, to the levels of scatological memorability achieved by John Bale. But implicit in these judgements is a more or less uncritical appeal to a canon of literary excellence and permanence drawn up by the victors. There is here a dismissal of the voices of the silenced that has excluded unread from the canon a large body of powerful Tudor writing and drama, an exclusion only now being challenged for the Elizabethan and early Stuart periods by literary historians.[23] That circular appeal to an exclusively protestant literary canon is explicit in Edward Baskerville's judgement that the protestant writers of Mary's reign included 'a number of skilled writers whose reputations are still familiar' – he cites Bale, Knox, Ponet and Goodman

– while 'the Roman catholic side had to rely on the talents of writers whose names were obscure before the century was out'.[24] But *naturally* their names were obscure because, in Elizabeth's England, the printing, importation and even possession of their books was a felony, they were defending a religion that, under direction from the Crown, the Elizabethan nation had come to reject, and, in the nineteenth century, there was no catholic equivalent of the Parker Society to bring their writings back to the attention of modern readers.

The themes of the pamphlets, printed sermons and treatises of the Marian apologists were of course the doctrines and practices contested by the protestant reformers and overturned under Henry and Edward. Above all, these were the real presence of Christ in the eucharist and the doctrine of the sacrifice of the Mass; the spiritual primacy of the pope; the antiquity, unity and holiness of the visible catholic church, embodied in European Christendom generally, and specifically in the restored church of England; the sole authority of the church to interpret scripture; the value of penance and good works for salvation; and the freedom of the human will. These positive affirmations were matched by a polemic against the reformation – the novelty, contradictions and confusions of protestant teaching; the lust, licentiousness and avarice of its founding fathers, from Luther to Henry VIII; the arrogance and ignorance of rank-and-file protestant believers; the singularity and lack of charity in their withdrawal from the parish and its ceremonial round; and the wedge that protestantism drove between its followers and the rest of society, indeed between people and their own parents. In the words of Bishop Hopton, 'Do you not believe as your father did? Was he not an honest man?'[25]

As Hopton's words indicate, the themes of the printed literature were replicated in the themes of preaching and of verbal instruction, and in the debates with and examinations of the men and women accused of heresy in the ecclesiastical courts. Studies of Marian printed polemic have suffered seriously from a failure to link them to the theological and ecclesial preoccupations revealed in the examination of suspects.[26] To read through the interrogations meticulously recorded in the pages of Foxe is to come again and again upon the tropes, themes and even the very phrases that also recur in and shape the catholic polemical and pulpit literature, and that are repeated, *mutatis mutandis*, from pamphlet to pamphlet and sermon to sermon. This is a crucial perception, for the printed propaganda of the Marian church derived much of its cumulative force and persuasiveness not merely from the skill or cogency of individual writings or preachings – though, as we shall see, there was skill and cogency in plenty – but also from the fact that their arguments and rhetoric drew on and helped fashion a much broader, familiar and all-pervasive discourse of persuasion and invective.

It is important, too, to register that, while much of this material was official, and commissioned by the leaders of the regime, some was the result of freelance activity, a fact that can make it difficult to assess just how carefully the Marian apologetic effort as a whole was orchestrated. The defenders of catholicism under Mary included commissioned gladiators such as John Christopherson, John Proctor and the Harpsfield brothers, all of them close to the court or the Cardinal and quite evidently writing on behalf of the regime. But they also included blatant opportunists, such as that doctrinal chameleon, John Standish. Standish had been a polemicist against the recently executed protestant Robert Barnes under Henry VIII, but had become an ardent evangelical under Edward. He was Ridley's only married canon of St Paul's and was rewarded for his allegiance to the new religion by being appointed archdeacon of Colchester in January 1553. On Mary's accession, he was ousted from that and all his other preferments, and deprived as a married priest in 1554. It is just possible that his subsequent return to catholicism was sincere – part of the tidal wave of evangelical re-conversions in response to the apparently providential establishment of what John Proctor called 'this newe and miraculous reign of mercifull Mary'.[27] But Standish's later career suggests otherwise. That same year he published a *Discourse Wherein is Debated Whether the Scripture Should be in English*, addressed to Parliament. In it, he urged fifty reasons why it was 'everie faithfull christians duety, being in authoritie, to lay his helping hande to the taking awaie quite (and that with al spede) the English [Bible] translations, with all hereticall Englyshe bookes'.[28]

No other Marian writer argued for the total withdrawal of the English Bible, and this extremist volte-face by a former evangelical enthusiast suggests that Standish had adopted this ultra-catholic position to ingratiate himself with the regime. Standish did not dare put his name to the first edition of the *Discourse*, since he knew that, because of his protestantism under Edward and his marriage, 'he had grevouslye offended, and bene a sclaunder to Christes true religion'. Within a year, however, he evidently felt that he had sufficiently re-established himself, 'beynge received agayne into Peter's shippe the catholycke churche, all hys former wykednes quyte forgiven', and he issued a second edition under his own name. Both editions were published by Robert Caly, an indication that the work was, at any rate, acceptable to the regime. The following year, Standish pressed home his campaign for recognition and favour by publishing *The Tryall of the Supremacy*, an attack on the Royal Supremacy and defence of the unity of the church under the papacy, with a fulsome dedication to Cardinal Pole, lamenting (in tones derived from Pole himself) England's descent into heresy and chaos ever since Henry 'through counsel of some wicked men' had usurped the chair of Peter.[29] Standish's choice of publisher for this work, Thomas Marshe – a specialist in almanacs and school and legal textbooks, whose rather disparate handful of religious publications look like purely commercial speculations – indicates that Standish was still, in 1556, working without official countenance.[30] Nevertheless, his re-conversion to catholicism and self-appointed role as a champion of orthodoxy was evidently persuasive enough for him to be restored to the archdeaconry of Colchester in 1558, a sensitive front-line position that would have involved the active pursuit and prosecution of heretics. Yet, on Elizabeth's accession, Standish promptly changed sides once more, took the Oath of Supremacy and, despite his recent papistical publications, managed to retain some at least of his preferments.

Not every Marian writer, therefore, was equally sincere or necessarily always entirely on message. But a broadly agreed Marian platform of tropes, themes and emphases soon emerged, and the persuasive power of any individual work derived from, and was enhanced by, its reworking of material familiar from many other outlets, both written and oral. This wider oral discourse provided the broader context for the regime's printed polemical effort and, although it has largely been ignored in discussions of Marian apologetic, it is essential to any realistic appraisal of the regime's argumentative impact. There is no space here for an exhaustive survey of the Marian apologetic and catechetical effort, which, as we have seen, has often been dismissed by historians of the reign.[31] But we need to register the real strength and impressiveness of that effort. This emerges from even a brief scrutiny of the nearest thing that the Marian church produced to a comprehensive defence of the catholic faith, Bonner's *Profitable and Necessarye Doctryne* of 1555 with its accompanying

Homilies. Although produced for the London diocese, this took on national significance when it was authorised for use in the rest of the country by Pole in 1556, pending the completion of the catechetical and homilitic texts commissioned by the Legatine Synod. It is easy to see why Pole approved Bonner's book for general use, since it offered a comprehensive statement of catholic belief, markedly superior to anything comparable produced by the Edwardine regime. A direct comparison is possible here because these Marian formularies retained the format and doctrinal rhetoric of the formularies of faith approved under Henry, while drastically revising their actual content.

Bonner's *Profitable and Necessarye Doctryne* was, in fact, an expanded reworking of the 1543 *Necessary Doctrine and Erudicion for any Chrysten Man*, the so-called *King's Book*, the work of a committee headed by Stephen Gardiner, Mary's Lord Chancellor.[32] The *King's Book* was the statement of belief around which the Henrician conservatives had rallied in Edward's reign, a fact that no doubt explains why it was retained as a framework for its Marian replacement. But the *King's Book* had been a compromise, and reluctant evangelical acquiescence in a basically catholic book had been achieved at the cost of silence about many individual points of catholic belief, including such central issues as the sacrificial character of the Mass. As a statement of catholic faith, therefore, it was radically defective. Accordingly, though much of the text of the *King's Book* was retained in Bonner's *Profitable and Necessarye Doctryne*, its content was greatly expanded and totally overhauled. Naturally, its teaching on the evils of the papacy and the rights of the Royal Supremacy was reversed, but it was also enormously expanded and enriched across the whole range of catholic doctrine. The new book was specially notable in providing extended discussion and citation of the biblical and patristic sources for contested teachings. It thus became both a resource for parish clergy needing sermon and catechetical material, and a controversial handbook for priests and interested laity anxious to weigh the competing claims of catholic and protestant teaching. The extensive biblical and patristic extracts, moreover, added a warmth and devotional earnestness to the new book that was wholly lacking in the dryer *King's Book*.

A sense of the differences between the two texts can be gauged by comparing the discussion of the sacrament of the altar in both. In the *King's Book*, the section on the Mass occupied thirteen pages. The discussion began with the institution of the eucharist by Christ, insisted on the transformation of the substance of bread and wine into the body and blood of Christ, condemned rationalist questioning of the real presence, pressed the need to remember Christ's bitter passion in receiving, and justified administering communion to the laity in one kind only. The book then drew on Christ's words about the bread that comes down from heaven in the sixth chapter of St John's gospel to urge reverence in receiving, and to remind the reader briefly of the benefits of communion, by which 'we be made heavenly, spiritual and strong against all wickedness'. Finally, the *King's Book* emphasised that communicants should receive this heavenly food fasting, and warned against irreverent behaviour and chatter or unnecessary walking around in church during Mass. Nothing whatever was said about the sacrificial character of the eucharist, or its benefits for anyone, living or dead, apart from those present and receiving: there were no references to patristic teaching, and few direct biblical citations.[33]

The comparable section in the *Profitable and Necessarye Doctryne* included most of the words of the earlier formulary, but these were now absorbed and recast into a much longer treatment of the Sacrament, extending over fifty-two pages, and far more comprehensive and exhaustive in scope. The eucharist was to be treated 'diligently and fully', it was explained, both for its own dignity above all other sacraments, and 'also that of late yeres it hath most of all other bene assaulted, and impugned, and yet of no good manne, but of the wretched sort alone'. At every stage of the discussion, full biblical citations and proof texts were provided in Latin and English, and each doctrinal point was supported in addition by 'many and most evident Authorities and testimonyes of the auncient holy fathers, aswell of the greke as of the Latyne Churche', with the Greek Fathers stressed to emphasise the universality of the church's teaching. All the ground covered in the *King's Book* was treated at much greater length, but the *Profitable and Necessarye Doctryne* also added new material on such issues as the reformers' rejection of the word 'Mass' itself, which it demonstrated had been employed by St Ambrose and other Fathers,

> so it maye greatly be marveyled, that this word Masse, being so auncient in the catholyke churche and so termed amongst the auncient fathers thereof shuld be taken for so great an eye soore, or soo odyouse a thing, as amongst our late scysmaticall preachers, it hath bene impudentlye taughte.

The scope of the whole discussion was now greatly extended to include a careful defence of contested topics such as the sacrificial character of the Mass and the efficacy of the Mass on behalf of the dead as well as the living.[34]

The thirteen *Homilies* that accompanied the *Profitable and Necessarye Doctryne*, the work of Henry Pendleton and especially John Harpsfield, also preserved something of the same diction and persuasive style as Henrician and Edwardine official publications, and indeed included revised versions of two homilies on non-doctrinal topics that Bonner and John Harpsfield had contributed to Cranmer's book. The new book of homilies, however, differed even more dramatically from its predecessor both in doctrine and in theological comprehensiveness. The grim and negative anthropology that pervaded Cranmer's protestant collection was decisively set aside, and a new homily 'On the Redemption of Man' drew on Greek patristic theology to set out the dignity of human nature ennobled by the incarnation. The equivalent Edwardine homily had presented the crucifixion as designed 'to aswage God's wrath and indignation conceived against us'.[35] By contrast, the Marian homily of redemption presented the crucifixion as 'a moost parfyt myrrour and glasse for us, therein to beholde the excedyng great love of God towarde us'. It celebrated the fact that human nature in Christ had been 'taken and joyned in him to the Godhead in unitie of person' so that 'by his innocencie and through death, willingly suffered in that his most innocent body, not only himself [should] become immortal man, and have glory everlasting, but make so many also, partakers of like blessedness'. This participatory and incarnational account of salvation has no parallel in any protestant formulary of the mid-Tudor period, and it marks the more deliberate embrace of patristic scholarship, and the more humane theological outlook of the Marian Homilists.[36]

Bonner was also responsible for one aspect of the Marian church's concern with instruction that has been largely overlooked, namely its awareness of the special need to secure the proper instruction of the young. In 1556, the bishop issued *An Honest Godlye Instruction and Information for the Tradynge, and Bringinge vp of Children*, with strict instructions to schoolmasters and parents that they 'neither teach, or use any other maner A B C, catechisme or rudiments, than this, made for the first instruction of youth'.[37] This little schoolbook was explicitly designed as a tool to undo the damage that five years of heretical teaching had done to the young in particular:

> seyng of late dates, the youth of this realme hath ben nouseled with ungodly Catechismes, and pernicious evil doctrine, whiche is to be feared, they wyl not forget, in as much as the new vessel long doth kepe the sent or savoure, of the firste liquore, wherewith it was seasoned.

The *Profitable and Necessarye Doctryne* had catered for the catechetical needs of adults and so, 'seynge the elder age is provided for in necessary doctrine already set furthe', it was appropriate 'that the saide youth should also have some helpe herein'. Bonner's little catechism was a compact collection of Christian fundamentals, but it began with a very practical 'criss-cross line' page, containing six different alphabets as well as short reference charts of vowels, syllables, diphthongs and standard abbreviations, designed as a textbook of reading and writing. To this was added the specifically religious material, 'such wordes, sentences and matters . . . as is judged to be most necessary, apte and requisite' for children to learn. These included the basic catholic prayers in English – the Our Father, Hail Mary, the Confiteor and the Latin responses needed for altar-boys 'to answere the Priest at Masse', grace before and after meals, the *De profundis* psalm to say for the dead – and the basic rudiments of catechesis – the creed, the commandments of God and of the church, lists of the seven corporal and spiritual works of mercy, the seven sacraments, the seven deadly sins, the seven gifts of the Holy Ghost and the eight beatitudes. The same year saw two editions of a shortened and somewhat simplified version of the Primer or Book of Hours in English, designed for older children, and introducing them to the Office of the Virgin, which had provided the basic framework of educated lay piety before the Edwardine revolution.[38]

Bonner's books provided a more than serviceable interim basis for catechesis and preaching, but, in December 1555, Pole's Legatine Synod commissioned replacement texts on a far more ambitious scale. These included an Erasmian catechism by the Dominican Bartolomé Carranza, which was to be translated into English,[39] and sets of model sermons structured around the traditional catechetical divisions of creed, commandments and sacraments. Pole later identified two of the '*piis et doctiise viris*' (pious and learned men) charged with producing these commissioned sermons as John Boxall, dean of Peterborough and Windsor and the Queen's principal secretary, and Thomas Watson, a Cambridge-trained humanist, Master of St John's College and Marian bishop of Lincoln.[40] Both their parts of the project were apparently complete by the summer of 1558, though only Watson's reached print. Published by Caly in June 1558, Watson's *Holsome and Catholyke Doctryne Concernynge the Seven Sacraments of Chrystes Churche* quickly ran through three official editions and one pirated one, a mark of the avid demand for this, the first of the official synodical texts, which of course every parish would have had to acquire.[41]

These thirty sermons on the sacraments are a remarkable achievement, a sustained and lucid exploration in the plain style of the best of contemporary catholic theology of the sacraments. The text reflects Watson's own formation in Fisher's seminary for preachers, St John's College, in the reliance of his sermons on a scriptural and patristic base with a special debt to the writings of St Augustine and St John Chrysostom. Watson, reflecting the ethos of mid-Tudor Cambridge, shows a relative lack of interest in scholastic theology, though he occasionally quotes St Thomas. The sermons, which would have taken between fifteen and twenty minutes to read aloud, were unevenly distributed, taking most time over controversial topics – three on baptism, two on confirmation, seven on the Mass, eleven on the sacrament of penance, two on ordination, three on matrimony, one on extreme unction, and a prefatory sermon on the number of the sacraments.

The tone of Watson's book is quite different from those authorised by Bonner. There is virtually no overt polemic, and the scriptural and patristic material is seamlessly absorbed into the plain and sober texture of the writing, with no hard words and no potentially off-putting display of learning to trouble the parish congregations for whom the sermons were intended. Bonner's texts were clearly the product of a fraught crisis situation. Watson's are designed to be more durable: calmly informative and hortatory addresses made for the long haul, setting out the catholic faith without reference to protestant contestation. The scriptural basis, meaning, ceremonies and fruits of each sacrament are described, with a good deal of attention to the inner disposition needed for their fruitful reception. In the long series on penance, for example, entire sermons are devoted to the danger of despair over sin, to the opposite danger of presumption on God's mercy, to the nature and need for true contrition, to the inward confession of the sinner direct to God, to auricular confession to the priest, to the penitent's preparation for confession, to the nature and need for amendment of life, to reconciliation with one's neighbours, to the satisfaction or penance for sin needed after confession, and to the means to avoid sin in future. In the sermon on satisfaction, Watson translates part of the decree on that subject passed at the sixth session of the Council of Trent, though this had not yet been formally promulgated. Watson's text is also fully attuned to contemporary spiritual reforms in advocating frequent communion. The medieval custom whereby most people received only once a year, he considered, was the result of spiritual decline:

> Suche was the fervente charitie of the people in the begynnynge of the Churche, that came every daye, or in a maner every daye to this holy Sacrament, and afterward when devotion decreased, they came everye sondaye, and further as the charitie of the people waxed colde the fewer tymes they prepared themselves to receive this Sacrament . . . it was decreed . . . that he that came not thrise a yere . . . shoulde not be taken as a Catholyke manne.

This fatal spiritual coldness had now to be reversed by more frequent and ardent participation in the sacraments, so that

> I shall moste earnestlye exhorte every man and woman as they love theyr owne soules, and to be preserved in grace and the favor of God, to dispose themselves often tymes effectuallye to receive the bodye of oure Sauvyour Christe, whiche is every daye bothe offered to God the father for the synnes and infirmytyes of the people, and also is prepared and offered to all them that wyll with a pure harte receyve it.[42]

This earnest, lucid, unspectacular writing in fact embodied a rich and sophisticatedly contemporary spirituality, well adapted to its pastoral purpose. In range, thoroughness and spiritual depth, Watson's collection contrasts favourably with the tiresome and contentious Elizabethan *Homilies* of 1563. The production of material of this calibre and durability so soon after the restoration of catholicism suggests that dismissive judgements on the quality and effectiveness of the Marian church's teaching need revision.

However, it is the ability of the Marian regime to produce lively propaganda rather than sustained instruction that has been most often called into question, and so we must turn now to its performance on that front. But, in doing so, we need to remind ourselves first that the very qualities of satire and invective that have led twentieth- and twenty-first-century historians to award the literary laurels to protestant writing – its attack on tradition, its entertaining scurrility, its lack of reverence – were much more equivocal assets in the eyes of sixteenth-century people. Catholic polemicists, indeed, homed in on this ribald dimension of protestantism, its alleged contempt for order and deference, and its consequent undermining of the social order. The reformation cause had received a body blow in this regard in the Duke of Northumberland's execution speech, acknowledging the insincerity of his own protestant profession and attributing his own rebellion and all the ills of England 'synce afore the dethe of kynge Henrye the eyghth' to 'seditious preachers and teachers of newe doctryne'.[43] Wyatt's rebellion had consolidated the case against the reformation as a dangerous social solvent, destroying loyalty and order, and catholic apologists exploited this to the hilt, homing in on the socially disruptive dimensions of reformation polemic as proof of its diabolic origins. So I will focus here on one of the commonest themes of Marian catholic polemic: the changeability and destructive power of protestantism, and the new religion's alleged tendency to destabilise traditional order, whether that order was manifested in the ancient ceremonial framework of catholic worship, the due obedience of subjects to their sovereign, or the respect that children or apprentices or social inferiors owed to parents or masters.

Pole gave explicit instructions that, whenever the benefits of the reconciliation with Rome were preached, the many evils that had afflicted England because of the schism were to be emphasised as well. But, even before Pole's arrival, the reformation as the destruction of order was one of the major themes of catholic polemic. Here is John Christopherson, in his *Exhortation to All Menne to Take Hede . . . of Rebellion*, one of the two official responses to Wyatt's rebellion of 1554:

> The devil for the better furtheraunce of heresye, piked out two sortes of people, that shuld in taverns and innes, at commen tables, and in open stretes set forward his purpose, as wel as false preachers dyd in the pulpet: that is to say, minstrels and players of enterludes. The one to singe pestilente and abhominable songes, and the other to set forth openly before mens eyes the wicked blasphemye, that they had contrived for the defacing of all rites, ceremonies and the whole order, used in the administration of the blessed Sacramentes.

And so

> Was not all thynges, through [heresy] brought so farre out of order, that
> vice ruled vertue, and folishnes ruled wisdome, lightness ruled gravitie,
> and youth ruled age. So that the olde mens saying was herein verified,
> that when the Antichrist should come, the rootes of the trees shulde
> growe upwarde. . . . the sonne hated hys owne father, the sister her
> brother, the wife her husband, the servante hys mayster, the subject
> the ruler. And in every house, at every mans table, in every corner, in
> every strete, at every taverne and inne, at all tymes was there suche
> unreverent reasonynge of God's highe mysteries, that those that mette
> together frendes, departed enemyes, and sometyme were at daggers
> drawyng for the matter. And then you shoulde have herde, thou
> Papiste, and thou heretike. And in a small number of yeares it came to
> passe, that no neighbour could love another. . . . Thus were the
> members of Christes Churche by such devilishe discorde, miserably
> rent asunder.[44]

This invective against protestantism as a socially destructive force is
pervasive in Marian writing.[45] The same theme surfaced continually in
the face-to-face confrontation with protestants in the trials.
Christopherson's bitter indictment of the destructive power of
reformation, for example, was echoed in Thomas Martin's devastating
prosecution case against Cranmer in 1555. Here Martin is speaking
directly to Cranmer, and commenting on Satan's temptation of Jesus in
the wilderness:

> marke the Deuils language well, it agreed wyth your proceedinges
> moste truelye. For *Mitte te deorsum*, Caste thy selfe downeward, sayde
> hee, and so taught you to cast all thinges downeward. Downe with
> the Sacramente, downe with the masse, downe with the Aultars,
> downe with the Armes of Chryste, and vpp with a Lyon and a Dog,
> downe with Abbeyes, downe with Chauntreys, downe with
> Hospitalles and Colledges, downe with fasting, and Prayer, yea downe
> with all that good and godly is. All your proceedinges and preachynges
> tended to no other, but to fulfill the Deuils request, *Mitte te deorsum.*
> And therefore tell not vs that you haue Gods worde.[46]

Martin there targets in particular the reformers' destruction of the
catholic liturgy, and preachers and writers in general recognised an issue

here that resonated with the conservative instincts of the majority of the population. Martin's sharp eye for Edwardine reforms with a high shock factor – the reformers' wives, or their long beards, for example (both unpopular with the laity), or the substitution of the royal arms for the crucifix in churches (in Martin's words, 'downe with the Armes of Chryste, and vpp with a Lyon and a Dog') – are recurrent and telling features of Marian polemic.[47]

The fact that Cranmer had produced two communion services in rapid succession, differing dramatically from each other and from the familiar Mass, provided a powerful example of the instability and doctrinal chaos of the new religion. Many people had been alienated by the escalating radicalisation of protestant liturgical practice under Edward, spearheaded at St Paul's Cathedral by Bishop Ridley. His restless liturgical experimentation, moving the table from the old high altar steps down into the upper choir and blocking the sight of the communion bread with veils and even brick screens to prevent adoration, had elicited the adverse comment of London chroniclers, and was bitterly controversial. Marian preachers and polemicists tuned in to this conservative outrage. At Ridley's trial, John White, bishop of Lincoln, had reproached him for his liturgical experiments:

A godly receiuing I promise you, to set an Oyster table in steede of an Altar, and to come from Puddynges at Westminster to receiue: and yet when your table was constituted, you coulde neuer be content, in placing the same now East, nowe North, nowe one way, nowe another, vntill it pleased GOD of his goodnesse to place it cleane out of the Church.[48]

That same theme was eagerly elaborated by pamphleteers and preachers. James Brookes appealed to his audience at Paul's Cross in November 1553:

Have not we had chaunge in doctrine, chaunge in bookes, chaunge in tounges, chaunge in aultars, chaunge in placing, chaunge in gesture, chaunge in apparaile, chaunge in breade, chaunge in gevynge, chaunge in receyvyng with many changes mo, so that we had still chaunge upon chaunge and lyke never to have lefte chaungyng, til al the hole world had cleane been changed?[49]

John Proctor, royal chaplain, and one of the regime's most effective writers, demanded in 1556, 'What orders, what forme of religion have they set furth sins their firste raigne, that shortly after they altered not? Which three of them amongst them all, that agreed together in their matters?'[50] It was a telling question to a public which had endured the unfamiliarities of two progressively more radical English Prayer Books in three years. The liturgical and doctrinal inconstancy of reformation therefore became a favourite theme for catholic polemic. In Miles Hogarde's brilliant journalistic squib of 1556, *The Displaying of the Protestantes*, liturgical change became proof of the wavering inconstancy of the 'effeminate' (that is, married) bishops 'which were ever learning and never able to come to the truth'. First, he wrote, they placed the table

> alofte where the hygh altare stode. Then must it be set from the walle that one mighte go betwene, the mynysters beinge in contention on whether parte to turne their faces, either towards the West, the North, or south . . . Thus turning every waye, they myste the right waye . . . For such Sacrament, suche minister, such carpenters, suche toles.

The Holy Ghost had taught the catholic church the true use of the sacrament of the altar in the Mass 'till these bunglers toke in hand the same, meaning as thei thought to amend it. But as their presumption was vayne so in thende it proved. For God seing their inconstant vanities in misusing his sacramentes, brought all their attemptes to a vaine effect.'[51] Marian polemicists were quick to apply these generalities to specific cases: James Cancellar, writing in the months immediately after Cranmer's execution, saw the 'inconstancie' of the reformers and 'the variete of order that was in their religion' grimly fulfilled in 'that execrable man's' own wavering uncertainty, his multiple recantations and his ultimate return to his 'shamefull heresies'.[52]

Hogarde and his colleagues knew that they were playing a strong suit in targeting successive transformations of protestant eucharistic practice, an area where old loyalties died hard and where they could be confident of appealing to conservative lay feeling. As one broadside ballad put it,

> O heresy, thou walkest a-wrye
> Abrode to gadde or raunge:
> Like false brethren, deceave children,
> This Churche nowe for to chaunge;
> Her prayer by night to banish quite
> With new inventions straunge.[53]

'New inventions straunge' was a hard-worked trope in catholic polemic, therefore, both preached and printed. There is no doubt of its powerful appeal. The Yorkshire parish priest Robert Parkyn homed in on precisely the same variations in practice between Cranmer's two Prayer Books:

> for the table . . . was hadde down in to the bodie of the churche in many places and sett in the mydde allee emonge the people . . . upon wich table a loaf of whytte bread such as men use in their howses with meate and a cuppe of wyne was sette without any corporax . . . the priest orr minister . . . straightly forbidding that any adoration should be done there unto, for that were idolatrie, said the boke, and to be abhorride of al faithfull Christians . . . Oh how abhominable heresie, and unsemynge ordre was this, let every man ponder in his owne conscience.[54]

On the other side of England, in the twentieth of the sermons he published in 1557, the Bristol preacher Roger Edgeworth pressed home the same message. This, he told his hearers and readers, 'is the verie property of Heresies, thei be ever unstedfast and not agreing amonge theim selves, but some take one way and some another, for example, how manie maners and divers wayes of ministeringe the Communion have we hadde among us?' And he launched into a description whose essential features will now be familiar – common bread laid irreverently direct onto the tablecloth, the people driven out of the chancel lest they see and worship, 'and anone that way seemed not best, and therefore was there veils or curtens drawn . . . to hide it', the tables placed in the nave, the ministers themselves turning north or south or east or west. This 'pulling down of altars and setting up of boards', he told his hearers, had been the mark of the Arian heretics in the early church also. But now, if we 'convert ourselves to the God of Grace, he will solidate, stay and settle us sure, contrary to all such inconstancy'.[55]

As the attentive reader will have noted, my illustrative material here has been drawn from a range of sources – sermons, heresy trials, journalistic pamphlets, private diaries, official propaganda tracts. The point I want to stress is that the force of Marian polemic was not derived from an isolated pamphlet here or a sermon there. Instead, it worked as a form of carpet bombing, driving its message home in many forms, but achieving a remarkable consistency across genre and occasion, and a powerful cumulative effect. In the process, its proponents generated a sustained catholic rhetoric, and a battery of forceful arguments.

The *Displaying of the Protestantes*, the best-known of the sources I have just quoted, was first published in June 1556 by the plebeian London tradesman Miles Hogarde and has generally been considered the single most effective piece of Marian propaganda.[56] As I hope the drift of this chapter has indicated, however, Hogarde's writing (while certainly among the most vivid produced in Mary's reign) is by no means isolated, either in its targets and procedures or in its kind and quality, contrary to what is often asserted. Hogarde's work was, however, a particularly effective *London* polemic. He was a close observer of the progress of heresy in the city, and used the detailed and gossipy knowledge that he shared with his London readers to highlight and discredit the infinite divisions of the reformers. Hogarde seems to have had the run of Bishop Bonner's house, and himself participated in the interrogation of heretics. His publisher, Robert Caly, who had taken over the printing shop of the disgraced Richard Grafton, was similarly active in the campaign of arrests of London heretics, and was satirised by Foxe as 'Papist Robin' or 'Robin the Promoter' for his activities as informer and arresting officer. He never held any official patent or privilege as a printer, but he published many of the regime's best polemical works, and was responsible for printing several official or semi-official works, such as Bonner's little catechism for children, Thomas Martin's attack on the marriages of priests, the writings of John Proctor and all of Hogarde's writings. This suggests a degree of coordination between the campaign in the press and the actual search for and arrest of heretics which it would be good to know more about.

Hogarde has attracted more attention than any other Marian writer. But, in fact, perhaps the regime's most remarkable propagandist venture was the powerful defence of the physical repression of heresy, published in 1555 during the first summer of the campaign of burnings. This work anticipated many features of Hogarde's *Displaying of the Protestantes*. Because of the peculiar circumstances of its publication, however, it certainly reached a much larger audience than any of Hogarde's books, and indeed more than any other single-author Marian book. The anonymous pamphlet, *A Plaine and Godlye Treatise Concerning the Masse, for the Instructyon of the Simple and Unlearned People*, first appeared in June or early July 1555, when the executions were intensifying. It very rapidly went into a second printing. More remarkably, it was then included as an additional item at the back of the official Marian Primer, or prayer book for lay people, published that year under the imprint of John

Wayland. The Primer, published 'with the assent of the most reverende father in god the Lord Cardynall Pole hys grace', had unequivocal official status, and the treatise, being sold along with the Primer, shared in this status.[57] In this extraordinary form, bound up with a prayer book, the *Treatise* went through three further editions, achieving a remarkable five editions in six months by the end of 1555, more than any other controversial work of the period, and enough to make clear both the regime's awareness that the burnings needed justification, and their determination to provide it.[58] The linking of a defence of the campaign against heresy with the doctrine of the Mass was natural enough, of course, since the Mass was the principal target of protestant hostility, and the doctrine of the Sacrament the main topic in the examinations of heretics. But the inclusion of a fiercely controversial justification of the burning of heretics between the same covers as the regime's one official devotional manual was a daring step, a bold joining of piety, catechesis and polemic, designed to ensure maximum circulation for the *Treatise*, and a uniquely receptive readership.

The first forty pages or so of this fifty-five-page pamphlet are devoted to a detailed defence of catholic teaching on the Mass, the key issue in contention between the regime and the protestants, reviewing the scriptural, patristic and rational arguments on both sides. The points made are well organised and well illustrated, drawing on some of the same material deployed in Bonner's *Profitable and Necessarye Doctryne*, but given extra force by the author's colourful gift for invective, equally unsparing of the heretics in their 'develyshe dryfts and pestilent persuasions', and of their gullible dupes, the 'fraile foly and fond madness of such beatle blynde people that so redely and so fondely would beleve and credite . . . such a rude Railying rablemente against not only the universal Church, but also against the very manifest and open Scripture'. Protestant preaching was 'pestilent and pernicious unto people, seditious to a shrewde sort', the author claimed, and it not only falsified doctrine, but undermined the very fabric of society. We have met this kind of rhetoric before, though this author brings his own distinctive alliterative relish to it:

> settynge the world at such losenes and leude libertie that no lawe could let lust, all good order broken, the magistrates contempned, and the people so farre divided that the father dread the childe, the marchaunt hys prentyse, the master hys man, the misteres her mayde, the wyfe

her husband. No man durst trust his next neighbour. Amitie and friendship was fled the realme, truth and trust was outtroden, al good maners and nurture in youth exiled, the very norishe of chastetee in maydens cast of cleane, so that what eche man liked and lusted, that he thought lawful.[59]

The tone sharpened even further in the final quarter of the work, a detailed attempt to neutralise evangelical exploitation of the burnings as propaganda. The details of the *Treatise*'s defence of the burnings will be considered in their proper place elsewhere.[60] Here, it is enough to note that this vigorous and, to judge by its multiple editions, widely read pamphlet took the propaganda battle into the enemy camp, mounting a forceful and even aggressive justification for the campaign of repression as that campaign gathered momentum through the summer of 1555.

Marian polemic and apologetic writings have been seriously underrated. When restored to their proper place within a broader campaign of persuasion and repression, they look altogether more focused and more formidable than has been allowed. This was a regime fully alert to the power of the press, with the theological and literary resources to generate a formidable body of catechetical and hortatory material making a positive case for catholicism, and with talented polemical writers able to land telling blows on the soft underbelly of protestantism, targeting its association with rebellion, irreverence and social disruption. The almost universal assumption of historians of the reign that protestant writers and polemicists had the best of the argument is, to say the least, not proven.

CHAPTER 4

From Persuasion to Force

Nothing has done more to colour attitudes to the religious history of Mary Tudor's England than the four-year campaign for the forcible suppression of heresy, in the course of which 284 protestants, 56 of them women, were burned alive for their beliefs, and approximately 30 more died in prison.[1] The smoke from the fires of Smithfield is in all our eyes, not least because it is impossible to read through our principal source for the history of the persecution, John Foxe's great martyrological polemic, *Actes and Monuments*, without a mounting sense of pity for the victims, and of revulsion at the process in which they were caught up. Even historians, intent on exorcising myth and redressing earlier hostile perceptions of the regime, have concluded, in Gina Alexander's words, that, in these burnings, the Marian church was using 'the wrong weapons . . . in a fight it could not win'.[2]

Any civilised twenty-first-century person will of course agree that burning men and women alive for their fidelity to deeply held beliefs must be both obviously and profoundly 'the wrong weapon' in a struggle for religious reconstruction. But that consensus is a matter of moral hindsight, attained this side of the Enlightenment, and, strictly speaking, is hardly a historical judgement at all. Nor, in terms of the effective containment of dissent in early modern society, does it seem so very obvious that the execution of heretics *was* 'the wrong weapon'. It is hard to see how the Marian regime – or any other sixteenth-century regime, for that matter – could have avoided confrontation with an ideology so inimical as Marian protestantism was to its religious objectives and its political stability and social cohesion. As John Christopherson wrote, 'nothing there is, that bredeth so deadly hatred, as diversitie of myndes touching religion',[3] a perception almost universally shared by his contemporaries. No sixteenth-century European state willingly accepted or could easily imagine the peaceful coexistence of differing religious confessions, and such a coexistence does not seem a particularly realistic aspiration for Mary's England. Consider, for example, the verbal violence of Rowland Taylor's ferociously anti-catholic prayer, written before any protestant had as yet been burned, for the deliverance of England from

this Babylonicall stewish spirituall whoredome, conspiracie, tyranny, detestable enormities, false doctrine, heresie, hardnes of hart. . . . euident and open idolatry, sacriledge, simonie, blasphemy, superstition, hypocrisie, transubstantiate angell of lyght and day deuill, kyngdome of lyes, foule vayne schismes, sects, sedition, apostasie, gay sweete poyson, honied and sugred viperous venome, wily woluishnesse, sathanicall subtletie, and abhomination in the sight of God . . .[4]

Nor is it at all obvious that the Marian regime 'could not win' its battle against heresy or, indeed, that by 1558 it was not in fact winning. The perception that it could not and was not is based largely on the fact that, as things turned out, it *did not*. On the contrary, however, I shall argue that while it seems clear that persecution, however systematic, was unlikely to have eliminated protestantism entirely as an underground movement, the exile or execution of its leaders, and the determined clampdown on the most intransigent members of the evangelical rank and file, had in fact frightened most members of the movement into outward conformity, and had created disarray in the relatively few Tudor communities in which protestantism had established a significant presence.

Yet the conviction that so repugnant a campaign *cannot* have been effective, and must have been a mistake, even from the regime's point of view, is deeply entrenched in the historiography of the period. Professor Andrew Pettegree, in his valuable study of protestantism in Mary Tudor's England, epitomises a long historiographical tradition in characterising the Marian burnings as not only brutal but anachronistic, ill-considered, ill-organised and politically and religiously counterproductive. Mary's government, he considers, adopted this policy of forcible repression just as the rest of Europe was turning away from wholesale persecution. By 1558, the English government '*doggedly* pursuing the campaign of conversion by execution'[5] would have seemed 'decidedly old fashioned as well as brutal'. Moreover, according to Pettegree, the regime miscalculated from the very beginning in attempting to 'terrorise evangelicals into conformity through the execution of high-profile preachers and bishops', because 'the execution of well-educated and respectable citizens by such a barbaric means was never popular', a fact attested by the large and sympathetic crowds attending the burnings of such men. Even Charles V in his campaign against dissent in the Netherlands, Pettegree argues, grasped the folly of executing respected local figures in their own communities, and he thinks it significant that Philip II's Spanish advisers cautioned the King against the English burnings.[6] The regime also lacked the imagination or insight, Pettegree claims, to exploit the burnings effectively for propaganda purposes. Though some of the victims were heterodox even by evangelical standards, rejecting mainstream doctrines such as the Trinity and practices such as infant baptism, or were acrimoniously at odds with orthodox protestants on the relationship between free will and salvation, the Marian regime failed to highlight this heterodoxy to discredit the victims or justify the burnings; this failure to exploit protestant divisions was, he considers, 'a critical lost opportunity'. Pettegree also articulates a fairly generally held perception of the impact of the executions in suggesting that they were increasingly counterproductive, causing widespread alienation among ordinary people. He argues that, in 'stark contrast' to the beginning of the campaign, when evangelical leaders might have been perceived as disturbers of the peace, by 1557 the 'social consensus underpinning support for the regime's religious policies was dangerously weak', it now being the agents of the persecution who were perceived as socially disruptive. In support of this judgement, he cites 'open dissent at the place of execution, the need for heavily armed guards to prevent tumult and protect those charged with executing the sentence, even daring prison raids to liberate imprisoned evangelicals'.[7]

There are some striking inconsistencies in this argument – Pettegree's acknowledgement that evangelical leaders targeted early in the campaign were perceived as disturbers of the peace and hence did not evoke sympathy, is hard to reconcile with his argument about the reluctance of local communities to see otherwise respectable men and women executed. He argues simultaneously that the regime was doggedly brutal in pursuing its campaign of violence, and 'remarkably lenient' in dealing with purveyors of heretical literature.[8] But, in any case, the general picture of incompetence and lost opportunities in the regime's handling of the campaign is, I shall argue, misleading. Incompetence and lost opportunities there were, perhaps the greatest of them the handling of the execution of Thomas Cranmer. The very decision to burn him, despite his multiple recantations, was probably Mary's own, and was one of the Queen's greatest mistakes, however understandable given his role in her unhappy early life. It drove the desperate old man to try to salvage his integrity by a last-minute volte-face, and a courageous death. In the process, it robbed the regime of its most spectacular trophy convert, and neutralised a potentially devastating blow against the protestant cause. But the particular shortcomings pointed to by Pettegree seem to me largely imaginary. Mary's government was intensely aware, for example, of protestant divisions, both at home and abroad. The regime investigated the issues in contest between warring factions among protestant prisoners in the London gaols, and trumpeted those divisions and variations in the sermons against heretics and heresy that accompanied the trials and executions.

Similarly, Pettegree's suggestion that the burnings would have struck contemporaries as anachronistic, or that European regimes in the 1550s were on the verge of a revolution in sensibility that made brutal punishments for belief repugnant and therefore increasingly rare, has a whiff of historical whiggery about it. It is not borne out by the history of European persecution in the mid-sixteenth century. Savage religious persecution had been in progress in both France and the Low Countries for more than a generation, and would continue for another, in the course of which France would descend into religiously driven civil war. More than 270 protestants would be executed for their beliefs in the Spanish Netherlands in the late 1560s, 46 in Italy, 38 in Spain, 26 in France.[9]

Religious persecution remained a viable government option, frequently resorted to all over Europe, well into the seventeenth century. Nor were barbaric forms of execution going out of fashion, least of all in England. Elizabeth I burned no catholics, but she strangled, disembowelled and dismembered more than 200. I should not myself care to allocate marks for brutality between these different methods of slow killing. Nor should we make too much of Spanish concern about the campaign against heresy in England in the spring of 1555. It is perfectly true that Philip's confessor, Fray Alfonso de Castro, preached at court against the burnings on Sunday 10 February that year, but, as we shall see, Castro was in fact a supporter of heresy trials *and* executions, and this sermon was almost certainly a tactical gesture, undertaken at Philip's command. Charles V's ambassador, Simon Renard, was initially panic-stricken about public hostility to the burnings, which he overestimated on the basis of alarmist reports of the early demonstrations in London and Essex, and which he feared would be blamed on Habsburg influence. But after the spring of 1555, despite the mounting pace of the campaign, there are no other indications of any Spanish reservations about the burnings. Castro himself reissued his standard guide to the punishment of heretics in 1556. That same year he also reissued his larger text-book on heresy with a dedicatory epistle commending Philip and Mary's restoration of catholicism in England. Bartolomé Carranza, the most important Spanish churchman in Mary's England, later claimed to have supported the executions.[10]

Nor can the notion of a progressive breakdown of public acceptance of the campaign against heresy be sustained. It is certainly the case that there were gestures of sympathy or support for the victims at many burnings, and this remained a matter of intense concern to the authorities to the very end of the reign. But such demonstrations were geographically limited to a few communities, recurring in a small number of centres of heresy (London and Colchester, in particular). Many of the really alarming demonstrations of this kind came early in the campaign, and most were demonstrably orchestrated by protestant activists rather than spontaneous manifestations of popular opinion. Worrying as they undoubtedly were for the regime, none of them came near to being as menacing as the protestant riot at Paul's Cross on 13 October 1553, long before there was any question of burnings. Understandably, Foxe lovingly recorded every scrap of evidence of popular support for the martyrs at their arrest or execution. But crowds with protestants in them are not necessarily protestant crowds, and, as we shall see, closer scrutiny of Foxe's pyre-side narratives suggests that, allowing for his own authorial agenda, there were just as often overt signs of hostility or indifference towards the victim as gestures of sympathy. The make-up and motives of the crowds at Tudor public executions were rarely simple.

Even by Foxe's account, the vast majority of executions passed off quietly. Certainly there is nothing to suggest an upward curve of disapproval, nor any evidence that resistance was stronger to the burnings in 1558 than it had been in 1555. Many of the victims themselves were indeed by then more determined and more vehement, for by 1558 there had been a fiery winnowing of the half-hearted from among the gospellers. The regime was now dealing with the committed hard core. But there is no sign of the spreading religious disaffection that Pettegree suggests was a feature of Mary's last years. Of the 81 burnings (comprising 221 victims in all) carried out between January 1556 and November 1558, so far as can be deduced from Foxe's accounts, there were significant disturbances at fewer than half a dozen.[11] One of these, the only specific example of popular *resistance* to the campaign cited by Pettegree, was the burning of John Noyes in his home village of Laxfield in Suffolk, when all his neighbours deliberately doused their fires to deprive the sheriff's men of hot coals for kindling. But this execution was, in fact, misdated by Foxe: it occurred in September 1556, not 1557, and so provides no evidence for the popular mood in the last two years of the burnings. Nor does it offer unambiguous evidence of local disaffection. Noyes had been arrested by local constables, and the reluctance of the householders in his village to assist the executioners actively in the death of even a heretical neighbour was hardly surprising.

No such sensitivities were on display at most executions, which, outside London and Colchester, were more often than not conducted somewhere other than the victim's home community. The Laxfield incident will simply not bear the weight of a theory of wide and widening disapproval of the campaign against heresy as a whole. As we shall see, most of Foxe's examples of discontent among spectators at the burnings can and should be understood as manifestations of protestant support for the victims, the solidarity of a minority with its own members. They cannot safely be taken as an indication of the views of the population at large. In what follows, therefore, I want to consider the origin, direction and conduct of the campaign of burnings; to try to put aside twenty-first-century humanitarian sensibilities and assess soberly the effectiveness of that campaign as an instrument of counter-reformation; to see what can be said about the shifting nature of mid-Tudor public reaction to it; and to determine what the campaign reveals about the aims, methods and competence of the Marian religious establishment.

Preaching at Paul's Cross against Mary's title to the throne on 9 July 1553, Bishop Nicholas Ridley regaled his audience with anecdotes of his own fruitless efforts to budge the princess from her stiff-necked popery, and warned that, if she became queen, she would betray the kingdom to a foreign power and persecute true religion. Three days later, one of London's most gifted evangelical preachers, John Bradford, published a call to national repentance, with a preface warning that 'a grievous and bytter cuppe of Goddes vengeaunce is readye to be powred oute for us Englyshmen to drynke of'. For the nation's ingratitude, impiety and lack of zeal towards the Gospel, God had taken away King Edward, and 'so wil he take awaye his Gospel . . . now he begynneth to brew such a brewing, wherein one of us is like to destroy an other, and so make an open gappe for foren enemies to devoure us, and destroy us'.[12] Within weeks, Ridley would be deposed from his bishopric, and Bradford from his prebend at St Paul's. The rehabilitation of the imprisoned catholic bishops, and the appointment as Lord Chancellor of Stephen Gardiner – whose opposition to religious radicalism under Henry VIII had already earned him a place in protestant demonology as a persecutor of the saints, the 'common Cuttethrote of Englaunde'[13] – confirmed the worst protestant fears. Evangelical activists began to exhort their listeners to stand fast in the storm that was coming. At Paul's Cross on 6 August, John Rogers made a 'godly and vehement Sermon', 'confirmyng suche true doctrine as he and other had there taught in K. Edwards dayes, exhortyng the people constantly to remayne in the same, and to beware of all pestilent Popery, Idolatry, and superstition'.[14]

To begin with, the Queen's own utterances on the subject of compulsion were carefully emollient. Mary's first proclamation about the likely shape of her religious settlement, issued on 18 August, acknowledged her own adherence to 'that religion which God and the world knoweth she hath ever professed from her infancy', and her hope that 'the same were of all her subjectes quietly and charitably embraced', while promising that the Queen 'mindeth not to compel any her said subjects thereunto unto such time as further order by common assent may be taken therein'.[15] But the proclamation also denounced the sedition and false rumours spread by 'evil-disposed' preachers, and forbade sermons, biblical exposition and the playing of interludes, while its careful limitation of tolerance until 'further order by common assent be taken' signalled the likelihood of the parliamentary imposition of a catholic settlement. This was more cautiously phrased than the Queen's more open-ended declaration to the Council on 12 August, when she had said that 'she meaneth graciously not to compel or constreyne other mennes consciences otherwise than God shall (as she trusteth) putte in their harts a persuasion of the truth that she is in, through thopeninge of the Wurde unto them by godleye, vertuouse and lerned preachers'.[16]

That initial resolve to rely on persuasion and preaching alone, if it was ever seriously intended, was to be tested to breaking point the very next day, when the first public catholic sermon of the reign at Paul's Cross, by Bishop Bonner's protégé Dr Gilbert Bourne, was disrupted by a protestant riot. A hostile crowd howled down the preacher when he began to denounce the maltreatment of Bishop Bonner and the religious innovations in Edward's reign, a dagger was thrown at the pulpit, and Bourne himself had to be hustled away to safety in St Paul's school.[17] The incident, stoked by protestant activists in the crowd, was a warning to the regime of the hold that the reformation had established among some sections of the citizens of London; it marked the end of the honeymoon of unqualified rejoicing that had greeted Mary's accession. It was also to provoke a draconian act 'Against offenders of preachers, and other ministers of the Church' in Mary's first Parliament, imposing indefinite imprisonment on disturbers of divine worship, on magistrates and local officials who failed to apprehend offenders, and on anyone abetting or concealing them.[18] One of the most prominent of the Sussex martyrs, Richard Woodman, was first arrested under the provisions of this Act.[19] More immediately, the Paul's Cross tumult provoked a crackdown on protestant preaching and scripture exposition in the city churches, and an ominous demand from the Council that the Lord Mayor and aldermen provide immediate and circumstantial demonstration whether 'they be able or no by their authorite to kepe the Citie committed to their charge without sediciouse tumults'.[20] The round-up of culprits suspected of involvement in the riot widened over the next month into the arrest of 'seditious preachers' as far afield as Coventry, Leicester and Canterbury: those arrested included Thomas Becon, Miles Coverdale and John Hooper.[21] Archbishop Cranmer was committed to the Tower on 14 September, though only after his Declaration against the Mass, designed to scotch damaging rumours that he had conformed, broke the studied silence he had maintained since the Queen's accession, and despite his own treasonous complicity in Northumberland's coup.[22]

If protestant defiance had provided the trigger for the regime's resort to force, no one could seriously have doubted the inevitability of such an outcome. Some protestants, including several future victims of the burnings, would challenge the very idea that a government should 'in a matter of faith use compulsion, nor violence, because faith is a gift of

God, and cometh not of man, neither of man's laws, neither at such time as men require it'. Both the layman Thomas Haukes and the cleric John Bradford would challenge Bishop Bonner in almost identical words: 'where prove you that Christ or his Apostles killed any man for his faith?'[23] Such opinions are hardly surprising from the mouths of men facing execution for their beliefs. In fact, however, most protestant leaders agreed with their catholic counterparts that false faith was worse than no faith at all, and that those stubbornly adhering to religious error were rightly condemned to death.

In Edward's reign, Cranmer himself had been instrumental in persuading the Duke of Somerset to proceed with the burning of the Kentish Anabaptist Joan Butcher. John Foxe, the martyrologist, one of the very few sixteenth-century clerics who opposed burning even for stubborn heretics, had tried to persuade the preacher John Rogers, who was a royal chaplain, to intercede on Butcher's behalf, if only to commute her sentence to hanging. Rogers, ironically destined to be the first victim of the Marian burnings in February 1555, refused to help, justifying the execution of unrepentant heretics, and specifically defending burning, despite its popish associations, as the least agonising of options and 'sufficiently mild' for so heinous a crime. No doubt improving the story with the benefit of hindsight, Foxe later claimed that he had left their meeting expressing the grimly prophetic hope that Rogers himself might never have to contend with 'this same gentle burning'.[24]

Rogers's tough line was by no means exceptional: the same uncompromising support for the use of force was stoutly maintained by the last of the protestant leaders to be executed in 1555, John Philpot. In November 1555, Richard, Lord Rich compared Philpot's refusal to recant to Joan Butcher's intransigence – 'she went wilfully unto the fire . . . and so do you now'. Philpot denied the parallel: Joan Butcher, he declared, 'was a vain woman (I knew her well), and a heretic indeed, well worthy to be burnt'. In a vehement treatise against Trinitarian heresy, written in prison, Philpot insisted that it was the duty of all Christians to be fierce against the enemies of God's truth, 'whom the Divel hath shyten out in these days, to defyll the Gospel'.[25] And, in 1556, Miles Hogarde would exploit this evangelical hostility to more radical heresy by quoting, in defence of the Marian burnings of protestants, a passage from a sermon preached by Bishop Latimer before Edward VI, justifying the burning of Anabaptists and Arians.[26] The issue was therefore not whether heretics should be burned, but who qualified as a heretic. The duty of every Christian to uphold God's truth applied above all to the prince. Sixteenth-century rulers expected, and were expected by others, to enforce their own religious beliefs on their subjects. Cranmer had told Edward VI at his coronation that princes were God's anointed, whose duty it was to see 'God truly worshipped, and idolatry destroyed'.[27] Substitute heresy for idolatry, and these sentiments applied equally to catholic monarchs. As early as August 1553, Cardinal Pole himself had urged Mary not to be afraid to use the sword. God had put it into her hand 'for no other reason than that ribaldry and disobedience to the holy laws may be punished and the seditious receive their reward': it was her duty not only to honour God herself but to 'compel her subjects to do likewise'.[28]

In presenting the new faith as a legitimate target of forcible suppression, the regime was handed a huge propaganda coup in its very first weeks when, at his execution, the Duke of Northumberland, before a large crowd 'full of curiousity to hear what [he] would say, especially on matters of religion', made a full, explicit and allegedly spontaneous repudiation of protestantism. From the scaffold, the Duke attributed the ruin of England and his own corruption to the heresy into which the country had been led 'theis xvi yeres past' (a significant extension of the sin of schism back beyond Edward's overturning days into Henry's reign) by 'seditious preachers and teachers of newe doctrine'. He called on those present 'to remember the ould learning' and return to the faith and unity of the catholic church. Exultant catholics immediately grasped the propaganda value of such a speech from such a source, which 'had edified the people more than if all the Catholics in the land had preached for ten years'. According to one dismayed protestant observer, 'There were a greate number turned with his words.'[29] Mary's Council had maximised the effect of Northumberland's confession by rounding up the leading elite city gospellers to be witnesses on the morning that Northumberland attended Mass and made his admissions, and Pole saw to it that Northumberland's speech was widely publicised in Europe.[30] And, as we have seen, Mary's astonishing and, as many thought, miraculous defeat of Northumberland's conspiracy, and her initial rapturous popular reception as Queen, led scores of prominent evangelicals to abandon their reformed opinions, seeing in her triumph the direct hand of God.[31]

The association of the new religion with social disruption and open sedition was of course strengthened by Wyatt's rebellion, which Mary's government consistently (and plausibly) presented as inspired by a protestant agenda.[32] For the first six months or so of the reign the regime indeed avoided the adjective 'heretical' where possible, preferring to characterise protestant preaching and preachers as 'lewde' or 'seditious' instead. But, by the end of 1553, the Lower House of Convocation had formally endorsed a return to catholic teaching on the key question of transubstantiation, and was urging episcopal action against all who had preached 'any heretical, erroneous, or seditious doctrine', the suppression of protestant books, the revival of the laws against heresy and the restoration of the church's 'pristine jurisdiction against heretics, schismaticks and their fautors'.[33] In the wake of the rebellion, Gardiner himself called explicitly for repressive measures against heretics: the commonwealth could not be protected unless 'the rotten and hurtful members therof were cutt off and consumed'.[34] This readiness to eradicate dissent by blood and fire alarmed *politiques* such as Paget. Worries about the unknown extent of likely protestant backlash and about the financial implications of the regime's restoration of catholicism delayed the revival of the heresy laws until December 1554.[35] Yet, even before the legislation was in place, the regime's long-term intentions would have been clear to attentive readers of the official response to Wyatt's rebellion, in which John Christopherson denied that heretics who were banished or fled the country of their own accord were suffering persecution for the truth, or that a heretic who went 'gladlye . . . to the fyre, and patiently suffered' was dying as a martyr, from whose ashes 'twenty thowsande will rise'.[36] This ominous pre-emptive strike against the persuasive force of protestant martyrdom was written before a single dissident had been executed for the sake of religion. But the prisons were already full of men and women accused of heresy, and, given Christopherson's closeness to the regime, it was plainly only a matter of time before Parliament re-imposed the traditional sanctions.

Mass and daily offices in Latin became the only legal forms of worship in England from 20 December 1553. Conformity to catholic worship and teaching was now identified with allegiance to the regime, 'the Queen's proceedings'. From mid-January 1554, even before episcopal visitations had begun to enforce the new act, the Privy Council was stirring the Essex sheriffs and magistracy to arrest 'lewde' preachers and 'certayne lewde personnes in Colchester . . . and other places thereabouts, that have gone about to dissuade the Quenes people there from frequenting such Divine Service as is presentlie appointed by the lawes to be observed in the realme'.[37] At the end of February 1554, Bishop Bonner called on the people of his diocese to make their confessions in the approaching Lent, the necessary preliminary to formal reconciliation with the church, and instructed the clergy to submit to him lists of the names of all parishioners who failed to do so. The roster of suspected heretics thus generated expanded dramatically from September 1554, when a rigorous year-long visitation of the London diocese got under way. Most of the lay suspects brought before Archdeacon Harpsfield or other officials in the ensuing trawl capitulated and promised conformity. But many did not, and, of those who did, some subsequently thought better of their compliance and became non-conformist. Many of these hard-core resisters had a protestant past reaching back even beyond Edward's reign, to the last years of Henry VIII.

John Warne, the London upholsterer burned on 30 May 1555 alongside John Cardmaker, the high-profile minister of the reformed parish of St Bride's, Fleet Street, had been formally condemned as a sacramentary by Bishop Bonner as early as 1546, but had been rescued from execution by a royal pardon. Warne came under suspicion again in September 1553 when, in one of the earliest of what proved to be a series of blasphemous practical jokes in the city mocking the sacraments and clergy, his dog, 'a great rough water Spaniell', was discovered 'shorne in the hed, & . . . a crowne like a Priest made in the same'. It was later established that the culprit was not Warne himself, but a tailor of St Giles in the Fields. As his accusers pointed out, however, 'thou diddest laugh at it, and like it, though thou diddest it not thy selfe'. He was arrested yet again at New Year 1555 with his wife Elizabeth, while they were attending a secret protestant service in a house in Bow churchyard. Warne's track record as a protestant recidivist ensured that proceedings were taken against him first, but his wife and step-daughter both followed him in due course to the flames.[38]

The growing numbers of lay and clerical hardliners in the London gaols and in episcopal custody in 1554 thus left the ecclesiastical authorities in no doubt that drastic exemplary action was essential if they were to enforce conformity. However, the parliamentary failure of Gardiner's attempt to revive the heresy laws in April 1554 left the regime without sanctions other than imprisonment, public penance and excommunication. Tudor prison conditions could be bestial, and many of the accused were to die in gaol. Nevertheless, considerable freedom of access and movement might be allowed to prisoners with influential friends, or money to pay their way, not least because some of the prison officials were Edwardine appointees sympathetic to their protestant inmates. In the course of 1554, therefore, several of the London prisons, especially the King's Bench, the Marshalsea and the Bread Street Counter, became centres of protestant identity, influence and even recruitment. During John Bradford's year-long confinement first in the Tower (where he shared a cell with Cranmer, Ridley and Latimer) and then in the King's Bench (where his companions included Bishop Robert Ferrar, Dr Rowland Taylor and John Philpot), he was able to conduct an extraordinary ministry, receiving visitors, preaching, administering communion according to the second Edwardine Prayer Book and despatching letters to individuals and congregations as far away as his native Lancashire. The prison letter, deliberately larded with New Testament phraseology evoking the early church under pagan persecution, became a distinctive new protestant genre, and such letters might be widely circulated. Questions were raised in Parliament about the harm that Bradford's letters were held to be doing in the north-west, while the 'godly, learned and comfortable conferences' between Ridley and Latimer in their shared imprisonment would be issued in pamphlet form after their executions, to stiffen protestant resolve. One of Bradford's fellow prisoners, the Sussex lay activist, Richard Woodman, would look back to his long London imprisonment in 1554 as a time of encouragement and grace, 'amongst our brethren and my olde prison fellowes'.[39] This difficulty in monitoring and controlling the activities of prisoners in the secular gaols led Bishop Bonner to make increasing use of the Lollard's Tower at St Paul's, and even of his own windowless coal-house, as places of closer confinement and scrutiny for ideologically dangerous inmates.

The reconciliation of the country to the Holy See on 30 November 1554, and the accompanying settlement of the question of church property, removed the only serious parliamentary resistance to the revival of the heresy laws, which came back into force on 20 January 1555.[40] As if to underline their timeliness, on New Year's night 1555 a conventicle of more than thirty Londoners, John and Elizabeth Warne among them, was discovered in a house in Bow churchyard. Their leader, the priest Thomas Rose, was sent to the Tower, and later moved to Norwich (where he had held a living in Edward's reign) for trial by the bishop there. Confronted with the prospect of the fire, he recanted on 13 June 1555, but soon after escaped to exile in Frankfurt. The members of his congregation were distributed between the city's two Counter prisons. On 28 January, a panel of bishops led by the Lord Chancellor, Stephen Gardiner, began the process of emptying the gaols by initiating formal heresy processes against the leading preachers. The first of them, John Rogers, had been examined by the Privy Council the week before. He was formally condemned, along with Bishop Hooper, on 29 January and burned at Smithfield on 4 February, the first victim to go to the fire.

John Foxe thought that Gardiner and his episcopal colleagues were acting on a commission from Cardinal Pole, but no trace of any such commission survives, and the bishops taking part in these London trials operated under royal authority. Royal patents establishing national and diocesan heresy commissions with powers of search and arrest against heretics, distributors of heretical books and those suspected of sacrilege and other religious crimes survive from 1556 and 1557. The revived heresy laws stipulated that heretics were to be tried by their ordinary, and a *pro forma* patent for diocesan heresy commissions, consisting of the bishop with a small staff of officials, survives from February 1556. This, however, must be a formalisation or refinement of the system operating from February 1555. The patent of 1556 stipulated that local episcopal commissions should handle only straightforward heresy cases that clearly fell within diocesan jurisdiction. Anything more complicated was to be referred to the commission exercising wider powers in London under the chairmanship of Edmund Bonner, who seems to have inherited this invidious role from Gardiner, who very quickly ceased to handle heresy cases himself.[41]

Alongside the bishops, however, other groups of commissioners were at work, made up of highly committed lawyers and magistrates, active in seeking out and arresting suspects, and reporting directly to the Privy Council. In 1555, these commissioners included Thomas More's son-in-law, William Roper, who was sheriff of Kent but active against heresy well beyond the borders of his county. With him were Sir Nicholas Hare,

Master of the Rolls, the civil lawyer Sir Richard Rede and the canon lawyer William Cooke. They were subsequently joined by the most notorious heresy hunter of the reign, Dr John Story, Regius Professor of Canon Law at Oxford, MP for various Sussex constituencies, a Middlesex JP and Chancellor of the dioceses of London and Oxford. Story, who used his house in Greyfriars as an interrogation centre for suspects, was passionate in pursuit of heresy, convinced that well-directed severity was the key to its elimination, and critical of what he saw as feeble episcopal inaction. According to John Foxe, Story boasted late in 1555 that 'there hath bene yet never a one burnte, but I have spoken with him, and have bene a cause of his dispatch'.[42] The wide remit of these commissioners can be gathered from the proclamation establishing an expanded commission, composed of Privy Councillors, great officers of state, grandees, lawyers and clerics in February 1557. The King and Queen granted the commissioners powers to search for and examine suspects for heresy, to seize heretical or blasphemous books, to enquire into cases of sacrilege, blasphemy and the retention of church goods, and to punish by fines or imprisonment. Those whom they were satisfied were heretics were to be referred to the ordinary for formal heresy proceedings.

Thomas Thirlby was the only bishop in this 1557 commission, and he may well have been included in his capacity as Privy Councillor rather than as bishop of Ely. A similarly mixed lay and clerical body was established for the diocese of Canterbury just before Pole's first archiepiscopal visitation of 1556. The Canterbury commission included, in addition to Pole himself, a range of local grandees and lay activists sympathetic to the Cardinal's priorities, including William Roper. It also included half a dozen of Pole's closest clerical collaborators in the diocesan administration and the campaign against heresy in particular. Both the national and the Canterbury commissions were quorate when three of the members acted together (out of twenty and twenty-two respectively), but at Canterbury the quorum had always to include at least one of Pole's clerical right-hand men. Pole's last heresy commission, established in March 1558, would consist entirely of trusted and suitably qualified clergy, a further indication of characteristically clericalist counter-reformation priorities.[43]

The campaign against heresy, therefore, though under increasingly tight clerical control in the cardinal legate's diocese, was for most of the reign never an exclusively clerical concern, and the Queen herself was anxious that it should be pressed carefully but inexorably forward. In a memorandum on the reform of the church written early in 1555, she outlined the essentials of the programme actually adopted, stipulating that the punishment of heretics should be done 'without rashness', directed first at 'such as by learning would seem to deceive the simple', and the rest 'so to be used that the people might well perceive them not to be condemned without just occasion, whereby they shall both understand the truth and beware to do the like'. In London in particular, because of the presence of a strong and vocal protestant minority, 'I would wish none to be burnt without some of the Council's presence', and to explain and justify the burnings and correct heretical error there should be 'good sermons at the same'.[44]

This document, with its emphasis on preaching at the burnings, has been taken to suggest that 'the Queen's priorities were rather different from Pole's, and from the policy which was subsequently followed'.[45] In fact, Pole himself probably helped draft it: at any rate, he would explicitly refer to and endorse Mary's instructions, in a letter to his suffragans in September 1555, and there is no reason whatever to think that there was any significant difference of opinion between Cardinal and Queen on religious policy. Indeed, Mary's reverence for Pole's opinion, his constant presence at court and her anxiety to keep him by her even at the risk of the neglect of his other pastoral responsibilities were all matters of pointed comment to contemporaries. Observers of the court, noting the regular two-hour audiences of Cardinal and Queen, believed that the Queen would not allow 'by any means . . . that [the Cardinal] should be the slightest distance from her', since, even in secular matters, 'she knows that none of her ministers can give more sincere or more prudent counsel than he does'. Pole himself was obliged to defend his presence at court rather than in his diocese in terms of the support and guidance that Mary needed from him to ensure that 'the church's affairs might be better ordered'. The suggestion of divergence on religious matters between Queen and Cardinal rests, among other things, on what we have seen is the mistaken assumption that Pole, unlike the Queen, was unenthusiastic about preaching. But, in any case, Mary began this same memorandum by insisting explicitly that those charged with the restoration of catholicism should regularly 'have recourse' to Pole 'to understand of him which way might be best to bring to good effect those matters that have begun concerning religion'. There seems little doubt, therefore, that, in all matters of religion, Mary took her lead from Pole. The sole exception to this rule appears to have been the decision to burn Thomas Cranmer (despite his recantations); this was almost certainly the result of the Queen's own deep loathing of the man who had divorced her parents and plunged a whole generation of her subjects into heresy.[46]

Nevertheless, if we can be sure that churchmen at the very highest level endorsed the persecution, some of this campaign of repression's most enthusiastic participants were laymen, commissioners working with local magistrates. The pursuit of heresy and heretics was closely supervised, and episodically urged on, by the Privy Council, who viewed heresy as a threat to the regime, and had, from the start of the reign, been concerned to galvanise local officials to decisive action against 'lewde and seditious' preaching and all forms of religious nonconformity.[47] A royal letter to the justices of the peace in Norfolk on 25 March 1555 spelled out how the regime envisaged the role of the local magistrates in the fight against heresy. The county was to be divided up into eight or twelve smaller units, allocated between them as appropriate. They were to assist and support with their presence the preachers who were to be sent down into the country 'to preach Catholic doctrine to the people'; and they were to search out those who, by absence from church or other tokens, showed their religious dissidence, to labour to persuade them where possible, and to punish the obstinate where necessary, paying special attention to 'preachers and teachers of heresy, and procurers of secret meetings for that purpose'. They were to recruit in every parish 'some one or more honest men, secretly instructed,' to act as informers. They were also to charge constables 'of the most honest and catholick of every parish' to vigilance against vagabonds, wanderers 'and such as may be probably suspected'.[48]

There are many examples of zealous magistrates willing to fulfil this role, such as Edmund Tyrrell, bailiff of St Osyth in Essex and MP for Maldon: a man, according to Foxe, ever eager to 'heape vp mo coales to this furious flame of persecution, whether of a blind zeale, or of a parasiticall flattery I knowe not'.[49] Tyrrell was to remain a very effective hammer of heretics for the rest of the reign, leading a sweep against Essex conventiclers in 1556, no doubt spurred on by the discovery that two groups of gospellers were meeting with the connivance of one of his herdsmen for sermons in woods near Hockley, on his own land. Like his namesake Sir John Tyrrell in Suffolk, he would become expert in organising nocturnal raids on the houses of suspected heretics.[50]

The activities of the informers and local officials who helped magistrates such as Tyrrell are harder to document, but it is clear that such informers, 'promoting neighbours', were common. Prominent among the London informers was one of the most important catholic printers and publishers of the reign, Robert Caly, 'Papist Robin the promoter', whose printing shop was close to Dr John Story's house in the Greyfriars. He seems to have exercised extensive powers of citizen's arrest, and to have kept a watching brief on fellow publishers.[51] Foxe prints a striking example of the information supplied by a group of such local 'promoters', presented to the heresy commissioners sitting at Ipswich in May 1556. Arranged under the various Ipswich parishes, the report gives the names of thirty-nine townsmen and women who had fled the town for religious reasons, 'and lurked in secret places'; twenty-three more who refused to receive the Sacrament; ten 'who observe not ceremonies' in varying ways, from refusing the pax at Mass to spitting out the host after receiving communion; named members of the town elite who had opposed the compilation of the report; and alerted the commissioners that a local curate, Ralph Carleton, 'by corruption of money' was failing to report some non-communicants.[52] This document was delivered to the commissioners while Bishop Hopton was also in the town, conducting a visitation and interviewing suspects,[53] which can hardly be a coincidence, and may suggest a pincer movement against heresy, involving the forces of both church and state. The report itself provides remarkable testimony both to the willingness of groups of local activists to collaborate with the regime's campaign of enforcement, and to the devastatingly disruptive effect that that campaign might have on protestants in communities such as Ipswich.

As we shall see, conciliar desire to involve magistrates and local officials in sharp and decisive action against heresy, to eliminate the evangelical hard core and to frighten the wavering back into conformity did not always sit easily with the pastoral concerns of the bishops and clergy to convert rather than kill the heretic, or with clerical squeamishness about proceeding to extremes. Though lay councillors could show themselves surprisingly well informed about doctrinal issues, most were impatient of theological niceties. Some were doubtful whether protestants would have the stomach to endure sustained persecution, believing (or at any rate hoping) that the mere threat of burning would reduce even the intransigent to compliance. During John Rogers's examination by the Privy Council, Sir Richard Southwell, himself no paragon of principle, sneered contemptuously 'thou wilt not burne in this geare when it commeth to the purpose, I know well that'.[54] Events were to prove him very wide of the mark, but Southwell might be forgiven for doubting the likelihood of protestant constancy, in the face of the sanction of a terrible death.

In accordance with the Queen's stipulation that 'such as by learning would seem to deceive the simple' should be particular targets, the most prominent protestant leaders and heresiarchs, Bishops Cranmer, Ridley and Latimer, were destined for show trials, including a turbulent public disputation involving the combined theology faculties of Oxford and Cambridge. A hostile audience of townspeople and members of the university hissed and booed the defendants, the whole sequence being designed to demonstrate that protestantism had lost the argument as well as the political initiative. Their catholic clerical opponents certainly hoped that these and other evangelical leaders could be brought to recant their 'fantasticall & deuilish' opinions, and in so doing 'winne many, and do much good'.[55] Their condemnations and deaths were therefore postponed, and they were endlessly reasoned with to bring them to conformity – in Cranmer's case, for more than a year. Meanwhile, and unsurprisingly, the first four victims of the revived laws, executed in February 1555, were also notable clerical leaders. All had been prominent in the establishment of the Edwardine reformation, and all were men whose determination and public reputation made some sort of showdown with them inevitable.

John Rogers, the first to die, was a noted London preacher, biblical translator, lecturer in divinity at St Paul's Cathedral and one of Bishop Ridley's most admired protégés. Immediately after Mary's accession, he had placed himself at the head of principled resistance to the new order, preaching a 'vehement and godly' attack on catholicism at Paul's Cross, and he had been a conspicuous presence at the Paul's Cross riot of 13 August 1553. Arrested as a seditious preacher three days later, he maintained that he had intervened at the preacher's urgent request, in order to restrain the crowd, and had thereby saved Bourne's life. The authorities appear to have believed, however, that his ability on that occasion 'to rule and lead the people malapartly' showed that he had helped foment the disturbance in the first place:[56] the two versions are not necessarily incompatible. Held for weeks under house arrest, Rogers had ample opportunity to escape to the Continent and the regime may well have hoped he would do so. He chose, however, to face the coming storm.

Lawrence Saunders, burned four days after Rogers at Coventry on 8 February, was another prominent preacher, rector of the prestigious London church of All Hallows, Bread Street, but a pluralist and a key figure in the reformation in the Lichfield diocese, where he had spent much of Edward's reign. Saunders deliberately returned to London after Mary's accession, determined to steady his London congregation and to witness against the restoration of antichrist proceeding so rapidly there. He was well aware that he was inviting retaliation and indeed told a friend that he was 'in prison till I be in prison'. Despite a pointed warning from Sir John Mordaunt, a Privy Councillor who had heard (and disapproved of) his fiery anti-catholic preaching, Saunders courted arrest by denouncing the abominations of popery from his London pulpit on 15 October, and was duly imprisoned along with the backsliding John Cardmaker, who had already recanted, in the Counter in Bread Street, just a stone's throw from his rectory. During their shared confinement, Saunders persuaded Cardmaker to renounce his recantation and ultimately embrace martyrdom.[57]

John Hooper, Edwardine bishop of Gloucester and Worcester, was theologically the most radical, pastorally the most energetic and personally the most rebarbative of all Edward's bishops, and on all three counts a natural target in the new order, despite his immediate public support for Mary's claims to the throne. His characterisation of Gardiner as 'God's enemy and mine' makes clear that there was also a personal history between Hooper and the chairman of the commission that was to try him.[58] Rowland Taylor, burned on 9 February, the same day as Hooper, was absentee rector of the rich Canterbury peculiar of Hadleigh in Suffolk. A protégé and close collaborator of Cranmer's, he had been one of the most active Edwardine reformers, serving as archdeacon both of Bury in Suffolk and of Cornwall on the other side of England, and as one of the Six Preachers at Canterbury. Arrested initially for his involvement in Northumberland's coup, he was released but subsequently rearrested, since his prominence under the previous regime, combined with his fiercely outspoken anti-popery, made him a marked man. Like Saunders and Rogers, he scorned flight. Preachers, he believed 'must be bowld and not mylk mowthd', and after his initial release he had refused to go into exile: 'Verbum Dei', he declared 'made us goo to London.'[59]

Other prominent evangelical clerics would follow these four to the stake in the months that followed.[60] More significantly, the scope of the campaign widened in March to include lay people, tried before their own bishops, rather than by Gardiner and the other episcopal commissioners. To begin with, the numbers of victims were comparatively small, but by the end of the year seventy-five had gone to the flames, the bulk of them in the summer months of June to September. Just four had died in February, ten in March (only one of them in London), two in April and another two in May. Many of these executions are poorly documented, but those whose cases we can reconstruct in any detail were tough-minded evangelicals, in many cases veterans, whose continued activism in defiance of the new regime perhaps surprised the authorities, and at any rate ensured that they became early targets.

By the time the burnings began, some, having resisted all attempts to persuade them to conformity or even quietness, had already been in gaol for a year or more. Rawlins White, an illiterate Cardiff fisherman and self-appointed roving evangelist in Edward's reign, became an active organiser of conventicles under Mary, resisted pressure from friends and family to go into hiding and was arrested by the town officers of Cardiff early in 1554. Bishop Kitchin of Llandaff, himself an incorrigible timeserver and the only bishop to remain in post under Henry, Edward, Mary and Elizabeth, made repeated attempts to persuade White to conformity, and kept him under very loose house arrest at Chepstow, perhaps in the hope that he would decamp. White, however, refused to oblige on either count. Transferred to secular jurisdiction, he spent a year in gaol in Cardiff, where he was sufficiently laxly imprisoned to be able to exhort visitors and conduct Sunday services (though a layman), and to maintain a vocal campaign against the 'false prophets' and wolves of Mary's church. With the heresy laws in place, he was once again brought defiantly before Kitchin, even appearing in the choir doorway of the bishop's chapel while Mass was being celebrated to call on any protestants in the congregation 'if there be but one Brother amongst you, the same one beare witnesse at the daye of iudgement, that I bowe not to this Idoll'.[61] He was executed at Cardiff sometime in March 1555.

The first layman to be burned in London was a Shoreditch weaver, Thomas Tomkins, executed at Smithfield on 16 March. Tomkins had been examined by Bonner for heresy in September 1554, before the revival of the heresy laws, and he appears to have been in the fairly relaxed custody of the bishop's house at Fulham since at least the hay harvest earlier in the summer (which he helped to get in, to pay for his keep). This suggests that he was probably one of those detected for refusal to communicate at Easter 1554. However he had come to Bonner's attention, Tomkins, like Rawlins White, undoubtedly had 'form'. He was an earnest and conspicuous gospeller of long standing, with a habit of aphoristic citation of scripture. He sported a flowing patriarchal beard, something of an evangelical trademark, which the irritated Bonner paid a barber to shave off, 'that so he wold loke like a catholike'. Tomkins was also given to overt and perhaps tiresome demonstrations of piety – he was, Foxe tells us, 'of such conuersation and disposition so godly, that if any woman had come vnto him with her web, as sometyme they did three or foure in a day, hee would alwayes begin with praier'.[62] Bonner made repeated attempts to coax this pious weaver to conformity, as did some of his most eloquent persuaders, Dean Feckenham, Dr Henry Pendleton and Dr William Chedsey, but Tomkins stood firm, and his dogged resistance evoked from the exasperated bishop one of the most notorious episodes in Foxe's *Acts and Monuments*. Apparently in an attempt to shock the weaver into a realisation of the appalling fate that awaited him unless he recanted, Bonner seized his hand and held it over a candle flame, a brutality that made the more squeamish Archdeacon Harpsfield cry out that 'he had tried him enough'.[63]

Tomkins was the only protestant executed in London in March 1555, but seven other members of Bonner's diocese, all but one of them lay people, were burned the same month at various locations in Essex. The geographical scatter of these first executions – at Rayleigh, Horndon on the Hill, Brentwood, Maldon, Braintree, Danbury and Colchester – was strikingly different from the pattern that would emerge the following year. As protestant resistance stiffened, the authorities manifested their corresponding determination to deal with dissent by moving from a policy of single executions in discretely separate locations to group executions in prominent centres (Maps 3 and 4). The victim in the best documented of these early burnings, William Hunter, was also the youngest, a nineteen-year-old London silk-weaver's apprentice from a staunchly protestant family in Brentwood. Hunter refused to go to Mass or to receive Communion at Easter 1554, and as a result was dismissed by his master, 'lest that he should come in daunger, because of him'. Returning to Brentwood, he fell foul of one 'father Atwel', the bishop's summoner, who found the young man reading aloud from the English Bible in a chapel in Brentwood. Hunter maintained that he was reading to himself for his own comfort, but it can hardly be a coincidence that he had chosen for his 'comfort' the sixth chapter of St John, one of the most controverted passages in debates between catholic and protestant about the Mass. Atwel's own religious position can be gauged from his declaration that 'it was never mery since the Bible came abroad in English'. He told Hunter that

> I perceiue your minde well enoughe, you are one of them that misliketh the Queenes lawes, and therefore you came from London, I heare say. You learned these waies at London, but for all that . . . you must turne an other leafe, or els you and a great sorte moe heretickes will broyle for this geare, I warrant you.

Atwel fetched a priest, Thomas Wood, from a nearby alehouse, and the acrimonious argument that followed exposed the full extent of Hunter's protestant beliefs, as well as his precocious self-assurance: as Wood declared 'It is a merye worlde when such as thou arte shall teache us what is the truth.'[64] The priest duly denounced Hunter to Sir Anthony Browne, MP for Maldon and one of the most active heresy-hunting magistrates on the Essex bench: though the lad went into hiding, Browne tracked him down and sent him to Bonner.

CHAPTER 5

The Theatre of Justice

The examination of suspected heretics culminated in a judicial process, designed to establish the guilt or innocence of the accused, and to excommunicate the incorrigible before handing them over to the secular arm for execution. But for both the catholic authorities and the protestants in the dock, it was also very much more. For the bishops, it was an opportunity to recall straying sheep to the unity of the church, to correct their errors and to set out authentic catholic teaching. And, since much of the examination, and invariably its final stage, was carried out before spectators in open court, it was also a public performance, a solemn piece of theatre in which justice was displayed. In London especially, it was an opportunity to demonstrate to a sometimes hostile lay audience that every effort was being made to win the accused over by persuasion – in the Queen's words, 'that the people might well perceive them not to be condemned without just occasion, whereby they shall both understand the truth and beware to do the like'.[1] For the accused, it was of course a tribunal with powers of life and death, a terrifying ordeal that, if they remained faithful to their convictions, could only end in an appalling and painful death. But it was also an evangelical opportunity to witness against the errors of antichrist, to vindicate their own fidelity to the Gospel, to prove the bloodthirsty cruelty of the bishops and to persuade the onlookers to embrace the protestant cause.

The official records of the processes from episcopal registers or court records are characteristically terse and uninformative: lists of articles put to, affirmed or denied by the accused, forms of recantation, and the text of the sentences read against those found guilty. They often survive only in the pages of Foxe or in his manuscript collections, for, in Elizabeth's reign, he pillaged the official archives for material for his government-sponsored *Acts and Monuments*, and thought nothing of cutting pages from the court books and registers to add to his dossier. But we owe our most vivid sense of the trials to a distinctive new protestant genre: the victims' own accounts of their arrests and especially their examinations,[2] rich in circumstantial detail and reported speech, conveyed so immediately and persuasively that we are often reminded that they were committed to paper on the eve of the age of Shakespeare. Their authors went to remarkable lengths to compile these accounts, to conceal them from their captors and to ensure their dissemination among fellow gospellers and hence their ultimate publication. Along with the letters of the martyrs and eye-witness accounts of the burnings, they constitute the core of Foxe's lurid portrait of Mary's reign. We have no choice but to rely on these accounts in trying to trace the progress of the Marian campaign against heresy, but we need to bear constantly in mind that we see that campaign and its personnel almost entirely through the eyes of its victims and opponents. We have to make inferences from this intensely hostile and tendentious material about the motives and intentions of those conducting that campaign. It is a testimony to both the integrity and the thoroughness of their compilers that we are able to do this at all.

The most famous examinations were, of course, those of the episcopal leaders of the protestant movement, Latimer, Ridley and Cranmer, which can be said to have begun with the full-scale academic disputation conducted with the three bishops by the theology faculties of both universities in April 1554. These became trials proper when Ridley and Latimer were summoned to Oxford in September 1555, before a legatine commission with power to judge, sentence, degrade and deliver them to the secular arm.[3] These were obviously high-profile events, carefully staged before large audiences. But, in London at any rate, the trials of even much humbler figures might also attract large crowds of spectators. The authorities were intensely aware that such examinations might provide publicity for the accused and their opinions, and displayed considerable anxiety about the possibly corrupting effects on the listeners. This concern was not, of course, peculiar to England. In 1547, Philip's chaplain, the Franciscan theologian Fray Alfonso de Castro, himself a participant in the examination of John Rogers, had composed what became the standard European textbook on the interrogation and punishment of heretics. In it, he warned that, though the authorities must do everything in their power to argue the heretic out of his or her error, such admonition should be held 'in private, and not before the people'.

Heretics loved nothing more than to debate while the common people stood by and listened, driven as they were by the lust for 'populist and empty glory' and the longing 'to be praised by everyone, and to be esteemed as more learned than anyone else'.[4]

Most of the fundamental doctrines contested between sixteenth-century catholics and protestants appeared somewhere in the articles alleged against suspected heretics or proposed to them for their assent – the real presence of Christ's body and blood in the eucharist; the authority and truthfulness of the catholic church, as embodied in European christendom and specifically in the Marian church in communion with the see of Rome; the sole right of that church to interpret scripture; the value of penance and good works for salvation; the freedom of the human will. Since many suspects came to the notice of the authorities by their absence from or irreverent behaviour during church services, many examinations focused on ritual issues and the externals of religious practice – the holiness and value of ceremonies, sacraments and sacramentals; refusal to carry a candle at Candlemas, to go to confession, to creep to the cross, to use holy water or holy bread, or to share the pax at Mass.[5] Of these issues, far and away the most important was the refusal to acknowledge the corporeal presence of Christ in the Mass, and, next to that, the rejection of the authority and ministry of the church. But the form and content of the articles varied greatly from diocese to diocese. In Norwich, the formula routinely used by Bishop Hopton and his chancellor began with the authority of the pope as 'supreme head immediately under Christ in earth of the universall Catholike Church'.[6] The pope was also routinely mentioned in the articles used by Ralph Baynes at Lichfield, and by William Geffrey at Salisbury. By contrast, the articles used in the London diocese treated the universality of the church of Rome's jurisdiction, but without explicitly mentioning the pope himself.

Since London saw more executions than any other diocese, the main outlines of the standard set of articles in use there are of special interest. These sought to elicit that the accused was resident in the London diocese (and so subject to the bishop's jurisdiction) and a baptised Christian, and so obliged to obey the authoritative teaching of the church. Suspects were asked to acknowledge that, at the time they had reached the age of discretion (fourteen), they themselves had followed the universally accepted teaching of the catholic church that Christ was truly present in the Blessed Sacrament, that this faith had been accepted by the accused's parents, ancestors and godparents, and that in denying it they had consciously departed from traditional Christian teaching. They had thereby aligned themselves with (and praised as martyrs) notorious heretics burned for their errors, whom the articles sometimes listed – Friar Barnes, Anne Askew, Bishop Hooper, Lawrence Saunders, John Bradford and many more. Finally, the articles declared that the fact of their heresy was notorious 'among the sad and good people of the citee of London and Dioces of the same' or at any rate in their own parish, where 'there is a common voice and fame therof'.[7] This general framework might be varied to meet specific issues, or to emphasise one aspect more than others. Bonner and his officials sometimes laid special stress on protestantism as a repudiation of family and community, asking 'doe you thinke, and steadfastly believe that your parentes, kinsfolke, frendes and acquaintance . . . had a true christen fayth, and were faythfull and true Christen people or no?' They might also emphasise catholic belief as part of the cement of society and of the body politic more generally, both national and European – whether

the King, and the Quene of thys Realme of England, and all the Nobilyty, Clergy, & Layty of this Realme professing and beleuinge the sayd Doctrine and faith, as other christian Realmes do, concernyng the . . . sacrament of the aulter, haue a trew Christian fayth, and beleue as the catholike, and true church of Christ hath alwais beleued, preached, and taught, or no

and whether the accused had any legitimate reason for embracing

the erroneous opinion or beliefe, that hath ben against the common order of the Church, brought in by certaine disordred persons of late, and at the vttermost within these 30. or 40. yeares last past.[8]

In the early stages of the campaign, the role of the examination in establishing that the condemned heretic had resisted every persuasion to conformity was highlighted, as in the formula subscribed by Thomas Tomkins in September 1554, acknowledging that

being many times and ofte called openly before my said Ordinarie, and talked withall touching all my sayd confessions and declarations, both by the saide mine Ordinarie & diuers other learned men, aswel his Chaplaines as other, and counselled by all them to embrace the truthe, and to recant mine errour . . . which they tolde me was plaine heresie and manifest errour: do testifie and declare hereby, that I do and wil . . . in no wise recant or go from any part of the same.[9]

The articles offered to Thomas Wattes of Billericay, whose reproachful allegations about their evangelical pasts had alarmed some of the leading Essex magistrates sitting in judgement on him, included a special mention of 'his erroneous and arrogant words before the . . . Commisioners . . . to the hurt of his soule and to the evill example of the people there present'.[10] Nicholas Harpsfield, in 1556 and 1557, found himself dealing in both London and Kent not only with mainstream protestant dissent, but also with groups of radicals with suspect views on the Trinity and the divinity of Christ. Additional articles were devised to take account of these beliefs.[11]

If the final judicial stages of a process were always held in open court, many of the initial examinations took the form of private or semi-private conversations between the prisoner and one or more commissioners, or the bishops and their officials. All of those who recorded examinations were involved in such conversations more than once, in some cases a dozen or more times, and most record the resort to experienced persuaders, often men who had themselves once professed evangelical convictions, to 'talk brotherly' with them. Thomas Haukes was counselled both by Richard Smith, who had recanted his catholicism in Edward's reign and resumed it in Mary's, and by John Bird, formerly bishop of Chester, deprived for marriage but now acting as Bonner's suffragen. Bird was old and half blind with 'a pearl in his eye', a kindly but not very effective persuader who urged Haukes to 'learn of your elders to beare somewhat'. During one such argument, Bird fell asleep in mid-sentence, providing Haukes – and Foxe – with an unforgettable vignette conveying the imagined senescence of the old religion – 'I suppose he is not yet awake.'[12] These encounters with converts might even be sought by the heretics themselves. John Bradford asked for a conversation with Dr Henry Pendleton in the Counter prison, explaining to him, no doubt ironically, that

> I remember that once you were (as farre as a man might iudge) of the Religion that I am of at this present, and I remember that you haue set forth the same earnestly. Gladly therfore would I learn of you what thing it was that moued your conscience to alter, and gladly would I see what thing it is that you haue sene sithen, which you saw not before.[13]

Episcopal residences, especially Bonner's, were public spaces, and so even these more private examinations might have witnesses, some of whom joined in debate or attempts at persuasion. Privy Councillors and commissioners routinely sat in on the examinations of major figures; the mathematician and astrologer Dr John Dee, 'the great Coniurer' (who was himself under suspicion for sorcery), took part in the preliminary examinations of John Philpot; and the London hosier and controversialist Miles Hogarde debated with Thomas Haukes. These preliminary examinations might go on for weeks or even months, depending on the importance of the accused, and often took on a gladiatorial character. This, as we have seen, was one of the drawbacks of the examinations from the regime's point of view, turning a pastoral instrument into a propaganda opportunity for error. John Philpot, former archdeacon of Winchester, was of gentry stock, with influential relatives, and had become notorious through his prominent role as spokesman on the protestant side in the debates about the Sacrament during the first Convocation of Mary's reign. The process against him was therefore spun out for months in the hope of winning him round, to the mounting exasperation of many. Bonner complained to Philpot a month before his execution,

> I am blamed of the Lordes the Bishoppes, for that I haue not dispatched thee ere this. And in Faith I made sute to my Lorde Cardinal, and to all the Conuocation house, that they would heare thee. And my Lorde of Lincolne stode vp, and said that thou wert a frantike fellow, and a man that wil haue the last worde. And they all haue blamed me, because I haue brought thee so often before the Lordes openly: and they say it is meat & drinke to you to speake in an open audience, you glory so of your self.[14]

There was some truth in this accusation. Philpot was indeed chronically argumentative, with a strong sense of personal infallibility. Debating with the notable catholic champion Morgan Phillips, a veteran of the Oxford debates with Peter Martyr, Philpot told him

> I tell thee playne, thou art not able to answer that spirit of truth, which speaketh in me for the defence of Christes true Religion. I am able by the might therof, to driue thee round about this gallery before me: and if it would please the queenes maiesty and her Councell to heare thee and me, I woulde make thee for shame shrinke behinde the doore.[15]

This public dimension of the examinations was heightened once the process moved to its formal stages in the Consistory, which, in London at least, was often crowded with spectators. Both sides therefore often spoke for effect, their words designed not merely or even mainly to persuade or answer objections, but to engage the sympathy of the audience for or against the catholic cause. In one of the most brilliant passages of his consistently brilliant prosecution of Cranmer in Oxford, the civil lawyer Thomas Martin made just such a direct appeal to the spectators. As we have seen earlier, all Cranmer's actions, Martin argued, had fulfilled the Devil's temptation of Jesus,

> For . . . Cast thy selfe downeward, said he: and so taught you to cast all thinges downeward. . . . Whether these bee not the fruites of your Gospell, I referre mee to this worshipfull audience: whether the sayed Gospell began not with periurie, proceeded with adulterie, was maintained with heresie, and ended in conspiracy.[16]

It was cause for concern, however, when the accused attempted to make similar rhetorical appeals to the 'worshipfull audience'. In 1557, the same Bishop White who had warned against giving Philpot publicity was convinced that Richard Woodman was attempting to appeal over the heads of the Winchester consistory court, sitting in St Mary Overy, to the spectators present. This crowd evidently included vocal members of the London evangelical community, for the bishop warned:

> Do you not see how he looketh about for help: But I would see any man shewe thee a cheerful countenance, and especially you that be of my Dioces. If any of you bid God strengthen him, or take him by the hand, or embrace him, or shewe hym a chearefull countenance, you shall be excommunicated, and shall not bee receieved in agayne, till you have done open pennaunce, and therefore beware of it.[17]

In fact, the argumentativeness of the accused might alienate as well as elicit sympathy. Woodman was a long-standing suspect, who had spent months in hiding and had briefly gone into exile in Europe. He was arrested in a raid on his home as part of a sweep of heretics following the establishment of a new heresy commission in the spring of 1557. A prosperous ironmaster and employer of a hundred workmen, he was a man of substance, and received a good deal of local support, even among the religiously conservative county gentry of Sussex. Prominent among them was James Gage, brother of Sir John Gage, the sheriff responsible for his arrest. Gage eventually brought Alban Langdale, archdeacon of Chichester, to London to reason with Woodman. In addition to his role in detecting heresy in the diocese, Langdale was parish priest to Woodman's father, 'an honest man' and a devout catholic who, according to the archdeacon, had wept bitterly over the his son's evil opinions. Taking this as his cue, Langdale used a familiar apologetic ploy to warn Woodman against presumptuously damning his ancestors, 'and all that use the same [faith] that they did, throughout all Christendome, unless it be in Germany and here in England a few years'. Woodman replied with appropriate scriptural illustrations, that 'we must not follow a multitude to do evill . . . for the most goe the wrong way'. When the exasperated archdeacon declared that Woodman was 'the naughtiest man that ever I talked with in all my life: for he will have his owne way in all thinges', Gage directed a lecture on humility to the accused: 'Woodman, leave that pride . . . hearken to this man. This is a learned man, I tell you. He is known to be learned. For else hee shuld not be allowed to preach before the Queenes Majesty.'[18]

In the early months of the campaign, the Imperial ambassador in London, Simon Renard, accused the bishops of being too 'hot and hasty' against heresy. The evidence suggests, on the contrary, that the relatively small numbers proceeded against in the spring of 1555 reflected episcopal caution, informed not only by worries about the likely public reaction to the burnings, but also by concern for the spiritual welfare of the accused. Even after episcopal determination hardened in the face of perhaps unexpectedly sustained protestant resistance, a recurrent feature of the surviving examinations and trials was the manifestly sincere and sometimes long-drawn-out efforts made by bishops and their officers to convert rather than condemn the men and women before them. Foxe himself drew attention to these attempts to persuade the victims to conformity. He of course took the worst possible view of them, either as bids to discredit protestant constancy to the Gospel with 'some forged example of a shrinking brother, to lay in the dish of the rest who were to be examined',[19] or as devilish, last-ditch attempts to seduce the victims from their allegiance to Christ, and so to damn them.

The real motives were less lurid and, in part at least, more creditable. The judges were priests, charged with the salvation of souls, and they had for the most part a genuine horror of the eternity of torment that they believed awaited unrepentant heretics. Their frequent pleadings with the accused to 'cast not your selfe away' had eternal damnation in mind as well as the horror of the death sentence itself. In any case, a repentant heretic was a potent witness to the error and inconstancy of protestantism: a dead one might be deemed a martyr.

Such concerns were evident from the very first trials, but there were also more pragmatic reasons for this reluctance to proceed to extremes. By 1555, after a generation of government-sponsored anti-clericalism, Bonner and other clergy involved were understandably nervous about the likely reaction of even catholic-minded Tudor people to the spectacle of bishops and priests pronouncing excommunications that were, in practical terms, death sentences on lay people, especially when the victims were of gentry status. When Thomas Causton and Thomas Higbed were arrested by magistrates at Colchester in March 1555, the bishop, 'perceiuing these 2. Gentlemen to be of worshipful estate, & of great estimation in that countrey, least any tumult shoulde thereby arise', travelled himself to Colchester with a team of persuaders, including the gentle and golden-tongued dean of St Paul's, John Feckenham, in the vain hope of reconciling them to the church, and so avoiding resort to the death sentence.[20] But Bonner was prepared to go to extraordinary lengths with protestants of humbler status too: he told the apprentice William Hunter

> I thinke thou art ashamed to beare a fagot and recant openly, but if thou wilt recante thy sayinges, I will promise thee, that thou shalt not be putte to open shame: but speake the worde here nowe betwene me and thee, and I wil promise thee, it shal go no further, and thou shalt goe home againe without any hurt.

He stipulated that Hunter might simply go to his parish church, make his confession and accept absolution as the price of release, an offer that Hunter refused. Even after the boy's formal condemnation, Bonner continued to try to persuade him, telling him that

> I wil make thee a free man in the Citie, & geue thee 40. pound in good money to sette vp thine occupation withall: or I will make thee Steward of my house and set thee in office, for I like thee well, thou hast witte inough, and I will preferre thee, if thou recant.[21]

Bonner's attempts to win over this dissident apprentice certainly sprang in part from ordinary human compassion, the sense of the tragic waste of a young life – and an immortal soul – for persistence in what Bonner and his colleagues inevitably regarded as perverse and pernicious error. Even dedicated officials, convinced of the necessity of rooting out heresy, when faced not with the abstraction but with men and women of flesh and blood, might feel the horror of the fate awaiting the condemned. Dr Michael Dunning, chancellor of the Norwich diocese, showed himself a dedicated and tough-minded scourge of protestants in Norfolk and Suffolk, eventually involved in more than two dozen of the thirty-three capital cases in the diocese. In May 1556, however, the first occasion on which he rather than Bishop Hopton had to pass sentence of condemnation, he was faced by three defendants, one of whom was a farm labourer only nineteen years old. Unable to budge them from their fatal confession of protestant beliefs, the seasoned chancellor 'burst out in teares, intreatyng them to remember themselues, and to turne agayne to the holy mother church, for that they were deceiued and out of the truth, and that they should not wilfully cast away themselues'. The diocesan registrar, tougher-minded and impatient of such squeamishness, called out testily 'in hast to ridde them out of the way, and make an end', and Dunning eventually passed sentence.[22]

Foxe, our principal source for the trials, was inclined to treat all such examples of judicial compassion for the men and women convicted of heresy as mere crocodile tears. And, even if one accepts their sincerity, there is to a modern sensibility something revolting in even the relatively humane implementation of a law that could offer mercy to the hapless men and women accused only at the price of their renunciation or concealment of deeply held beliefs. Such revulsion is inevitably intensified when one considers that many of the accusers and judges had themselves not long before professed and, in some cases, promoted the very same beliefs for which the accused were now to be condemned. It became almost routine for prisoners to challenge their judges on this score.

Bishops or officials who had renounced the pope, served under heretic kings and used the Edwardine Prayer Books, might attempt to deflect the reproaches of those on whom they now stood in judgement, with admissions such as that of Bishop Day of Chichester to John Bradford, when he told him that, in accepting the Henrician reformation, 'I went with the world, but, I tell you, it was always against my conscience.'[23]

Indeed, repented apostasy was often turned to positive advantage as a persuasive tool, as when Nicholas Shaxton invoked his own protestant past to persuade William Wolsey and Robert Pygot to recant as he had done – 'brethren remember your selues and become new men, for I my self was in this fond opinion that you are nowe in, but I am now become a new man'.[24] This cut little ice with the victims of the heresy laws, and some catholics as well as condemned dissidents believed that a compromised past of this kind stripped the judges of moral authority.

The Essex fuller George Ambrose, examined for heresy in March 1556, told Lord Chancellor Heath, himself a former Henrician conformist, that 'after he had read the late Byshop of Winchesters booke, intituled *De vera obedientia*, with Boners preface thereunto annexed, inueying (both) against the authority of the Bishop of Rome, he did much lesse set by theyr doinges then before'.[25] Interrogating Thomas Drowry, a blind boy with a track record of public dissidence, the chancellor of Gloucester diocese, John Williams, demanded to know who had taught the boy his heresies. To his confusion, the boy replied that he had learned them from Williams himself, citing in detail a cathedral sermon in Edward's reign in which Williams had taught that the Sacrament was to be received spiritually by faith, 'and not carnally and really, as the papistes haue heretofore taught'. The abashed Williams urged the boy 'Then do as I haue done, and thou shalt lyue as I do, and escape burning.' When Drowry refused to recant, Williams gave sentence against him, though the diocesan registrar, also present, later claimed that he had protested, 'Fie for shame man, will you read the sentence against hym, and condemne your selfe?'[26]

Whatever considerations of compassion or personal compunction might have given pause to those charged with the pursuit and punishment of heresy, in the spring of 1555 the likelihood of a public backlash against the campaign was an even more pressing concern. At the very start of Mary's reign, the Paul's Cross riot had signalled the volatility of public opinion in London, and the ability of the city evangelicals to mobilise frightening forces of disorder against a regime conscious of its recent and perhaps precarious accession to power. Although the suppression of Wyatt's revolt and the steady consolidation of catholic observance in the City of London as everywhere else encouraged the regime to firmness in dealing with dissent, the numerical weight and influence of evangelicalism remained an unknown quantity. Gospellers were certainly present in strength in the crowds who flocked to see John Rogers burned at Smithfield on 4 February 1555. Vociferous demonstrations of support for the condemned man alarmed onlookers such as the Imperial ambassador, who told King Philip that 'Some of the onlookers wept, others prayed to God to give him strength, perseverance and patience to bear the pain and not to recant, others gathered the ashes and bones and wrapped them up in paper to preserve them, yet others threatening the bishops.' Renard feared that 'the haste with which the bishops have proceeded in this matter may well cause a revolt' and urged Philip to suspend the burnings for the time being and to consider carrying out any further executions for heresy in secret.[27] Though such demonstrations remained a threat to the end of the reign, this was certainly an overreaction. However volatile the City of London, with its entrenched and influential protestant minority, and its specially strong support base of rowdy apprentices, protestantism was a minority faith everywhere in England, except possibly in one or two of the villages of the Stour valley. After Wyatt, support for the victims was never likely to escalate into revolt.

But however inflated, Renard's fears were, to begin with at least, widely shared. As we have already noted, on 10 February, Philip's confessor, Alfonso de Castro, preached a sermon at court, in which, according to Foxe, 'he did earnestly inuey against the bishops for burning of men, saying plainly that they learned it not in scripture to burne any for his conscience: but the contrary, that they should lyue & be conuerted, with many other things more to the same purport.'[28] This sermon was almost certainly preached on Philip's orders, reflecting his fear that the executions might turn popular opinion even further against the Spanish in England. But Castro himself cannot have objected on principle to the execution of heretics.

In 1547, Castro had published a treatise entitled *De Iusta Haereticorum Punitione* – as its title suggests, a powerful justification of the use of force in matters of religion, including the death penalty – and he was to reissue it in 1556, with a dedication to Charles V urging him to keep up the good work in his dominions. In May 1556, moreover, Castro dedicated a revised edition of another massive treatise on the detection and definition of heresy to Philip himself, with a laudatory dedication crediting Philip with the restoration of papal catholicism in England, and betraying not the slightest hint of misgiving in that year of many burnings.[29] But Castro may well have criticised burning in particular as a form of execution in the spring of 1555 – he had maintained in *De Iusta Haereticorum Punitione* that, though an apt enough symbol of the vehemence of God's hatred of heresy, the employment of fire against heretics was a matter of mere human policy, for which some other form of capital punishment might licitly be substituted. This was perhaps an indication of his own dislike of the cruelty involved in execution by fire. And, like every other conscientious priest, Castro believed that every effort had to be made to persuade heretics, before they were condemned as incorrigible.[30] If his sermon implied, however, that the bishops had rushed bloodthirstily to condemn the first victims of the new policy in 1555, he did them an injustice for, as we have seen, the processes against the condemned men had been in train for months, in some cases for more than a year.

The pressure for action was coming not from the bishops, but from the Council and the Queen, and, behind the Queen, very probably from the Cardinal and his circle. All observers agreed that Mary depended heavily on Pole's advice, and, in her detailed instructions to the Council about the handling of the burnings, she insisted that regular weekly recourse be had to Pole, 'to understand of him which way might be best to bring to good effect these matters that have been begun concerning religion'.[31] The sermon should therefore be seen as a Spanish political gesture, a ceremonial hand-washing inspired by Renard's panic. But the charge of bloodthirstiness would stick. Protestant pamphleteers poured out execrations against 'bite-sheep' bishops, and one of the most effective pieces of visual propaganda of the whole Tudor period was a magnificently macabre print depicting Gardiner, Bonner, Tunstall and other bishops robed for Mass, Gardiner at the altar, biting out the throat of a sacrificial protestant sheep and drinking its blood. Engraved in Germany in 1555, it was used as an illustration in the first edition of William Turner's *The Huntyng of the Romyshe Wolfe* the same year, and would have a long afterlife into the seventeenth century as a staple of anti-catholic polemic (Plates 28, 29).[32]

However that may be, in the wake of the demonstrations at Rogers's burning, extreme care was taken about the movement of the other clergy burned that month outside London. The sheriff charged with taking Rowland Taylor to Hadleigh for execution overreacted when a

Plate 1. Queen Mary, by Hans Eworth, 1554. Society of Antiquaries, London.

Hans Eworth's portrait, painted in Mary's first year as queen, proclaims the queen's intense piety. She wears a Tau cross on a choker of pearls at her neck , and hanging from her girdle is a gilt-enamel reliquary with emblems of the Four Evangelists, the 'Tablet de Burbyone' listed among Henry VIII's jewel collection in 1521. Relics were denounced and destroyed by Mary's father and her brother: to display this restored reliquary in an official portrait was an overt declaration of the queen's religious agenda. The huge diamond on her breast was given by the Emperor Charles V: its pendant pearl, 'La Pelegrina', was bought by the actor Richard Burton in 1969, as a Valentine's Day present for Elizabeth Taylor.

Plate 2. Cardinal Pole, by Sebastiano del Piombo, mid 1540s? Hermitage Museum, St Petersburg.

This portrait was probably painted while Pole was governor of the Papal State of Viterbo, and leader of the circle of Italian catholic reformers known as the 'Spirituali', which included Michelangelo on its fringes. The portrait catches the watchful taciturnity for which Pole was renowned. Flowing beards were common among Italian churchmen, though in England were often considered a mark of protestantism.

Plate 3. Stephen Gardiner, Bishop of Winchester and Lord Chancellor, artist unknown. Corpus Christi College, Oxford

Before Pole's arrival in England, Gardiner was the driving force behind the restoration of catholicism. An apologist for the Royal Supremacy under Henry, but increasingly alienated by the radicalisation of the Reformation under Edward, he defended both the cult of images and the catholic doctrine of the Mass, and spent most of Edward's reign in the Tower. In 1554 he worked both for the return to papal obedience and for the revival of the heresy laws, but his opposition to the marriage with Philip II probably cost him the Queen's confidence.

Plate 4. Medal of Pope Julius III with allegorical scene of the restoration of England to Catholic Communion, 1554. British Museum.

The return of England to papal obedience was eagerly greeted as a turning-point for the catholic cause in northern Europe. Reported back to Rome especially by members of Pole's circle, events in England were publicised both by the papal court and in the Habsburg empire. On this commemorative medal by the Paduan medallist (and forger) Giovanni Cavino, the symbolic figure of Anglia kneels and raises a suppliant hand to the pope. Ranged around are Cardinal Pole with his Legatine Cross and Red Hat, the Emperor Charles V, and King Philip and Queen Mary. The inscription, *Anglia Resurges*, declares 'England, you shall arise'.

IL FELICISSIMO,
RITORNO DEL REGNO D'IN=
GHILTERRA ALLA CATHOLICA
Vnione, & alla obedientia della Sede
APOSTOLICA.

COPIA DELLE LETTERE

Del Sereniff. Re d'Inghilterra, & del Reuerendiff.
Card. Polo Legato della. S. Sede Apoftolica
alla Santità di .N.S. Iulio Papa III. fopra
la riduttione di ql Regno alla vnione
della Santa Madre Chiefa, &
obedienza della Sede
Apoftolica.

In Roma per Valerio, & Luigi Dorici
Con Priuilegio.

Plate 5. Title-page, *Il Felecismo Ritorno del Regno d'Inghilterra alla Catholica Unione & alla obedientia della Sede Apostolica*, Rome 1555. Lambeth Palace Library H5134.F3.

A description by a member of Pole's household (Alvise Priuli?) of the reconciliation of the kingdom to the catholic church in November 1554, for circulation by the papacy through Europe. The arms of pope, crown and cardinal adorn the title-page.

Plate 6. *Copia delle lettere del sereniss. Re d'Inghelterra & del Reverendiss. Card. Polo …sopra Obedientia della sede Apostolica*. Lambeth Palace Library.

This pamphlet printed letters from King Philip and Cardinal Pole to Pope Julius III announcing the reconciliation of the England to the Holy See. The Order of the Golden Fleece and the Habsburg Eagle alongside the Papal arms signal the importance of events in England for catholic Europe.

Plates 7 and 8. The Tomb of Stephen Gardiner, Winchester Cathedral

Completed early in 1556, Gardiner's chantry-chapel in Winchester Cathedral combines typical 'gothic' features, including a cadaver effigy of the dead bishop, with the fluted columns of French-style renaissance classicism. The images of Ecclesia and Synagoga above the altar flank a niche which probably contained either a crucifix or an image of the Trinity. This restrained blend of tradition and modernity is characteristic of the Marian church, which Gardiner had helped to shape.

Plate 9. Habsburg Catholicism: the Philip and Mary Window, Sint Janskerk, Gouda, 1557

Philip II contributed this window to the reconstruction of the greatest church in the North Netherlands, after a catastrophic fire in 1552. The subjects – Solomon's dedication of the Temple in Jerusalem, and the Last Supper – allude to the rebuilding of the Janskerk, but were probably also a conscious allusion to the royal couple's wider project to reconstruct catholicism in England. Philip and Mary kneel at the Last Supper, an affirmation of the catholic doctrine of the Mass.

Plate 10. Catholicism Renascent: the shrine of St Edward, Westminster Abbey, 1556–7.

Mary revived monastic life, refounding houses of the Dominicans (friars and nuns), Observant Franciscans, Carthusians and Bridgetine nuns. She was especially moved by the voluntary return to the habit in 1556 of sixteen Benedictines, led by Abbot John Feckenham, till then Dean of St Pauls and a favourite at court. Westminster Abbey, a collegiate church and (briefly) cathedral under Henry and Edward, became once more a monastery. The monks restored the relics and shrine of St Edward the Confessor, and the Abbey became one of the focal points of catholic display in the capital. The Marian shrine crowning the reassembled medieval tomb is still in place.

Plate 11. Catholicism Renascent: panelling from the choir of Worcester Cathedral, 1556–7, now in Holy Trinity, Sutton Coldfield.

Like most other churches in England, Worcester Cathedral had been stripped of its medieval altars and decoration in the reign of Edward VI. The Marian Dean and Chapter, and Bishop Richard Pate, formerly a member of Pole's Italian household, restored the choir for Catholic worship, with financial help from the Queen herself. The Queen and Cardinal came to Worcester in 1557 to see the new screens, stalls and organ, of which this panelling, removed from the Cathedral by Victorian 'restorers' rather than Elizabethan iconoclasts, is all that remains.

Plates 12 and 13. Catholicism Renascent: Printed Missal (Paris 1555) donated to the parish of St Peter, Tempsford, Bedfordshire. Cambridge University Library.

Richard Perkyn the elder donated this magnificent folio Missal to his parish church in November 1557, an example of the gradual elaboration of worship funded by lay donations once the basic infrastructure of catholic worship had been restored. The inscription on the title page requests prayers for Perkyn's 'good prosperitie and welfare'. A second inscription under the crucifix before the Canon of the Mass indicates that he had died in the interval.

Plates 14 and 15. Catholicism Renascent: Screen Panels from Lessingham, Norfolk, c. 1555–6, St Peter Hungate, Norwich.

Under Edward VI, the rood-screen in the small coastal parish of Lessingham had been scraped and whitewashed. Under Mary, parishioners restored the screen panel by pane, replacing the ruined images of Apostles with the Four Latin Doctors, i.e. Saints Gregory, Jerome, Ambrose, and Augustine. These were the founding theologians of the Latin Church, but were also Pope, Cardinal, Archbishop and Bishop respectively, symbolizing both the hierarchy and the teaching authority of the church. Also included was St Roche, invoked against plague. Epidemic was sweeping England in the 1550s, and Roche's presence suggests that belief in his protective power had survived into Mary's reign.

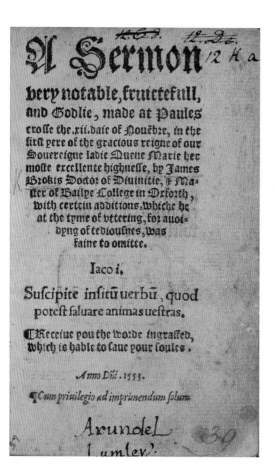

A Sermon

very notable, fruictefull,

and Godlie, made at Paules
croſſe the .xii. daie of Nouēbre, in the
firſt pere of the gracious reigne of our
Souereigne ladie Quene Marie her
moſte excellente highneſſe, by James
Brokis Doctor of Diuinitie, & Ma-
ſter of Bailpe College in Orforth,
with certein additions, whiche be
at the tyme of vttering, for auoi-
dyng of tediouſnes, was
faine to omitte.

Iaco i.

Suſcipite inſitū uerbū, quod
poteſt ſaluare animas ueſtras.

¶Receiue pou the worde ingraffed,
which is hable to ſaue pour ſoules.

Anno Dīi . 1553.

¶Cum priuilegio ad imprimendum ſolum.

Arundel

Lumley.

Plate 16. Title-page, James Brookes, *A Sermon Very Notable*, Robert Caly, London 1553. RSTC 3238-3239.3.

An expanded version of a sermon on the authority of the church preached at Paul's Cross in November 1553, this was one of the most successful catholic polemical efforts of Mary's first year, widely read and debated. Brookes became Bishop of Gloucester and presided as Papal delegate at the trial of Archbishop Cranmer. The house style of the title-page, announcing 'A sermon very notable fruitful and godlie', became standard for Paul's Cross Sermons printed by Robert Caly, and was used for the 1554 reissue of St John Fisher's famous Paul's Cross sermon against Luther.

¶A notable

and learned Sermon or
Homilie, made vpon ſaint An-
drewes daye laſt paſt 1556. in the
Cathedral churche of S. Paule
in London, by Mayſter Jhon
Harpeſſeild doctour of diuinitie
and Canon reſidenciary of
the ſayd churche, Set
furth by the biſhop
of London.

Vltima Decembris,
1556.

¶Cum priuilegio ad impri-
mendum ſolum.

Plate 17. Title-page, John Harpsfield, *Sermon for St Andrew's Day*, 1556. RSTC 12795.

Pole's Legatine Synod ordered an annual procession, Mass and sermon on St Andrew's Day (30 November) in thanksgiving for the restoration of unity with the Papacy: attendance by clergy and parishioners was compulsory. Harpsfield's sermon on papal primacy was intended for use by clergy unable to write their own. Designed to drive home the importance of papal authority, these annual celebrations ironically provided the model for later protestant commemorations, such as Guy Fawkes day.

Plate 18. Edmund Bonner, *A profitable and cecessarye Doctrine*, 1555, RSTC 3283.3.

Bonner's compendium of catholic doctrine was a complete reworking of the 1543 King's Book, elaborating and correcting its teaching. It was adopted by Cardinal Pole in 1556 for use throughout England as the basis for teaching and preaching, pending the completion of the more elaborate works commissioned by the Legatine Synod.

Plate 19. The burning of John Rogers at Smithfield, 4 February 1555.
Foxe, 1570, p. 1662, Trinity College, Cambridge, c.17.25.

Rogers, a bible translator and friend of Coverdale and Tyndale, led the resistance to Mary's restoration of catholicism with a 'godly and vehement sermon' at Paul's Cross in August 1553. A married incumbent of the city parish of St Sepulchre's, he was the first victim of the revived heresy laws, and his burning at Smithfield attracted turbulent crowds. Some protestants interpreted the pigeons disturbed by the flames and smoke as a manifestation of the Holy Spirit.

The burning of Maister Iohn Rogers, Vicar of S. Pulchers and Reader at Paules in London.

Plate 20. The burning of Bishop Hooper at Gloucester, 9 February 1555.
Foxe, 1570, p. 1684.

The unprecedented public execution of a bishop in his cathedral city for heresy aroused avid public interest. The burning was horrifyingly botched : the wood was wet, the wind high, and the bladders of gunpowder provided to shorten his suffering failed to explode. Hooper called out repeatedly 'for Gods loue (good people) let me haue more fire'.

Plate 21. The execution of Cardmaker and Warne, Smithfield 20 May 1555.
Foxe, 1570, p. 1752.

John Cardmaker, ex-Franciscan incumbent of St Bride's, Fleet Street, recanted when first arrested, and his constancy was in doubt up till the moment when he walked to the pyre he shared with John Warne, a London upholsterer. Cardmaker is portrayed talking to the sheriff, a conversation which alarmed protestant spectators, fearful he would recant again. When he did not, relieved evangelical sympathisers called out 'God be praised, the Lord strengthen thee, Cardmaker'. Cardmaker's long white shirt was a deliberate allusion to the white-robed martyrs in the Book of Revelation.

Plate 22. The execution of Hugh Latimer and Nicholas Ridley, Oxford 16 October 1555.
Foxe, 1570, p. 1938

The execution of Latimer and Ridley after a show trial was intended to signal the regime's determination to pursue heresy even at the highest level. Every household in Oxford was required to send a representative to witness it, and a sermon against the victims' errors was preached by one of Oxford's leading theologians, Dr Richard Smith. In Foxe's picture, Cranmer watches from the ramparts of the town Gaol, Bocardo. Note the open-air pulpit close to the pyre, the usual arrangement, and Smith's text from I Corinthians 13:3, much used against condemned heretics: 'Though I give my body to be burned, but have not charity, it availeth me nothing'.

The Martyrdome of Iohn Cardmaker Preacher, and Iohn Warne Vpholſter, An. 1555. May. 30.

Beware of Idolatry.

M. Cardmaker.

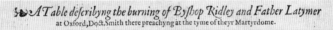

A Table deſcribyng the burning of Byſhop Ridley and Father Latymer at Oxford, Doct. Smith there preachyng at the tyme of theyr Martyrdome.

If I yelde my body to the ſyre to be burnt & haue not charitie, I ſhell gaine nothyng therby. 1. Cor. 13.

Smith.

O Lozd ſtrégthen them.

Cranmar.

Father of heauen receiue my ſoule.

Latimer. Ridley.

I cō̄mit into thy handes. etc.

M. Ridley I will remēber your ſute.

Plate 23. The burning of John Denley at Uxbridge, Middlesex, 8 August 1555. Foxe, 1570, p. 1867

At his execution Denley sang a psalm while the flames rose round him. Dr John Story, a notoriously zealous heresy Commissioner, ordered an attendant to fling a faggot at Denley, wounding his face and silencing him. Under Elizabeth, Story had to defend this notorious action in the Commons. Foxe's illustration, which first appeared in 1570, identified Story with a prominent label. Story had fled to the Low Countries, where he become a searcher of ships for heretical books. He was kidnapped, brought back to England, and executed for treason, with great savagery, in 1571, before a crowd shouting reproaches at him for his cruelty in Mary's reign.

Plate 24. Cranmer pulled down. St Mary the Virgin, Oxford, 21 March 1556. Foxe, 1570, p. 2065.

The decision to execute Cranmer despite six recantations was a major tactical error, for which the Queen was probably directly responsible. A living and penitent Cranmer would have been a huge propaganda asset for the regime: dead, he gave evangelicals an inspiring martyr. Cranmer spectacularly revoked his recantations after listening to a sermon on the morning of his execution, in which Dr Henry Cole explained that the archbishop had to die because he had granted Henry VIII's divorce, because he had led the nation into heresy, and to atone for the execution of John Fisher in Henry's reign. Cardinal Pole was consecrated Archbishop of Canterbury next day.

Plate 25. Thirteen evangelicals burned at Stratford-le-Bow, 27 June 1556. Foxe, 1570, p. 2096.

The campaign against heresy intensified in the summer of 1556. The largest burning of the reign took place at Stratford le Bow, Essex, two miles outside London, when thirteen evangelicals, mostly Essex artisans and their wives, were burned in a single fire. The men were chained to stakes, the women stood untied among them. Gruesome executions like this were staged to shock waverers into conformity. But evangelical leaders became expert at exploiting such events for their own cause, and the authorities eventually opted for less spectacular executions, providing fewer opportunities for organised demonstrations of support.

The burning of Simon Miller, and Elizabeth Cooper, at Norwich.

Sim. Miller. Elizab. Cooper.

Plate 26. The execution of Simon Miller and Elizabeth Cooper, Norwich 13(?) July 1557.
Foxe, 1570, p. 2198.

As waverers and the timid fell away, the hard-core became increasingly committed. By the summer of 1557 many of those being executed had already recanted at least once. Simon Miller provoked his own arrest outside a church in Norwich by asking the people coming out of Mass for directions to a protestant communion-service. Elizabeth Cooper, a Norwich pewterer's wife, had recanted once, but becoming conscience-stricken, she revoked her recantation publicly during Mass in her parish church.

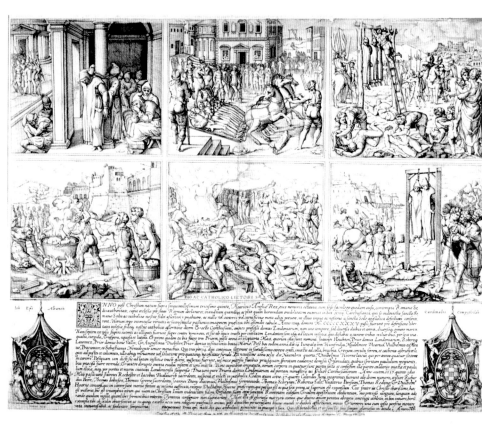

Plates 28–29. 'The Lambe Speaketh': anonymous print, Emden(?) 1555.

This powerfully gruesome print first appeared with Latin captions in William Turner's *The Huntyng of the Romyshe Wolfe*, printed at Emden in 1555. Later translated into English, it laid the blame for the Marian persecution firmly on the shoulders of the bishops under Stephen Gardiner, who here leads the nobility by the nose, despite attempts to restrain him. Protestant jibes against 'bite-sheep' bishops as wolves in sheep's clothing shape the central image of the horrifying feast on the blood of slaughtered protestant victims. Adapted the same year in a much less sophisticated German rhymed broadsheet, the print testifies to European protestant interest in the beleaguered reformation in Marian England.

Plate 27. Six Scenes of the Martyrdom of the English Carthusians in 1535.

This celebration of the Carthusians martyred under Henry VIII appeared in 1555, and was commissioned by the Roman Inquisitor, Juan Alvarez de Toledo, Cardinal Protector of the Carthusian Order. It incorporated imagery from Michelangelo's Vatican frescoes for the Capella Paulina, and Pope Julius III's favourite, Cardinal Innocente del Monte, solicited Cardinal Pole's help for the project in checking details of the martyrdoms in English archives. The print testifies to Papal Rome's intense interest in English affairs, triggered by Mary and Pole's restoration of catholicism. The print also represents a growing catholic awareness of the need for an orthodox martyrology to offset protestant claims to a monopoly on Christian heroism, and Cardinal Pole and his circle took steps to promote the cult of the Henrician catholic martyrs, especially that of Thomas More.

Plate 30. St John's College, Oxford, Banner.

The re-establishment of catholicism in the universities was one of the major successes of Mary's reign, especially at Oxford, where two new colleges were created to promote Counter-Reformation. Both Gregory Martin, translator of the Catholic Rheims–Douai Bible, and the Jesuit martyr, Edmund Campion, were foundation scholars of St John's College, established in 1555 by the wealthy London cloth-merchant, Sir Thomas White. This banner was presented to the college by Thomas Campyon, a London Grocer and tenant of White's, and probably the martyr's father. In addition to the central figure of the Virgin assumed into heaven, the banner bears images of the Trinity (dedication of the other Oxford Marian foundation), the college's (and Merchant Taylors') patron St John the Baptist, the arms of the Merchant Taylors, and the emblem of the Five Wounds of Christ, badge of catholic resistance to the religious reforms of Henry and Edward.

former parishioner encountered at Brentwood recognised Taylor, shook his hand and spoke to him: Taylor was hooded for the rest of the journey.[33] When Bishop Hooper was taken under arrest through the City of London to Newgate by night, sergeants were sent ahead to dowse the costermongers' candles in the city streets, and he too was hooded for his final journey from London to Gloucester. But, although there were some gestures of support from gospellers at both places of execution, there was no disorder.[34] As the burnings of lay protestants began in March, the Privy Council followed Mary's directions and took steps to ensure that local grandees such as the Earl of Oxford and Richard, Lord Rich were present 'at the burnyng of suche obstinate personnes as presently are sent doune to be bourned in diverse partes of the countie . . . and to be adying to the shirief of the said shire therein'.[35] Processions of the local gentry flanking the sheriff and his officers, like those Foxe noted at the burning of Christopher Wade at Dartford,[36] became a routine feature of the executions, a gesture of solidarity with the regime, which, in specially sensitive cases, the Privy Council both demanded and rewarded.[37]

For the regime, there was a delicate balance of advantage and danger to be weighed in the publicity surrounding the trials and burnings. Public executions of the protestant hard core were seen as an essential manifestation of the determination and irreversibility of the government's commitment to the catholic restoration. They were part of the 'theatre of justice' that underpinned law and order in a society too thinly policed for force alone to suffice in the implementation of controversial policy. The Queen gave specific instructions that Bishop Hooper was to be burned in Gloucester, 'for the example and terror of suche as he hath there seduced and mistaught, and bycause he hath done moste harme there'.[38] More generally, if the burnings were to fulfil their deterrent purpose fully, they had to be staged where protestantism had established a hold. So, as we have seen, although in 1555, at the start of the campaign, Essex heretics were burned at a range of locations spread across the county, from 1556 onwards *all* the executions in the county were carried out in Colchester, not despite the fact that the opposition to the regime's religious policies was most vociferous there but *because* of it. Gruesome deaths such as the botched slow roastings of the wretched Hooper at Gloucester and of Ridley at Oxford certainly awakened pity among onlookers, just as they harrow Foxe's modern reader. Moreover, burning was certainly the rarest and most spectacular, if not necessarily the most excruciating, form of Tudor public execution. Those who witnessed a burning, and especially perhaps mass burnings such as that of eleven men and two women at a single execution in Stratford-le-Bow on 27 June 1556, are unlikely ever to have forgotten it.[39]

But we need to bear in mind that public torment of condemned criminals was a hugely popular spectator entertainment in Tudor England, and we should not project modern sensibilities on to the people of the past. Many of the crowds attending burnings would have been mixed assemblies of evangelical sympathisers, hostile catholics and the great unwashed in search of entertainment. When George Tankerfield was burned at St Albans in August 1555, there was a 'great concourse of people to see and heare the prisoner', and Foxe tells us that

> among the which multitude some were sory to see so godly a man brought to be burned, others praised God for his constancy and perseuerance in the trueth. Contrarywyse some there were which said it was pity he did stand in such opinions, and others both old women & men cried against him one called him hereticke, & sayd it was pity that he lyued.[40]

Similarly, when Christopher Wade was burned outside Dartford in the summer of 1555, a large crowd assembled to watch, but evidently in holiday rather than sympathetic mood, 'so muche that thither came dyuers Fruiterers wyth horse loades of Cherries, and sold them', like popcorn or ice cream at a modern sporting event. When Wade attempted to shout down the catholic preacher stationed near the pyre, some of the bystanders pelted the condemned man with faggots, wounding him in the face, a gesture of hostility to the victim replicated at other burnings.[41] A crowd of seven thousand turned out to witness the burning of Bishop Hooper at Gloucester in February 1555, and Professor Pettegree sees them as a crowd of sympathisers, who 'were not there to demonstrate their approval of this aspect of Marian policy'.[42] Perhaps, and perhaps not: caution is needed here. The burning of a bishop for heresy was an event without precedent in English history and Hooper, the most abrasive of new brooms, had been a controversial and, in many quarters, an unpopular bishop in both his midland dioceses. Foxe himself tells us that the size of the crowd was due in part to the fact that it was market day, and that 'manye also came to see his behauiour towards death':

curiosity was at least as likely a motive in gathering spectators as sympathy.[43] Nevertheless, the ardently catholic Lord Chandos and his son Sir Edmund Brydges, who oversaw Hooper's execution, were sufficiently conscious of moving into uncharted territory and sufficiently uncertain of public opinion to provide a large guard, armed with 'bills, glaves and weapons'. They prevented Hooper making a speech and, when he launched into a long and pointed prayer on the 'cruel torments' he was about to undergo, the Mayor of Gloucester chased away two bystanders who were taking notes.[44]

As that suggests, the first burnings were carried out in a fraught and jittery atmosphere, as both sides sought to make the most of the propaganda value of the theatre of justice. Throughout the Tudor period, public executions for ideological reasons would remain 'inherently unstable events, a species of dialogue, a partly scripted, partly extemporised series of exchanges between the . . . victim, the secular and clerical representatives of . . . authority, and the crowd'.[45] In the early stages of the burnings, opinions differed about who had the advantage, but the authorities were certainly concerned about public reaction. The seven executions in Essex in March 1555 had provoked alarming demonstrations from evangelical sympathisers there, leading the Spanish ambassador to think that the burnings had 'hardened many hearts'.[46] At a cluster of executions at the end of the month, the victims 'vehemently exhorted the multitude', and the Privy Council complained that fragments of burnt bone from one of them, William Pygott, were being carried round Suffolk to 'shewe the same to the people as reliques and perswade them to stande in their errour'.[47] Through the first half of 1555, therefore, demonstrations of protestant feeling multiplied, one of the most striking occurring not at a burning but at the execution of a common felon, John Tooley, hanged at Westminster for robbing a Spaniard (as events were to demonstrate, a popular crime) on 26 April 1555. The crowd at Tooley's execution included many evangelicals, who responded with a thunderous 'Amen' when he read out from the cart a prepared statement concluding with the petition from the Edwardine litany, 'From the tyranny of the Bishop of Rome and all his detestable enormities, good Lord deliver us'. The incident had, in fact, been carefully stage-managed by protestant activists in the Marshalsea, one of whom had supplied Tooley with his script. The subsequent declaration of another sympathiser at the Bread Street

Counter prison that 'I cannot see but that this man died well, and like a Christian man', showed that, in that fraught spring, even a thieving thug invoking the protestant cause might, in some circles at least, take on the aura of martyrdom. That remark had been uncovered in the course of thorough investigation ordered by the Privy Council and carried out by the vicar-general of the diocese, Nicholas Harpsfield. It is perhaps worth reminding ourselves, however, that the same investigation revealed that William Walton, a chandler of Old Fish Street, standing close to the gallows had remonstrated with Tooley, 'good fellowe remember thy selfe: for thou arte not in the vnitie of the true faith. For thou oughtest to praye for the Pope'. London was a divided city, in which evangelicals remained a minority, if an effectively vociferous one.[48]

Tooley, whose body would subsequently be exhumed and burned by order of the Council, was hanged two days after the burning of another high-profile heretic and felon in Westminster. William Flower was a former monk of Ely who had become a radical protestant, married, and practised both as a surgeon and a schoolmaster. On Easter Day, 14 April 1555, he walked into St Margaret's, Westminster, wearing a Latin placard with the words 'Fear God, flee from the idol', while the congregation were receiving their Easter communion. Flower produced a large machete-like wood-knife and hacked at the head and arms of one of the Abbey clergy who was helping with the distribution of communion, seriously wounding him and soaking the consecrated hosts in blood. Flower was also carrying a paper with a declaration of his protestant beliefs, which he had provided in case the crowd in the church should lynch him, so that 'they might in the sayde writing have seen my hope'.[49] This demented suicide-mission profoundly shocked conservative Londoners and stiffened the determination of the Council to clamp down on religious dissidence. Both Bishop Bonner and the Middlesex magistrates were ordered to proceed against Flower with exemplary rigour, and he was burned outside the church he had polluted (because of the spilt blood, it had to be reconsecrated) on 24 April, his hand being hacked off at the stake before flame was set to him. His death was gruesome, for, either by omission or design, not enough wood was provided for the usual comparatively merciful 'quick fire'. The executioners tried to push him with their bills and staves into the small centre of flame but he fell forward, and his lower body was burned away while he was still conscious and his tongue still moved in his head.[50] Whether many apart from determinedly protestant Londoners pitied him, in the light of his murderous act of sacrilege, does not appear from the narratives, but one evangelical fellow prisoner, the future martyr Robert Smith, went to considerable lengths to establish and publish that Flower had at least died a sincere and penitent protestant. Even a crazed would-be assassin might be a warrior in the battle against antichrist, if his death could be presented as martyrdom.[51]

The bishops, and Bonner in particular, now found themselves in an invidious position. Widely perceived as provoking resistance by precipitate action, they had in fact proceeded as slowly against the protestants in their custody as the Privy Council would allow, repeatedly examining them even after condemnation, and manifestly more concerned with their conversion than their quick despatch. No one except Flower was executed for heresy in London that April. Energetic magistrates in the heretical badlands of Essex, busy rounding up dissidents, and the Council and Queen alike fumed at this apparent episcopal inactivity, and pressed for greater vigour. Three days after Flower's execution, the Essex justices sitting at Chelmsford sent Thomas Wattes, a Billericay linen draper, under guard to Bonner. The accompanying letter, dripping with careful deference, declared that

> in our opinion he is one of the most arrogant heretikes that hath bene heard speake, or euer came before you, & not meet to be kept here in any Gaole, as well for feare of corrupting others, as for diuers & sundry other speciall causes hereafter to be more declared.

As that last clause implies, however, there was a good deal more to this than met the eye. The magistrates were especially anxious to get Wattes out of Essex because he was an embarrassment to their leader, Richard, Lord Rich. At Wattes's examination before them, he had been asked by Sir Anthony Browne where he had learned his heresies and, to Browne's consternation, Wattes had declared 'euen of you Sir: you taught it me, and none more then you. For in K. Edwards dayes in open sessions you spake against this Religion now vsed, no preacher more. You then sayd, the masse was abhominable, & all their trumpery besides'. What basis there was for this claim is impossible to say. Browne, who, even in Elizabeth's reign, would remain a conservative catholic, vigorously denied it, declaring to Lord Rich, chairman of the bench, that Wattes had 'belied' him. Rich tersely replied 'I dare say he does', but he himself must have been in some anxiety about what further revelations might be forthcoming. Wattes had avowedly been converted and confirmed in his protestant views by a circle of Essex evangelical clergy, all of whom owed their Edwardine position and influence in the county to Rich's patronage. Rich himself presided at Wattes's burning, and Wattes then accused him directly: 'My Lord . . . beware, beware, for you doe against your owne conscience herein, and without you repent, the Lord will reuenge it: For you are the cause of this my death.' Rich, a consummate opportunist, had certainly never been a convinced gospeller at any time, but to be thus reminded of his inconvenient recent past was intolerable. Wattes was therefore bundled away to be dealt with by Bonner.[52]

If the Essex magistracy was busy sweeping the county clean of its Edwardine religious legacy and its attendant embarrassments, monarch and Council were concerned with the threat that heresy seemed to pose to the regime as a whole, and with which clerical scruple and the niceties of ecclesiastical court procedure seemed to collude. On 24 May, the King and Queen sent Bonner and his fellow bishops what can only be described as a savage rebuke, demanding more vigorous action against heresy. They had discovered, they declared, 'to our no lytle maruayle', that many heretics,

> being by the Iustices of the peace for their contempt & obstinacye, brought to the Ordinaries . . . are eyther refused to be receiued at their hands, or if they be receiued, are neyther so trauayled wyth, as Christian charity requireth, nor yet proceeded wyth all according to the order of Iustice, but are suffred to continue in their errours, to the dishonor of almighty God, and daungerous example of others.

This 'very straunge' inactivity was to be rectified, and Bonner and his colleagues were commanded forthwith

> to haue in thys behalfe suche regarde henceforth to the office of a good Pastor and byshop, as when any such offenders shalbe by the sayde officers or Iustices of peace broughte vnto you, you do vse your good wisedome and discretion in procuring to remoue them from their errours if it it may be, or els in proceding against them (if they shal continue obstinate) according to the order of the lawes.

It was all very different in tone from the Spanish court sermons of only three months earlier.[53]

Bonner was understandably rattled by this letter. Among the accused heretics he was due to see in consistory the next day (Saturday) were two Essex husbandmen who had been under examination on and off most of that month. The Mayor sat with the bishop in court that day, the processes were now hastily brought to a conclusion and the accused men duly condemned. The London Consistory Court routinely sat in a side chapel on the north side of St Paul's and an unusually large crowd had gathered just outside the screens, perhaps because another of the cases being dealt with that day was that of John Cardmaker, the famous preacher who had recanted but then reaffirmed his protestant beliefs. Bonner and his entourage, already nervous about the worryingly large numbers, panicked altogether when the spectators, thinking that the prisoners were about to be taken away to Newgate, rushed noisily for the exits to catch sight of them. Fearing that this was the start of a riot, everyone in court bolted for the connecting door to the bishop's residence and Bonner, slower than the rest, found himself locked out of his own house, while his officers, safely within, called ineffectually 'Save my lord, save my lord'.[54]

There is, in fact, no indication that the crowd in St Paul's was specially hostile to this court or its officers, and even Foxe thought the panic absurd, but the whole farcical incident illustrates the nervy atmosphere in which the campaign against heresy was being conducted. Bonner was well aware that he was blamed in the city for the campaign of burnings, and was worried enough to take steps to exculpate himself. The next day was Sunday, and Archdeacon William Chedsey, preaching at Paul's Cross before the Lord Mayor, aldermen and sheriffs, took the extraordinary step of displaying the royal letter to Bonner in the pulpit, explaining how the bishop had been rebuked by King Philip and Queen Mary for 'remisnes and negligence in instructinge the people, infected with heresye, yf they will be taught, and in punishing them yf they will be obstinate and willfull'. As a loyal subject, Chedsey told the crowd, Bonner would obey the royal will in this matter, and 'will trauayle and take payne with all that be of his iurisdiction for theire amendement: and sorye he is that anye is in pryson for any such matter'. But, he went on, 'he willed me to tel you that he is not so cruell or hastye to sende men to pryson, as some be slaunderous, and wilful to do naught, and laye theire faultes on other mens shoulders.'[55]

The royal rebuke left Bonner and the City officials with no option but to move against Cardmaker, who now, with John Warne, went to the stake at Smithfield on 30 May. Inevitably, London's gospellers turned out in strength at the execution, worried that Cardmaker would once again disgrace the cause of the Gospel by another last-minute recantation. A series of prolonged and earnest conversations between him and the sheriffs, while his companion John Warne stood chained to the stake, threw evangelical spectators into 'a meruailous dumpe and sadnes, thinkyng in deede that Cardmaker should now recant at the burning of Warne'. At last, however, Cardmaker cast aside his outer clothing, walked away from the sheriffs to the stake and embraced it, to the thunderous relief of the crowd, members of which shouted 'God be praised, the Lord strengthen thee Cardmaker, the Lord Jesus receive thy spirit' (see Plate 21).[56]

That cold wet summer was the worst for fifty years, when the crops rotted in the fields, culminating with freak storms in late September, flooding Westminster Abbey and Hall. London wherrymen rowed *over* Westminster bridge into the streets around it. Through it all, the pace of the burnings quickened, urged on by the Council[57] and by zealous local magistrates – seven in June (all in Essex), twelve in July, eighteen in August, twelve in September. Many of these executions passed without incident, like the series of burnings in the diocese and especially the city of Canterbury. There a concentrated campaign of multiple burnings had begun that would continue into the new year, and whose conservative citizens evidently cared little for the earnest gospellers of the Wealden villages from which the victims were mostly drawn.[58] Elsewhere, particularly in Essex, evangelicals used the burnings as opportunities to publicise their cause, and in London the crowds were out again in July at another celebrity burning at Smithfield, that of John Bradford.[59]

The regime was, of course, intensely conscious of the seductive effect of protestant courage and eloquence at the stake. The Queen's instructions for Hooper's burning warned that he was 'as heretiques be, a vainglorious person, and delyteth in his tongue, and having liberty, may use his sayd tongue to perswade such as he hath seduced, to persist in the myserable opinion that he hath sowen among them'. Neither at the place of execution nor on the way there was he to be allowed to 'speak at large', therefore, but 'thither to be ledde quietly, and in silence, for eschynge of further infection'.[60]

All the clerical leaders executed in the first half of 1555 seem to have been required to give undertakings not to speak controversially at the stake, and by and large they kept their promise. But lay victims had no such restraints and, as time went by, victims used the stake as a pulpit from which to denounce the pope, the idol of the Mass, the deceits of the whore of Babylon and her false prophets the clergy, especially those preaching or present at the burnings.[61] There soon emerged a symbolic code of behaviour at the point of execution, designed to underline the claim that the victims were martyrs for Christian truth. Lawrence Saunders, Rawlins White, Christopher Wade and John Bradford all went to their deaths dressed in long white shirts specially made for the occasion. There was a gruesomely practical dimension to this gesture: thick clothing prolonged the pain. But the white robes were also a deliberate allusion to the white-robed army of martyrs in the book of Revelation, who lay under the altar and whose blood cried out to God for vengeance.[62] Some of the victims kissed the stake and the faggots, as Cardmaker had done, and John Bradford and his disciple John Leafe elaborated this gesture by prostrating themselves in prayer for a minute on either side of the stake before going to it and kissing it, in what looks like a deliberate reminiscence of the Good Friday liturgy of the Passion, which began in just this way. Elaborate prayer or psalm-singing at the place of execution were other elements in the symbolics of martyrdom (see Plates 21, 23).

Notoriously, when John Denley was burned at Uxbridge on 8 August 1555, he sang a psalm in the midst of the flames, until one of the executioners silenced him by flinging a faggot at his head. Foxe recorded the brutally cynical comment of Commissioner Dr John Story, who oversaw the execution – 'Truly', Story jovially told the man who had thrown the faggot, 'thou hast mard a good old song.'[63] It was a brutality that would be remembered, and it would cost Story dear. The 1570 edition of Foxe's *Acts and Monuments* included a woodcut of the incident, in which Story was identified with a label above his head (see Plate 23).[64] One year later, bystanders shouted abuse at Story for his cruelty as he himself was dragged to execution for treason in June 1571. The notoriety that Foxe's narrative had given to Story's treatment of Denley and others almost certainly contributed to the excruciating savagery used in Story's own execution.[65] On both sides, this was an ideological struggle inscribed in the quivering flesh of suffering human beings.

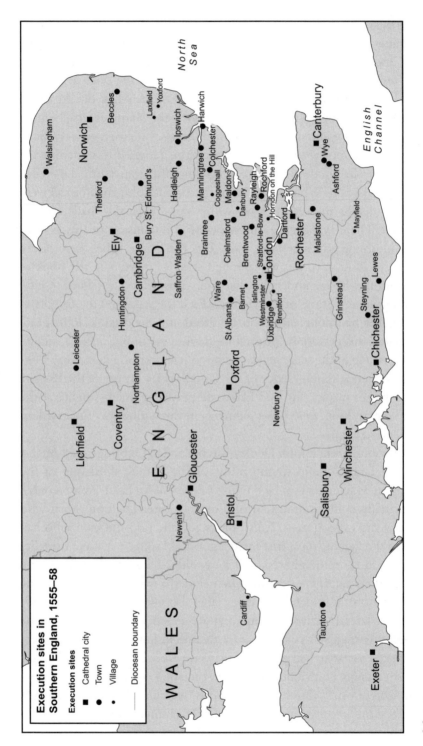

Execution sites in
Southern England, 1555–58

Execution sites

■ Cathedral city
● Town
• Village
— Diocesan boundary

North Sea

English Channel

WALES

ENGLAND

Walsingham
Beccles
Norwich ■
Laxfield •
Yoxford •
Thetford ●
Bury St. Edmund's ●
Hadleigh ●
Ipswich ●
Harwich
Manningtree ●
Colchester ●
Coggeshall
Maldon ●
Danbury
Braintree ●
Chelmsford ●
Brentwood ●
Rayleigh
Rochford ●
Horndon on the Hill
Dartford ●
Canterbury ■
Wye ●
Ashford ●
Mayfield •
Rochester ●
Maidstone ●
Ely ■
Cambridge ■
Saffron Walden ●
Ware ●
St Albans ●
Barnet ●
Islington
Westminster
Uxbridge ●
Brentford
Stratford-le-Bow
London ■
Huntingdon ●
Leicester ●
Northampton ●
Oxford ■
Newbury ●
Lewes ●
Steyning
Grinstead ●
Chichester ■
Lichfield ■
Coventry ■
Gloucester ■
Bristol ■
Newent ●
Winchester ■
Salisbury ■
Cardiff •
Taunton ●
Exeter ■

Map 1

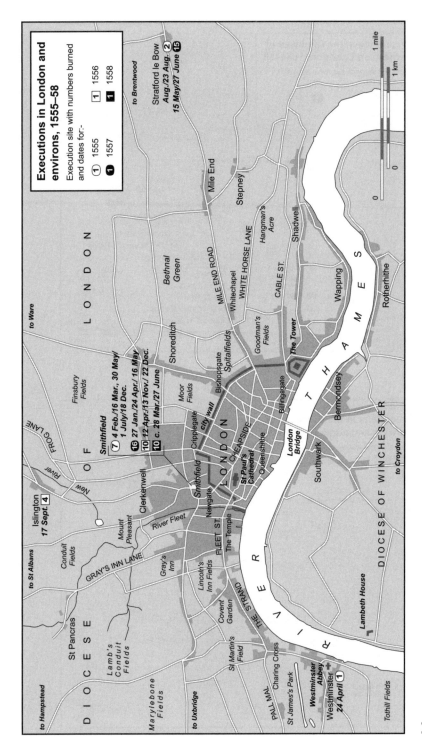

Map 2

125

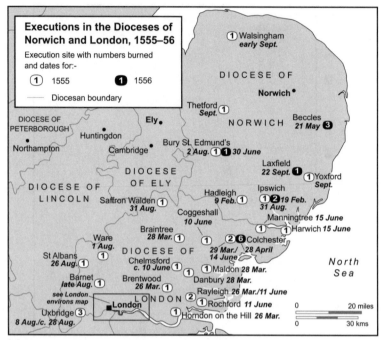

Executions in the Dioceses of Norwich and London, 1555–56

Execution site with numbers burned and dates for:-

① 1555   ❶ 1556

‑‑‑‑‑‑ Diocesan boundary

① Walsingham *early Sept.*

DIOCESE OF

Norwich •

NORWICH

DIOCESE OF PETERBOROUGH

• Northampton

Ely •

Huntingdon •

Cambridge •

Bury St. Edmund's *2 Aug.* ① ❶ *30 June*

Thetford ① *Sept.*

Beccles *21 May* ❸

DIOCESE OF ELY

Saffron Walden ① *31 Aug.*

Hadleigh *9 Feb.* ①

Coggeshall *10 June*

Laxfield *22 Sept.* ❶ ① Yoxford *Sept.*

Ipswich ① ❷ *19 Feb.* *31 Aug.*

Manningtree *15 June*

① ① Harwich *15 June*

DIOCESE OF LINCOLN

Ware *1 Aug.* ①

Braintree *28 Mar.* ①

St Albans *26 Aug.* ①

DIOCESE OF CHELMSFORD

Chelmsford *c. 10 June* ①

① ② ❻ Colchester

29 Mar./ 14 June *28 April*

① ① Maldon *28 Mar.*

Danbury *28 Mar.*

Rayleigh *26 Mar./11 June*

North Sea

Barnet *late Aug.* ①

Brentwood *26 Mar.* ①

see London environs map ■ London

L O N D O N ②

① Rochford *11 June*

Uxbridge ③ *8 Aug./c. 28 Aug.*

① Horndon on the Hill *26 Mar.*

0   20 miles
0   30 kms

Map 3

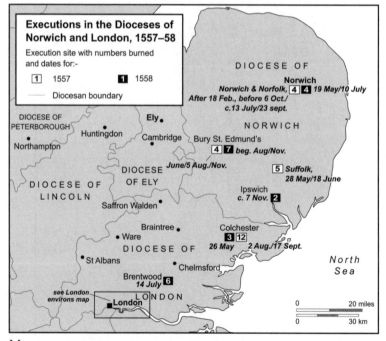

Executions in the Dioceses of Norwich and London, 1557–58

Execution site with numbers burned and dates for:-

1 1557   ■1 1558

‑‑‑‑‑‑ Diocesan boundary

DIOCESE OF

Norwich

Norwich & Norfolk, 4 ■4 *19 May/10 July After 18 Feb., before 6 Oct./ c.13 July/23 sept.*

NORWICH

DIOCESE OF PETERBOROUGH

• Northampton

Ely •

Huntingdon •

Cambridge •

Bury St. Edmund's 4 ■7 *beg. Aug/Nov.*

DIOCESE OF ELY

June/5 Aug./Nov.

5 *Suffolk, 28 May/18 June*

Ipswich *c. 7 Nov.* ■2

DIOCESE OF LINCOLN

Saffron Walden •

Braintree •

• Ware

Colchester 3 ■12 *26 May* *2 Aug./17 Sept.*

DIOCESE OF

• St Albans

Chelmsford •

Brentwood *14 July* ■6

North Sea

see London environs map ■ London

L O N D O N

0   20 miles
0   30 km

Map 4

126

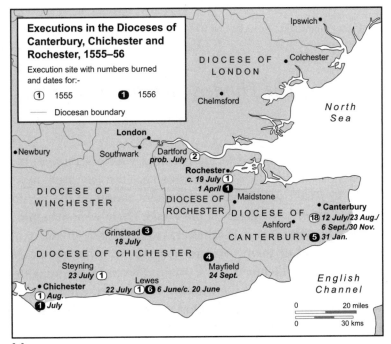

Map 5

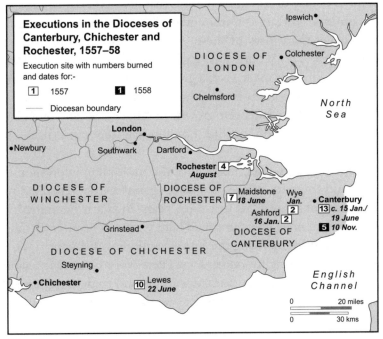

Map 6

CHAPTER 6

The Hunters and the Hunted

The geographical spread of the burnings was very uneven: 113 in the diocese of London, 65 of them in or near the city itself, most of the others in Essex; 52 in Canterbury, where almost all the victims came from the towns and villages of the Weald. There were nine more in the other Kent diocese of Rochester; twenty-seven in the diocese of Chichester, all of them men and women from the archdeaconry of Lewes; seven in Lichfield and Coventry; seven in Bristol; four in Ely; three in Oxford; three in the whole of Wales; and the rest of the dioceses with single executions or, as in Durham, none at all. There was probably a rough correspondence between these figures and the actual distribution of protestantism in the country, though the York and Lincoln dioceses were clearly underrepresented. The figures for London were of course distorted by the fact that it was the capital, and many of the processes for suspects from other dioceses were conducted there. In fact, fewer than forty of these victims qualify in some real sense as Londoners.[1] As Cardinal Pole starkly observed to the Lord Mayor and aldermen in November 1557, 'a greater multitude of these brambles and bryars were caste in the fyre here amonge you, than yn any place beside', but many of them had been 'growne in other places, and brought yn and burned amonge you', so that London had 'the worse name without your deserte'.[2]

Raw numbers alone might give the misleading impression that the scale and intensity of the campaign against heresy remained more or less constant through its first three years. In fact it intensified, both in ferocity and in its likely impact. There were seventy-five victims in the eleven months following the first executions in February 1555, eighty-five in 1556 and eighty-one in 1557. There was a significant scaling down only in 1558, a year of political disruption and epidemic disease. But the approximately constant numbers in the first three years conceal a dramatic change of direction and style from 1556. In the campaign's first year, no fewer than eighteen of the seventy-five victims were executed in Canterbury diocese. These Canterbury protestants all came from the villages and towns of the Weald, but they were all burned in the cathedral city, in four group executions between July and November that year. No citizen of Canterbury could have avoided witnessing at least one of these grisly spectacles. The majority of the other executions that first year (thirty-one out of fifty-seven) took place in the London diocese. Here, however, the approach of the authorities was quite different, with most of the victims being burned singly, often in small and relatively obscure sites, scattered widely through the diocese. Thus the fifty-seven victims from outside the Canterbury diocese were executed at forty different sites, and the public impact of these single executions must have been quite different from those in Canterbury (Maps 1 and 3).

This difference in method in the London diocese may well reflect concern and uncertainty about the likely public reaction to the burnings on the part of Bishop Bonner. If so, his doubts and those of the other bishops must either have been resolved by experience or overridden by authority, because from 1556 onwards the Canterbury pattern became normative in all the dioceses where dissenters were numerous. From the start of 1556 onwards the majority of those burned died in group executions of three or more, and the fires were concentrated at fewer

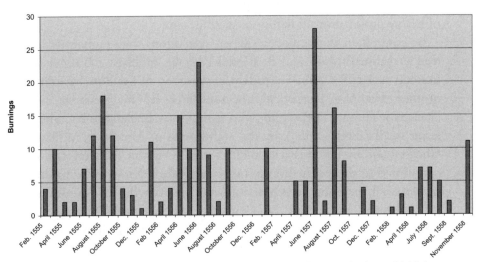

Executions by Burning 1555-58

This chart is based on figures compiled for the Foxe Project by Dr Thomas Freeman, to whom I am greatly indebted.

and fewer sites. So the forty-one places of execution used in 1555 were reduced to twenty-three in 1556, dropped again to fourteen in 1557 and finally to thirteen in 1558. There were specially gruesome mass burnings at Stratford-le-Bow, one of London's satellite villages, in June 1556, when eleven men and two women died in a single fire, at Lewes in Sussex in June 1557, when ten people were executed at once and at Colchester in Essex the same month, when another ten died in two fires on a single day. A few sites – Smithfield in London, Colchester, Lewes and to a lesser extent Bristol and Bury St Edmunds – served repeatedly as stages for these lethal dramas (Maps 1–4, Plates 19, 21, 25). The campaign was always fiercest in the summer months, peaking in June 1557, when a total of twenty-eight were executed in a single month.

Many factors helped to shape these grim statistics, chief among them the zeal or lack of it of the officials charged with the pursuit of heresy. The diocese of Durham saw no burnings, mainly no doubt because of the conservative nature of religion in the region, but in part at least because, from 1556, the aged Bishop Tunstall's right-hand man there was his archdeacon and great-nephew, Bernard Gilpin. Despite having spent part of Edward's reign in Paris to oversee publication of Tunstall's defence of the catholic doctrine of the Mass, Gilpin was a waverer between catholic and reformed beliefs, orthodox on the real presence, but decidedly shaky on papal primacy, the English Bible and the marriage of priests. He was sufficiently suspect among hardliners in the diocese to have set aside a 'long and comely' shirt, in case he himself should be brought to the stake.[3] With such an archdeacon, the absence of heresy prosecutions is hardly surprising.

By contrast, in all the dioceses where executions were numerous, we find a zealous bishop and dedicated catholic officials – Bonner in London assisted by John Harpsfield, archdeacon of London, by John's brother Nicholas Harpsfield, vicar-general, by his nephew and chancellor Thomas Darbyshire (who would leave England to become a Jesuit in Elizabeth's reign), by the archdeacon of Middlesex, William Chedsey, and by commissaries such as John Kingston. All were totally committed to the extirpation of heresy, and all of them were efficient. In Norwich, the bishop was Mary's former chaplain, the ex-Dominican John Hopton, assisted by his chancellor, Dr Michael Dunning. In Canterbury, Pole's team was headed by Nicholas Harpsfield again, as archdeacon, assisted by the suffragan, Bishop Richard Thornden, a man with a malodorous past that he was anxious to expiate by diligence against heresy. At Chichester, the key figure was John Christopherson, bishop from the summer of 1557; at Lichfield, Bishop Ralph Baynes and his chancellor, Dr Anthony Draycott. These men uncovered heresy in their dioceses in part by the vigorous use of the normal processes of visitation. The microscopic scrutiny that they could bring to communities harbouring evangelicals can be traced in the surviving documentation for the episcopal and legatine visitations of 1556 and 1557, and especially in the remarkable records of Nicholas Harpsfield's visitations of the diocese of Canterbury, even though, in these visitations, heresy was just one of many pastoral concerns.[4]

Cardinal Pole instigated a systematic legatine visitation of all the dioceses in April 1556.[5] Simultaneously, he established a heresy commission for his own diocese and, though the format for the Visitation Articles varied from diocese to diocese, it was clear that the detection of heresy was to be a major consideration in all the visitations. The emphasis was on *practical* indicators of orthodoxy – devout use of the sacraments and sacramentals such as holy water; the attendance of at least one adult member of every household at the intercessory processions with litany of the saints held on Mondays, Wednesdays and Fridays; devout behaviour during Mass, especially at the moment when the Host was elevated, when they must adore, 'not lurking behind pillars or holding down their head'.[6] Parishioners absenting themselves from church, failing to make their Easter communions, turning their backs on the elevated Host, or speaking irreverently about the Mass and other sacraments, were targeted and examined. Foxe tells a story of a heresy-hunting magistrate of Smarden in Kent, Justice Drayner, who was nicknamed 'Justice Nine-holes'. With the help of the parson and

> to shew himselfe diligent in seeking the trouble of his neighbors, Darayner made in the Rodeloft nyne hooles, that he might looke about the church in Masse tyme. In which place alway at the sacring therof, he would stand to see who looked not, or held not vp his hands therto: which persons so not doing, he would trouble & punish very sore.[7]

In Lincoln diocese Thomas More, a twenty-four-year-old serving man in Leicester had been reported within days of the commencement of the visitation for irreverent remarks made to a neighbour about the

Blessed Sacrament. He had subsequently left Leicester, perhaps to avoid arrest, but was traced to the country, where he was staying with relatives, and brought before Bishop White in St Margaret's Church, Leicester. White quizzed the young man in very concrete terms, asking 'what is yonder that thou seest aboue the aultar?' More answered, 'forsooth I cannot tell what you would haue me to see. I see there fine clothes, with golden tassels, and other gay gere hanging about the pixe. What is within I cannot see.' Refusing to acknowledge the presence of Christ in the pyx, he was condemned, and burned in Leicester on 26 June.[8] That pattern of detection was replicated everywhere.

In Kent, the fierce and sustained campaign against heresy that had sent a stream of dissidents to the fire in the second half of 1555 tailed off in the spring of 1556, but revived once Pole became archbishop, though the executions themselves halted for a while. In his new capacity as archbishop of Canterbury, Pole issued special instructions to his visitors on the detection and pursuit of heresy,[9] emphasising the culpability of Cranmer and other clergy in misleading the laity, and offering clemency to all who accepted doctrinal instruction from their catholic pastors.

In a renewed scrutiny, Archdeacon Nicholas Harpsfield had arrested at least fifteen plebeian lay people by the end of May 1556 – servants, sawyers, weavers, labourers. They held a variety of heretical opinions, from denial of the presence of Christ in the eucharist to the rejection of the divinity of Christ or the Holy Spirit. Appallingly, five of those arrested had died in gaol by November 1556: Foxe says they were starved to death by venal gaolers.[10] Ten more were burned in January 1557, and a further fourteen in June that year. Pole's accession had perhaps made his Kentish clerical administration more scrupulous in seeking recantations, but there had been no slackening in rigour against the stubborn. Exhaustive returns survive for Harpsfield's continuing visitation of Kent in 1557, and they provide us with an extraordinarily detailed view of the processes of detection from the point of view of the pursuers. Parish by parish, especially in the Weald, where protestantism had many adherents, Harpsfield enquired after the names of anyone who had not made their Easter communion, anyone who absented themselves from church, anyone refusing holy water or holy bread, or ceremonies such as creeping to the cross, and women who refused to confess and receive communion before childbirth. The (mostly plebeian) culprits were summoned before the archdeacon and quizzed on the beliefs underlying their deviant behaviour. Some escaped with a warning and a promise to conform themselves to the unity of the church and participate in sacraments and ceremonies. Their conformity was normally ordered to be certified to the archdeacon by the churchwardens, or in person by the offenders before the heresy commissioners in Canterbury.[11]

Habitual offenders or hard cases might be required to perform humiliating public penance. Margaret Geoffrie of Ashford, who had revealed her protestant beliefs by refusing to look at the elevated Host, was excommunicated, and only restored after swearing amendment on the book of the Gospels. Harpsfield ordered that, on the following Sunday, she should 'sitte in the myddes of the chancel upon her knees having beades in her handes and devoutlie behaving herself and that at the tyme of the elevacion she shall devoutlie and reverentlie worship the Blessed Sacrament'.[12] In communities with a persistent protestant presence, such as Hawkhurst or Cranbrook, Harpsfield required the incumbent to report anyone refusing to wear rosary beads or not participating in ceremonies. In such places, every adult was required to go to confession to the parish priest twice during Lent, and then 'to receave the Sacramente wekelie as the howsholdes shalbe appointed'. One adult member of every household was also required to take part in the processions and litany on Wednesdays and Fridays. Men known to have good voices and to have sung in church in King Edward's reign were listed and required to join the parish choir at Mass and other services.[13] Clergy were forbidden to bury anyone who had refused the sacraments in their last illness, and no one was to be given their Easter communion unless they took part in the veneration of the cross on Good Friday.[14]

The provisions against heresy in Harpsfield's returns represent only one concern among many other equally prominent issues. The archdeacon spent as much or more time ensuring that the parish churches were properly equipped with everything from the right books to the shovel needed to bury the dead, that priests were providing sermons, or that local adulterers were made to do public penance. Moreover, his first concern in dealing with heretical belief and practice was quite clearly a desire to reconcile the offenders to the church and secure their future conformity wherever possible, if necessary after due penance. But the returns also show an unflinching determination to track down every single deviant and to punish the recalcitrant. Wherever suspects failed to appear, Harpsfield issued orders to local constables to 'apprehende and attache thise persones following beinge suspected of heresie', and to bring them either to the heresy commissioners at Canterbury, of whom Harpsfield himself was one, or to Cranbrook, where a zealous local justice, Sir John Baker, was an ardent heresy hunter, maintaining his own gaol above the porch of the parish church.[15]

For the zeal of the bishops and their officials provided only one prong of the Marian assault on heresy. As we have seen, equally crucial were the activities of the royal commissioners and their agents, informants and supporters in the localities. From 1555 onwards, commissions against heresy were active in the heartlands of dissent – in Kent, in East Anglia and especially in Essex – galvanising and coordinating the activities of local JPs, constables and other officers. They had authority to enquire into all aspects of religious nonconformity, including non-attendance at church and the refusal of particular rites and sacraments, and the possession or dissemination of heretical or seditious books, and they had power to seize the possessions of religious exiles and fugitives for the Crown.[16]

The commissioners routinely sent batches of prisoners to the bishops for formal examination and, though their interventions were not always welcomed by diocesan officials, there does seem to have been some attempt to coordinate the activities of the commissioners and routine episcopal visitation. For example, the commission sitting at Beccles in Suffolk in May 1556, which considered, among other things, a detailed dossier on protestant dissent in Ipswich, coincided with Bishop Hopton's visitation of the town: this seems unlikely to have been a coincidence.[17] The sessions of these commissions in market towns and regional centres, headed by grandees such as Richard Lord Rich or Thomas Lord Darcy, emboldened local catholic activists and powerfully reinforced the drive against protestantism, especially while the leading commissioners were resident in the county. Thomas Tye, the zealously catholic former evangelical rector of 'Much' or Great Bentley in Essex, a parish plagued with nonconformity, told Lord Darcy in December 1556, after the departure of one such commission, that, 'whylest your good Lordship lay here in the country, the people were stayed in good order, to our great comfort: but since your Lordships departure, they haue made digression from good order in some places'.[18]

The Ipswich dossier for the commissioners had been compiled by a group of 'promoters' or informers against heresy, who included Philip Williams, a former chamberlain and future MP for the town, and Mathew Butler, town constable, 'a curious singyng man, a fine player of the Organes, a perfect papist, and a diligent promoter of good men'. This group was 'not many in number, but in heart and purpose mightily bent to impugne & impeach the growyng of Christes Gospell, & the fauourers of the same'. Their activities inevitably brought them into conflict with the local gospellers who, here as everywhere else, included individuals in positions that enabled them to hinder or subvert this aspect of the 'Queens proceedings'. Among the recommendations made by the Ipswich informers was a request that the town gaolor be called to account, since he was a gospeller 'who by euill counsel doth animate his prisoners of his secte', and who, with his wife, 'did checke vs openly with vnseemely woordes, tending almost to a tumult'.[19]

This desire for external support against local hostility was understandable. As the report showed, Ipswich had a substantial protestant presence among the artisans and tradesmen of the town, and the 'promoters' certainly made enemies. Their dossier, arranged parish by parish, listed nearly forty inhabitants who had 'fled out of the towne, and lurked in secret places' on account of religion, another twenty who would not receive the Sacrament, and a dozen who had conformed, but whose continuing heterodoxy was revealed by such gestures as looking away from the Host at the elevation in the Mass or spitting it out after receiving it. The document also threw light on some of the town's social groupings within which evangelical convictions had gained a hold. The list of religious fugitives included six shoemakers and three shoemakers' apprentices, together with assorted members of their families – one wonders where a catholic went to get his boots repaired in Ipswich. Those rejecting religious ceremonies included several midwives and women who 'refuse to have Childrenne dipped in Fontes', and the promoters urged the commissioners 'that none be suffred to be midwives, but such as are Catholike, because of evill counsel at suche times as the necessitie of womennes travaile, shall require a number of women assembled', a revealing sidelight on the processes by which reformed ideas might spread in gender groups and below the level of literacy. The Ipswich promoters did not confine their activities to laying information. Two months after they placed their dossier before the commissioners, Butler and his even more zealous colleague, the physician Dr Richard Argentine (who would be ordained priest on the death of his wife), raised the alarm when one of the fugitives on their list, Agnes Wardall, returned to her home for a secret visit. They organised and led a posse to raid the house, and Mistress Wardall only escaped by hiding first in a cupboard where she almost suffocated and then in a nettle-filled ditch where, fortunately for her, a kindly member of the town watch spotted her, warned her of her visibility by coughing and distracted his fellow pursuivants.[20]

The commissioners exerted their influence in the regions powerfully but episodically. The regime therefore sought to press home the attack on heresy through the more constant activities of county leaders, the justices of the peace, and borough and county officials, especially the sheriffs, who were responsible for overseeing the executions. In Kent, Suffolk and Essex, where dissent was at its most resistant, campaigning magistrates were crucial in the pursuit and arrest of suspects, and Sir John Tyrrell of Gipping Hall in Suffolk and Edmund Tyrrell of St Osyth's in Essex feature in Foxe's pages almost as luridly and as often as Bishop Bonner himself. Both Tyrrells organised midnight raids on the houses of suspects, pressured local constables and village headmen to name and pursue absentees from church, interrogated suspects at their own manor houses, sent heretics under arrest to the bishops for examination, and reported back to the commissioners or to Privy Councillors.

A letter from Edmund Tyrrell in June 1555 to one of the commissioners, perhaps Sir Richard Southwell, captures the intensity and range of his engagement with the campaign. On 11 June, he had, at the request of the Council, assisted the sheriff at two separate burnings in villages near Eastbourne. Returning home afterwards to St Osyth's, he encountered on the road John Denley, a gentleman, and John Newman, a pewterer, Kentish evangelicals from Maidstone (Denley had a record, having been arrested and examined, but apparently released after recanting by Richard Thornden, bishop of Dover). These two were travelling together as fugitives from their own county, and were on their way to visit and comfort beleaguered fellow gospellers in Essex. In a gesture repeated by other evangelicals who had once recanted and wished now to clinch a new-found willingness to die for the Gospel,

Denley had concealed about him an incriminating confession of faith. 'Euen as I sawe them, I suspected them', Tyrrell reported, 'and then I did examine them, and search them, and I did finde about them certaine letters, whych I haue sent you, and also a certaine wrytinge in paper, what their faith was'. Since they came from outside the county via London, he sent them to be examined by commissioners in London, 'so that their lewdnesse might be throughly knowen: for I thinke these haue caused many to trouble their consciences'. Both men were eventually executed in August 1555, in separate burnings at Uxbridge and Saffron Walden.[21] Their arrest in the aftermath of two other burnings was no freak event. Gospellers used burnings as opportunities for a show of protestant strength and solidarity, and the authorities routinely arrested or took the names of those involved in such demonstrations, a process designed either to deter such sympathisers or to secure their recantation.[22]

In the spring of 1556, Tyrrell's zeal against heresy became, if anything, fiercer, when he discovered a conventicle of about a hundred people using his own woods at Hockley for open-air preachings with the connivance of one of his servants, the herdsman John Gye. With a colleague on the Essex bench, the Privy Councillor and heresy commissioner Sir John Mordaunt, Tyrrell launched a sweep against Essex conventiclers that would lead to the execution, among others, of three uneducated women, Katherine Hut, Elizabeth Thackwell and Joan Horns, in May of that year.[23] Characteristically, in sending to Bonner prisoners arrested in this campaign as 'not conformable to the orders of the Churche, nor to the reall presence of Christes body and bloude in the Sacrament of the aultare', Tyrrell and Mordaunt nagged the bishop about the need for drastic action *pour encourager les autres*, 'not doubting with the punishment of these and the other before sent to your Lordship, but that the parishe of great Burstede and Billerica shall be broughte to good conformitye'.[24]

The tensions and problems that these parallel jurisdictions and separate initiatives could create for the episcopate were illustrated in August 1556. A commission headed by the Lord Chamberlain, John de Vere, sixteenth Earl of Oxford (a notorious philanderer and probably himself a secret protestant), and by Thomas, Lord Darcy, met in Colchester to seize the lands and goods of religious fugitives, to search for heretics and to oversee the restoration of church goods in the region.

The commission arrested twenty-three gospellers from Suffolk and Essex, 'apprehended at one clap', presumably at a conventicle. One was a heavily pregnant woman in no state to endure imprisonment. In a hearing conducted in the presence of the bailiffs, aldermen and town clerk, she quickly agreed to do penance in her parish church 'and to continue a Catholicke & a faythfull woman, as long as GOD shall send her lyfe': she was duly set free, on sureties from her husband, the gentlest possible outcome. The remaining twenty-two prisoners were to be handed over to the bishop's officials for examination. Bonner's commissary, John Kingston, in Colchester to inspect the local churches (another example of the apparent synchronisation of the activities of the commissioners and episcopal officers), agreed to 'discharge the town and country of these heretickes', but insisted that that he would need time to examine the prisoners, whose religious views he must establish, 'least I should punish the Catholicks'. It was therefore agreed that he would take them to London within ten days.

The arrest of so large a number, however, created intense interest in a town already so riven with religious differences that there were well-known protestant and catholic pubs. To Kingston's consternation, the commissioners suddenly decided on 30 August that the prisoners must be removed to London forthwith. Kingston had dismissed his armed escort, and was wary of the Colchester crowds, having on other occasions had to lead prisoners through the town 'in great preasse and daunger'. He hastily hired a new escort of four men, which included a bowman, the bailiff of Ipswich providing not only an additional armed escort through the town, but also the town clerk 'ready there with his booke to write the names of the most busie persons' in the event of any demonstration. In fact, there was no trouble, and Kingston led his eight female and fourteen male prisoners peacefully away, writing ahead to Bonner to complain of the unreasonableness of the commissioners, and to prepare the bishop for the reception (and maintenance) of so large a group of suspects.

The journey was uneventful, the prisoners so docile that they were allowed to walk free except when they came to a village, when they were given a rope to hold as if they were fettered. But as they approached the city *en route* to Aldgate, where they were to spend the last night of the journey, they began to acquire an escort of London conventiclers and sympathisers who had got wind of their arrival. Next morning, which was Saturday, Bonner wanted them brought for examination quietly before the city was astir. Instead, realising the propaganda potential of the situation, they delayed their walk to St Paul's until after 10 a.m., and insisted on going through Cheapside, exhorting passers-by as they went, gathering a crowd and receiving in return, as the bishop noted grumpily, 'much comfort *a promiscua plebe*'. By the time they arrived at St Paul's, they had an entourage that the alarmed Bonner estimated at a thousand, and he sent to the Mayor and sheriffs to complain that 'thys thing was not well suffred in the city'. Bonner duly examined the twenty-two, all of whom he considered 'desperate and very obstinate'. Despite his efforts, using 'al the honest meanes I could both by my self and other to haue wonne them, causing diuers learned men to talke with them', he found in them 'nothing but pride and wilfulness', and so was minded to take them out of the City to his house at Fulham, to pass sentence on them out of the public glare.[25]

Here, however, yet another jurisdictional delicacy complicated matters. It had been a fraught and tense summer of many burnings, peaking in June with twenty-six executions, thirteen of them on a single occasion in the London suburbs at Stratford-le-Bow on 27 June. The men and women executed that day had originally been sixteen in number and, after their condemnation, John Feckenham, dean of St Paul's, had preached against them at Paul's Cross, highlighting the divisiveness of protestantism by saying that among the sixteen there were sixteen different opinions about religion. They had retaliated by issuing a joint declaration of faith, reaffirming their shared convictions: that the true church was always the persecuted church 'by the death of Saints confirmed'; that the 'Sea of Rome is the sea of Antichrist . . . whereof the pope is head under the devill'; and that the Mass was a 'blasphemous Idoll', in which there was only bread and wine. Undeterred, Feckenham continued to visit the group in gaol and at length seems to have persuaded three of them to recant. The Cardinal duly absolved the three penitents, and secured their pardon from the Queen.[26]

Bonner emerged bruised from this episode, and may have felt himself to be cast unjustly in the invidious role of hanging judge. The details remain obscure, but the fact that Feckenham was able, at the eleventh hour, to pluck three brands from the burning might have suggested that Bonner on this occasion had acted too hastily in a matter of life and death, and more, of eternal salvation, and that he could have tried harder to persuade before condemning the sixteen. The Cardinal evidently thought something of the kind for, two months later, surrounded by the tumult of city gospellers and confronted with this embarrassingly large and intransigent group of twenty-two from Colchester, Bonner hesitated and wrote to Pole for instructions, 'perceiuing by my last doing that your grace was offended'.[27]

The matter was discussed by the Privy Council, and it was eventually agreed that the burning at this juncture in London of twenty-two men and women, however stubborn, 'at one clap', would invite tumult. They were offered and accepted the option of a loosely phrased recantation, in which they affirmed vaguely that Christ's body and blood were present in the sacrament of the Lord's supper, 'according as Christ's Church doth minister the same', declared their obedience to the catholic church (without being required to say what or where they thought that church was), and promised to obey superiors both spiritual and temporal. They were then released.[28]

This grim comedy of the Essex twenty-two, with its tangle of jurisdictions and personalities, was to have an even grimmer sequel. Most of the twenty-two disappear from the record after their dismissal by Bonner, presumably because, whether their submission was real or feigned, they gave no further cause for proceedings against them. But six of them, Richard Rothe, William Bongeor, Ellen Ewring, William and Alice Munt and their daughter Rose Allin, went to the stake within a year, all but Rothe on the same day in Colchester in August 1557. Having been dismissed by Bonner, the Munt family had returned to their home parish of Much Bentley, where they not only continued to absent themselves from church, but, as their parish priest complained, 'do dayly allure many other away from the same, which before did outwardly shew signes & tokens of obedience.' Emboldened by their release, they openly mocked those parishioners who did attend Mass, 'calling them church Owles, and blasphemouslye calling the blessed Sacrament of the altar a blynde God, with diuers suche lyke blasphemies'.[29]

Much Bentley was, in fact, the centre of a very active conventicle, sustained not only by the Munts, but especially by another layman named Ralph Allerton, who had himself recanted a year or so earlier and had been released by Bonner after another strategically vague profession of obedience to the catholic church at Paul's Cross, similar to that agreed by the Colchester twenty-two. Plagued by conscience, he was now once again propagating his evangelical beliefs in the parish, and, by the end of 1556, the Much Bentley gospellers were meeting regularly on Sundays, as the priest informed Bonner 'in the time of diuine seruice, sometimes in one house, sometime in an other, and there keepe theyr priuy conuenticles and scholes of heresy'.

The priest, Thomas Tye, knew what he was talking about. He himself had been an ardent evangelical in Edward's reign, and, for more than a year after Mary's accession, had been one of the many gospellers driven into hiding 'in woodes, barnes, and other solitary places'. Like many other evangelical clergy, however, he had somehow experienced a change of heart, and by 1556 was not merely a conformist, but an extremely determined and devastatingly well-informed heresy hunter. Tye blamed the softness of the central authorities for the brazenness of the conventiclers. In the light of their release, he declared, local officials would do nothing about the Munt family, or indeed any other conventiclers. As he told Bonner, 'the Quest men in your Archdeacons visitation alleadged that forasmuch as they were once presented & now sent home they haue no more to do with them nor none other'. Tye complained that he had received no satisfaction when he had raised the matter with Commissary John Kingston either, who had told him that the Council had released the Colchester twenty-two 'not without great consideration'. 'I pray God', he added darkly, 'some of your Officers proue not fauorers of hereticks.' All of this he considered disastrous for the morale of faithful catholics like himself 'which dayly prayeth to God for the profite, vnity, and restauration of his Church agayne', and it caused the heretics to rejoice: 'The rebels are stout in the Towne of Colchester.'[30]

Tye did not confine himself to lobbying the bishop and his officials. He himself engaged in preaching tours against heresy in Essex, in the course of which he was responsible for the reconciliation of a dozen ex-conventiclers at Harwich. But he also invoked the help of the secular arm. He organised a petition from leading parishioners addressed to Lord Darcy as commissioner for heresy, begging him

(for the loue of God, and for the tender zeale your good Lordshippe beareth to iustice, and common peace and quietnes of the kyng and Quenes maiesties louing subiects) to awarde out your warrant for the said Wylliam Mount his wife, and Rose her daughter, that they beinge attached and broughte before your good lordship, we trust the rest wyl feare to offend (theyr ryng leaders of sedition being apprehended).[31]

Darcy evidently passed the matter for action to Edmund Tyrrell, and the Munts were forced into hiding. On 7 March 1557, the first Sunday of Lent, Tyrrell staged one of his trademark nocturnal raids, with a posse led by the constables of Much Bentley, and captured the whole family. Refusing now any compromise with 'the members of Antichriste', William, Alice and Rose Munt were burned with seven others at Colchester on 2 August.[32] And, at Tye's prompting, Ralph Allerton was arrested and examined by Bonner in April: he was burned with Richard Rothe, another of the twenty-two, at Islington on 17 September 1557.[33]

The whole episode of the Colchester twenty-two and its aftermath at Much Bentley reveals a great deal about the progress and direction of the campaign against heresy in its final two years. By 1557, a high proportion of those being burned were recidivists who had survived at least one previous encounter with ecclesiastical authority, often because those authorities had bent over backwards to release them. The victims themselves were therefore increasingly intransigent, influenced by dismay at the progress of catholic restoration and the defection of former gospellers, by guilt-feelings over their own earlier compromises or recantations, by the example of more courageous brethren and by the steadily mounting pressure of anti-Nicodemite literature smuggled in from mainland Europe, denouncing all compromise with the synagogue of Satan and exhorting the faithful (from a safe distance) to make a stand. For their part, the regime, aware of the determined radicalism and increasingly entrenched separatist mentality of a protestant minority, now shorn by persecution of its weaker and less committed elements, was correspondingly determined to deal with this committed hard core.

The wide-ranging national heresy commission, established in February 1557

to enquyre and search out all such persons as obstinately do refuse to receiue the blessed sacrament of the aultar, to heare masse, or come to their parish Churches, . . . and all such as refuse to go on Procession, to take holy bread, or holy water, or otherwise doe misuse themselues in any church or other halowed place, raised the level of the campaign and, as Foxe observed, 'these new Inquisitours . . . beganne to ruffle and to take vpon them not a little: so that all quarters were full of persecution and prisons almost full of prisoners'.[34] The most fully documented case from this renewed push against heresy, that of Richard Woodman, burned at Lewes with nine others on 22 June 1557, illustrates both the growing instransigence of the gospellers and the corresponding determination of the regime to clamp down on dissent. It also illustrates the complexity of the problems facing the regime as it attempted to do so.

Woodman, as noted earlier, was a prosperous ironmaster employing more than a hundred workers in the village of Warbleton in East Sussex. An ardent gospeller in Edward's reign, he had first come to the attention of the Marian authorities early in 1554, when he stood up in church and denounced the parson of Warbleton. This was yet another married former evangelical who had conformed, and had not yet been deprived. Woodman publicly upbraided him for preaching 'clean contrary to that which he had been taught'. A panel of Sussex magistrates unsurprisingly decided Woodman was a heretic, and sent him up to London to be examined. He remained in the King's Bench prison in Southwark for eighteen months, questioned no fewer than twenty-six times by assorted commissioners, including William Roper and the formidable Dr John Story, who eventually transferred Woodman to the closer security and bleaker conditions of Bishop Bonner's coal-house, where he remained a further month.

Woodman's heretical convictions on the doctrine of the sacraments and the church were plain to all but, given the length of his imprisonment and the number of his examinations, it seems equally plain that the authorities were reluctant to condemn him. Despite threats by Bonner that he would soon be despatched, Woodman was eventually released on 18 December 1555, the day on that John Philpot was burned at Smithfield. Seeking some formula approximating to catholic belief that Woodman could affirm, the commissioners had asked him if Judas had received anything more than bare bread at the last supper (in contradiction of evangelical belief that there was no objective presence in the eucharist, so that only the believer received Christ by faith, and hence that the reprobate received bare bread). Woodman answered that Judas *had* received more than bread, meaning, as he later explained, not that Judas had received Christ's body, but that he had eaten the devil and damnation with the bread. On this occasion, however, the commissioners declined to listen to any further explanation and, on the strength of his ambiguous declaration, recommended his release to Bonner. The bishop duly dismissed him and several companions,

> requiring nothing els of us but that we should be honest men, and members of the true Catholike Church . . . the which all we affirmed that we were members of the true church, and purposed by God's helpe therein to die . . . But he willed us many tymes to speake good of hym.

Subsequently, rumours spread that those released had bought their freedom with a recantation, and 'the Papists sayd that I hadde consented to them'. Woodman set about vindicating his integrity by travelling round Sussex parishes 'to the number of 13 or 14, and that the chiefest in all the Countrey', summoning the priests to argue in the churchyards, since he would not enter the 'the idols' temple'. Warrants were soon out for his arrest again, and he was forced into weeks of hiding in a wood near his home, and then, for a short period, to flee abroad, his house being searched regularly, 'sometimes twice in a week'. In March 1557, in the wake of the establishment of the even tougher heresy commission, he was arrested after a spectacular chase, when a posse of twenty men besieged his house, acting, as Woodman believed, on a tip-off from his own conformist father and brother.[35]

Imprisoned once again in Bonner's coal-house and then in the Marshalsea, Woodman's case was complicated by the fact that the law required that he be tried by his ordinary, the bishop of Chichester. But, because of the hostility of the anti-Habsburg and half-mad Pope Paul IV to Pole and Queen Mary, John Christopherson, the bishop-elect, had not received faculties from Rome and so could not act, a technicality that Woodman understood and of which he made use. Christopherson nevertheless spent hours with the accused man, had him to dine at his own table, repeatedly assured him of his good will and strove, fruitlessly, to argue him into conformity.

A prolonged series of examinations produced only mounting exasperation on the part of Woodman's questioners, especially lay commissioners such as Story, who visibly chafed at the excessive patience of the examining clergy. 'My Lord', Story told Christopherson,

'I will tell you how you shall know an hereticke by his words, because I have bene more used to them then you have bene.' In a repetition of the pattern of his earlier examinations, the bishop of Winchester, John White, acting in place of Christopherson, chose to understand Woodman's original attack on the married parson of Warbleton as evidence of a *catholic* acceptance of the celibacy of the clergy. Once again, Woodman's eager attempts to set the record straight in case he should be suspected of papistry were ignored. The officers hustled him away before he incriminated himself, on the principle that, as White declared when Woodman had left the court, 'they would take me whilest I was somewhat good'.[36] But there was in the end no real room for a further fudge. A great mass of incriminating papers had been found in Woodman's house, including his own extended account of his 1556 examinations, and the process became increasingly confrontational as Woodman spelled out ever more explicitly his loathing of the catholic church. Eventually, the impasse caused by Christopherson's inability to act was resolved when the Cardinal used his legatine authority to appoint Nicholas Harpsfield as Woodman's temporary ordinary. He was condemned on 16 July 1557, and burned with nine others at Lewes on 22 August.

What strikes the reader from Foxe's account of all this, apart from the accused man's own determined refusal of ambiguity or compromise, is the extraordinary lengths to which the authorities went, both to arrest him in the first place, and then to win him over once he was in custody. Some of the heresy commissioners realised early on that Woodman was incorrigible and advocated summary condemnation. By contrast, the bishops, Christopherson especially, but even the less patient John White who manifestly loathed Woodman, laboured hard to conciliate and coax him into some sort of compliance. In part this was out of awareness of Woodman's standing in his county, as a family man of substance, a major employer, popular with his neighbours and members of the county elite, and so not lightly to be put to a shameful death. A stream of persuaders came to coax him. James Gage, brother to the high sheriff of the county, in whose house Woodman had been briefly a prisoner, told him 'I promise thee, my brother, neither I, nor no gentleman in the country . . . but would thou shouldest doe as well as their owne bodyes and soules, as a great many of them have sayd to thy face.'[37] But they were also conscious that he was a key leader and sustainer of dissent in Sussex, whose reconciliation to the church would set a powerful example: as Christopherson told him, 'if you would follow the lawes of the catholike church, it would be an occasion to bring a great many into the true church, that are out of it as you are'.[38] Such negotiations, like the displays of protestant courage at the stake, were moves in a propaganda war that historians have too readily assumed the regime was losing. That was not how it seemed to some of those most involved. Dr Story, who advocated summary treatment of Woodman, was one of the busiest and fiercest of the royal commissioners for heresy, his house at the old Greyfriars in London a hub for information and action against it. In a better position than most to judge, by mid-June 1555 he was confident that the campaign of repression was already working. London, 'the spectacle of this realm', he believed, was 'daily drawing, partly for love and partly for fear, to conformity'. And although

> of late through too much pity mixed with sinful civility, the inferior sort – yea in times of executions – began to be stout and seemed to glory in their malignity: now the sharpness of the sword, and other corrections, hath begun to bring forth that the Word, in stony hearts, could not do.

So that 'by discreet severity we have good hope of universal unity in religion'.[39] Not everyone shared this optimism about the effectiveness of 'discrete severity', or the new docility of 'the spectacle of the realm', however. Preaching at the obsequies of Philip's lunatic grandmother, Queen Joanna, on the very day on which Story wrote his upbeat assessment of the effectiveness of the campaign, John Feckenham, dean of St Paul's, rebuked the citizens of London for their 'slouthfull retourne from your wicked errours and heresies', and warned them to 'geve better eare to the voices of your shepardes'. They must 'retourne . . . into the unitie of Christes churche agayne', if they hoped to avoid the judgement of God and 'a miserable and lamentable death and endynge'.[40] Certainly feelings were running very high among London's gospellers. The bitterness that the burnings and other manifestations of resurgent catholicism could provoke showed itself murderously on the last Sunday of July. Two of the Greenwich Franciscans travelling from the city back to their convent by boat were badly injured in an ambush from the shore, when great stones were flung at them from a wharf 'by diverse lewd personnes'.[41]

Following a lead from, of all people, John Foxe himself, Pole has usually been exonerated from any direct responsibility for the persecutions, being seen as a gentle Erasmian figure, a tolerationist *manqué*, at one time (if not still by 1554) sympathetic to protestant views on justification, and himself, directly and through his Italian friends, the victim of the persecuting zeal of Pope Paul IV and the Roman Inquisition. Foxe himself claimed that Pole tried to restrain Bonner's zeal against protestants, and he did not himself preside directly at any heresy trials until the last month of his life.[42] All this is true as far as it goes. Nevertheless, there can be no serious doubt that Pole did back the campaign of repression, that he appointed as his close collaborators the most determined and efficient figures in the nationwide search and punishment of heretics, and that, from at least the end of 1555, his direct influence can be detected in the way that heresy was being handled.

Pole did indeed have a horror of killing heretics, not because of any squeamishness about the death penalty, but because he believed that an unrepentant heretic not only died in torment but went straight to hell for all eternity. Modern historians find it hard to credit such convictions as grounds for action, but they weighed heavily with sixteenth-century people. Many of the spectators at the burnings would certainly have shared Pole's horrified belief that the men and women at the stake were *vitandus*, contaminating presences already breathing the air of hell. In the second of two remarkable letters to Cranmer in 1555, Pole spelled out how deeply such thoughts affected him. Cranmer's judges had abandoned all hope of his recovery, Pole told him,

> whereof doith follow the moste horrible sentence of condempnation both of your bodie and soule, both your temporall death and eternall, which is to me so greate an horrour to here, that if there were ony way, or mean, or fashion, that I might fynd to remove you from errour, bryngeng yow to the knowledge of the treuthe, for your salvation: This I testifie to you afore God, apon the salvation of myne owne sowle, that I wold rather chuse to be that meane that yow might receive this benefyt by me, than to receive the greatest benefyt for my selfe that can be geven under heaven in this world: I esteem so moche the salvation of one sowle.[43]

Accordingly, Pole placed enormous emphasis on efforts to convert rather than to punish heretics. The most spectacular outcome of this policy came in the summer of 1556, when Edward VI's tutor and one of the key figures in the protestant diaspora in Europe, Sir John Cheke, was kidnapped and brought to England, where hand-picked theologians under Pole's direction argued him into submission. In October, Pole choreographed and probably drafted the text of a minutely detailed formal recantation by Cheke at court, in which Cheke praised the clemency that had forgiven him his treasons and that would win other heretics back to the church, 'drawn by . . . Mercy, and not plucked by extremity', because it showed that 'their Life and Mendment is sought, not their Death and shame'.[44]

Cheke's conversion, real or feigned, was a devastating blow to the protestant cause, duly exploited in the campaign against heresy in London, and, whether by design or coincidence, providing some compensation for the bungled handling of Cranmer's recantations and death earlier the same year. From the time of his recantation, Cheke was required to accompany Bonner when the bishop sat in consistory in heresy trials and, according to the Venetian ambassador, that recantation was instrumental in persuading thirty other imprisoned evangelicals to return to the unity of the church. The sincerity of Cheke's conversion was, of course, widely questioned by his former co-religionists but, according to Pole's companion Alvise Priuli, when reproached by one of them with having recanted only for fear of the fire, Cheke had retorted, 'Yes, for fear of *hell*-fire'.[45] It seems likely that Cheke's carefully composed recantation was intended for public circulation, but the fact that it did not find its way into print in the two years between the recantation and the end of the regime is a puzzle, and looks like a lost opportunity.

The myth of Pole's detachment from the campaign of repression has been propagated in part by the apparent rift that we have already noted between the Cardinal and Bishop Bonner over the handling of the Essex heretics in June 1556, not long after Cheke's capture, the worst month in a year of many burnings. The incident seems to have rankled with Bonner, and Foxe, who could not bring himself to admit that the reprieved men had escaped burning because they had recanted, based round it his claim that Pole was 'none of the bloody and cruel sort of papists'. In fact, however, the whole incident was entirely consistent with the Cardinal's general policy of doing all that was humanly possible to persuade heretics to recant. The same insistence on the superiority of securing recantations rather than executions is evident in the most up-to-date textbook on the punishment of heresy and heretics, Alfonso de Castro's much reprinted treatise *De Justa Punitione Haereticorum* of 1547, so Pole's concerns here reflect standard contemporary European thinking on the matter. We should note also that the unrepentant thirteen went to the fire.[46]

For there can be no doubt that Pole thought that heretics who would *not* repent were quite properly executed. Reporting the burning of Ridley and Latimer to King Philip in October 1555, he described the Spanish friar Peter de Soto's efforts to get them to recant. It did no good, Pole commented, since 'no one can save those whom God has rejected'. And so they were burned, 'the people looking on not unwillingly, since it was known that nothing had been neglected with regard to their salvation', an unmistakable echo of the Queen's own Directions in such matters. With a canny eye on the propaganda possibilities, as well as Cranmer's chances in the next world, he told Philip that the archbishop seemed less obstinate and that, if he could indeed be brought to recant, 'the Church will derive no little profit from the salvation of a single soul': had Pole's views prevailed with the Queen on this occasion as on most others, the outcome of Cranmer's case would no doubt have been very different.[47]

Pole's direct involvement in strategic thinking about the campaign of burnings, and the Queen's collaboration with him in this area in particular, was, however, made explicit in a circular letter to the bishops of his province in September 1555, written in the build-up to the Legatine Synod. Having requested detailed information about diocesan finances and clerical pensions, Pole went on to emphasise the need for careful and compassionate handling of the execution of heretics. One aspect in particular exercised him, he told his colleagues. This was a matter that he was pursuing with the cooperation of many pious men, and about which the Queen had already written individually to each bishop. This was almost certainly a reference to the well-known 'Directions of Queen Mary to her Council, Touching the Reformation of the Church', which we have already encountered, in which she insisted on a two-pronged policy of punishment of the recalcitrant and instruction of the ignorant.[48]

As we have seen, in those 'Directions' Mary had also insisted that no moves against heresy were to be undertaken without the direct advice of the Cardinal, and he now claimed the policy outlined in the Queen's directions as his own. The Queen had reminded them, he declared, of the crucial importance of ensuring that there was a preacher present at every execution, because heretics could harm the ignorant and rude multitude at least as much by their deaths as ever they did alive. It was important, Pole insisted, that the preachers should show that the heretics were being executed because of their evil life and stubborn intransigence, and that they should explain that the culprits had been offered every inducement to acknowledge their errors, and so escape death. And indeed, he went on, every motive for repentance had to be urged on the heretics up to the very last moment, 'that having the terror of divine judgement before their eyes, they might plead for the mercy of God'. It was never too late to repent, and God's mercy was never denied to the sincere penitent, however tardy. So, by this merciful course of action,

> even at the last the heretics may be overcome, and the people protected from scandal, to which they are all too prone if there is no preacher there to explain matters, and when they see these unhappy men bearing their torments with so much endurance, not recognising the Devil's strength underneath this false piety and bogus courage.[49]

The emphasis on the offer of mercy up to the last minute is entirely characteristic of Pole, but so too is the steely insistence on the need to justify the executions, and the concern that the propaganda advantage should not go to the devil's party.

Pole spelled out his attitude to the burning of unrepentant heretics in his own diocese in a remarkably explicit manuscript instruction, probably intended as guidance for the Canterbury commissioners in 1556. Pole was intensely conscious of the lapse of the entire Henrician episcopate into schism, Fisher only excepted, and that awareness undoubtedly put a barrier of reserve between him and the older bishops, which may well account for the occasional lack of cordiality in his relationship with Bonner, as it certainly coloured his relations with Gardiner.[50]

One consequence of this reserve towards the former Henrician bishops was a willingness to accept that the heretical beliefs of many of the laity were not culpable, but the result of evil teaching. As he told his commissioners, 'it ys nott the opinion alone that maketh a man to be an heretique be it never so much against the fayth, for it maketh him not to be iudged an heretique, yf he take nott the same of his owne iudgement & defend it not with pertynacite'. The simple faithful had been misled by bad bishops and priests such as Cranmer, 'the corruptions of the world being suche that many bysshops themselfes have more need to be taught than to teache other'. If an accused heretic pleaded that bad influence, therefore, and offered as a defence that he had 'learned his opinion of his busshope in deade', provided that he 'styketh not to his owne iudgement, butt to the iudgement of his busshope', then his defence 'ys to be admitted, he nott to be condemned, butt to be taught the waye, how having his busshope infected with heresye, which hath also infected him, he may be delivered of that infection'.[51] In practice, however, Pole realised, recent experience in England had shown that many heretics 'wyll do nothing that deservith pardon nother afor God nor man'. They had followed the false teaching of their bishops, not out of a laudable trust in their divinely appointed fathers-in-God, whose instruction as laymen they were obliged to obey, but because

> fynding the busshopes opinion such as seamith to be more conformable to their reason, which thei make iudge both of the bysshopes opinion and of all other, and for that cause thei cleave unto the bushops opinion, wych is their owne opinion, wherin thei shewe them selfes both to have hereticall opinions and to be heretiques in deade, most worthie to be condemned, depryving by this meanes themselfe of all kynde of iust defence.

All those, therefore, who refused correction from Pole as their legitimate bishop, revealed that they were no true children of the church. With such people, argument was wasted and 'S Paule wyll nott the busshope shuld spende tyme by disputing and reasonynge, thinking therbye to convert them, butt after one or two admonitions to separate himself from them, and to separate them from the rest of the bodye.'[52] For those thus separated, of course, the law prescribed death by fire. And once again, experience showed that those dying by fire were justly punished,

> as Satan ys punished to be cutt off from the body of lyffe, which their behaviour most shewith when they come to suffer that kynde of death that the lawes . . . doith ordain for such . . . that by their contempt of that death and by their wordes going to death they may

the sooner corrupt other in their pertinaciouse opinion to bring them also to the fyer as they be brought, in so much that yf thei be put to a lighter payne that ys nott so open to the worlde . . . thei take ytt sorer muche then the fyer.[53]

There is no ambiguity in these stern sentiments, and documents from the Canterbury heresy trials that Foxe chose to suppress make clear that Pole's assistants in the diocese followed his directions to the letter, and translated his admonitions directly into policy. Among the Kentish gospellers examined by Nicholas Harpsfield in February 1557, as a new phase of energetic repression began, was John Fishcocke of Headcorn, a radical separatist with a record of dissent stretching back to his teens in Henry VIII's reign. Fishcocke's comprehensive heresies on many issues, from the primacy of the pope to the value of sacraments and ceremonies, led to his burning in June 1557, but he was clearly aware of the guidelines that Pole had laid down for the Canterbury trials, and the particular emphasis in Pole's instruction on belief about the real presence. Fishcocke signed a declaration stating that

He doth desire to be respectuated because he humblye desirethe to be ascerteyned what my lord cardynalles graces consciyence and fayth ys in the said blessed sacrament, saying that he doth beleeve assuredly that his grace knowethe the trewthe, And therapon did faytheullye promise to receive my lordes graces iudgemente in good parte and that he will beleve itt accordinglye as his grace by his letters or writings shall advise him, in this part.[54]

John Strype, who first printed this document, misunderstood it, taking it to mean that Fishcocke suspected that, whatever the Cardinal outwardly pretended, 'he was indeed inwardly a protestant, and believed as they did on the doctrine of the sacrament'.[55] In fact, what Fishcocke's declaration demonstrates is that Harpsfield and his colleagues were operating to guidelines imposed by Pole himself, and were requiring suspects to demonstrate their sincerity by explicit adherence to their bishop's views on the real presence. In the declaration signed by Fishcocke, the phrase about Pole's 'conscience and faith' has been emended from the original 'conscience and *opinion*'. What was at stake here was precisely not Pole's *opinion* as a private individual, but the faith he taught as bishop, the divinely appointed guide for the priests and people of his diocese.

That Pole was willing to translate theory into practice on this matter is evident from the track records of the men whom he appointed to do the work in Canterbury and elsewhere, most notably of course Nicholas Harpsfield, his closest collaborator among the English clergy, whose zeal as archdeacon of Canterbury and vicar-general of the London diocese gives him a place alongside Bonner in Foxe's infernal pantheon of persecutors.[56] In fact, Harpsfield was thorough and determined rather than bloodthirsty, characteristics shared with Pole's other collaborators in the fight against heresy, such as Robert Collins, who had acted as Pole's agent before he arrived in England, served on many heresy commissions and, from March 1556, was Pole's commissary-general for heresy in the city and diocese.[57] Collins sat as judge in a series of Canterbury heresy trials, including that of John Bland, in which his patience and gentle speech towards the accused were noted.[58]

Pole's concern with the systematic pursuit of heresy was not confined to his own diocese. He was responsible for a series of equally effective appointments of vicars-general for vacant dioceses, all of whom distinguished themselves in the pursuit of heresy, notably William Dalbie in Bristol[59] and William Geffrie at Salisbury.[60] And these were no mere rubber stampings of routine appointments: Pole himself looked to these men to pursue a vigorous campaign against heresy. This emerges clearly from Pole's own intervention in Salisbury diocese over the appointment of Geffrie.

On 15 July 1555, Pole wrote to the bishop of Salisbury, John Salcot or Capon, a Henrician survivor who had been active as a commissioner in the national campaign against heresy, but whom Pole evidently thought lacking in zeal in his own diocese.[61] Pole admonished Salcot that he had heard that clergy who had attacked the doctrine of the Mass in sermons and by writing under Edward, but who had outwardly conformed on Mary's accession, were once again spreading their poisonous errors abroad in the diocese. The bishop must take care that such wolves did not wreak havoc among his flock. No priest must be allowed to exercise his ministry until the bishop was certain they had been sincerely reconciled to the church, and were firmly established in their adherence to catholic doctrine. And Salcot must not only expel the erring from the ministry, 'sed etiam severissime juxta canonicas sanctiones coerceantur'.[62]

On the very same day, Chancellor Geffrie began his serious pursuit of heresy in Salisbury, taking up residence at the cathedral and handling cases in the consistory court in person. This can hardly be a coincidence: Geffrie's arrival was clearly the advent of the archbishop's troubleshooter, to overcome local inertia. Pole's own writings make clear his pastoral anxiety to save souls, his eagerness to bring the doctrinally erring to repentance; but his commitment to silencing heresy at all costs is equally clear and, if the master is to be judged by his men, Pole was determined to eradicate dissent, by persuasion if at all possible, but, if not, then by compulsion.

CHAPTER 7

The Battle for Hearts and Minds

John Foxe's partisan artistry and the paucity of other sources has made it hard for the historian to assess the actual impact of the burnings on those who witnessed them. The most famous of the executions, that of Bishops Ridley and Latimer in the town ditch of Oxford on 16 October 1555, is a case in point. The culmination of a series of disputations involving theologians and canon lawyers from both universities, and of a show trial attended by a large lay audience, the execution itself was a carefully staged event, designed in part to silence the most influential of all the protestant leaders, and to focus the wavering mind of Thomas Cranmer, then imprisoned in the town gaol, 'Bocardo', on the wisdom of recantation. The Regius Professor of Divinity, Richard Smith, preached a short sermon beside the pyre on the text: 'If I yield my body to the fire to be burned, but have not charity, I gain nothing' (see Plate 24). In it, he compared Latimer and Ridley's deaths to the suicide of Judas, traced their heresies to the alien teachings of Luther, Oecolampadius and Zwingli, and warned the people against contamination from contact with or sympathy for those who died wilfully outside the church. The two victims themselves were prevented by the sheriff from making any reply, but commended themselves to God by crying out 'in a wonderful loud voice' the dying words of Jesus on the cross. But the most famous element in the scene, Latimer's ringing words to his companion at the stake, 'Be of good comfort maister Ridley, and play the man: wee shall this day light such a candle by Gods grace in England, as (I trust) shall neuer be put out', appears, sadly, to be pure invention, added by Foxe in the 1570 edition of *Acts and Monuments*, and modelled on the words of the early church martyr Polycarp at his burning by the pagan Roman authorities.[1] The impact of this execution at the time on those who watched it is therefore hard to judge. Cardinal Pole thought that the spectators had by and large accepted the justice of the execution.[2] Foxe, in contrast, attributed the conversion of the future martyr Julins Palmer, fellow of Magdalen College, to horror at this burning, on his return from which 'in the hearing of diuers of his frendes, he brast out into these woordes, and suche like: O raging crueltie, O tyrannie tragicall, and more than barbarous', and from that day forward 'studiously sought to vnderstand the truth'.[3] In fact, although in Edward's days he had been a stubborn papist whose views had cost him his college fellowship, by the beginning of Mary's reign Palmer had already changed his mind. A reading of Calvin's *Institutes* during his Edwardine exile had convinced him that all images were idols, the pope antichrist, and the catholic clergy 'the filthy sinke hole of hel'.[4] No doubt the deaths of Latimer and Ridley revolted him, therefore, but it was revulsion nourished by a change of heart and mind that had already taken place.

We may compare Palmer's reaction to the deaths of Ridley and Latimer with the response of another young Oxford academic, William Ely of Brasenose, to what is generally (and probably correctly) taken to be the greatest single propaganda disaster for the Marian regime: Cranmer's reversion to his evangelical convictions just before his execution on the same spot five months later. Ely had made friends with the archbishop during the last weeks in which he had appeared to be a sincere catholic penitent. Far from being impressed by Cranmer's last-minute determination to die in the protestant cause, however, when the old man offered to shake his hand as he mounted the pyre, Ely

> drewe backe his hande and refused, saying: it was not lawfull to salute heretickes, and specially such a one as falsly returned vnto the opinions that he had forsworne. And if he had knowen before that hee would haue done so, he would neuer haue vsed his company so familiarly, and chid those sergeants and Citizens, whiche had not refused to geue hym their hands.[5]

We have no way of assessing which response, Palmer's or Ely's, was the more typical, but it is certain that we cannot simply assume that the executions that horrify us provoked equal horror, or perhaps especially disapproval, in their sixteenth-century witnesses. As it happens, we have the remarkable testimony of another sensitive catholic eyewitness of Cranmer's death, the anonymous 'J. A.', whose often-quoted and apparently sympathetic account, and especially the remark that 'I think there was none that pitied not his case', has prompted many, including Cranmer's modern biographer, to the view that J. A. 'despite his religious views, found much to admire in Cranmer's last hours'.[6] In fact, however, J. A. was a good deal more ambivalent about Cranmer than that remark suggests. The pity that he displayed was not so much for Cranmer in himself, but reflected, rather, a fairly conventional Tudor meditation on the revolutions of the wheel of fortune, and the sordid end of a man who had held the greatest spiritual office in the land:

> For although his former life, and wretched end, deserves a greater misery, (if any greater might have chanced than chanced unto him,) yet, setting aside his offences to God and his country, and beholding the man without his faults, I think there was none that pitied not his case, and bewailed his fortune, and feared not his own chance, to see so noble a prelate . . . after so many dignities, in his old yeares to be deprived of his estate, adjudged to die, and in so painful a death to end his life.[7]

J. A. had no doubt, however, that Cranmer had deserved his terrible end, and he deplored rather than admired the courage of his final stand:

> His patience in the torment, his courage in dying, *if it had been taken either for the glory of God, the wealth of his country, or the testimony of truth, as it was for a pernicious error and subversion of true religion,* I could worthily have commended the example, and matched it with the fame of any father of ancient time.

As it was, however,

> seeing that not the death, but the cause and quarrel thereof, commendeth the sufferer, I cannot but much dispraise his obstinate stubbornness and sturdiness in dying, and specially in so evil a cause.

In a careful appraisal of the impact of Cranmer's death, J. A. remarked that it had indeed 'much grieved every man', but 'not after one sort'. Some onlookers 'pitied to see his body so tormented with fire raging upon the silly [simple] carcass, that counted not the folly'. Others, 'that passed not much of the body, lamented to see him spill his soul wretchedly, without redemption, to be plagued for ever'. It is clear that J. A. was one of the latter, and he believed that, by his last-minute stand, Cranmer had condemned himself to an eternity of torment in hell. Nevertheless, reflecting that Cranmer's friends 'sorrowed for love; his enemies for pity', he acknowledged that 'strangers', those who were uninvolved, also sorrowed 'for a common kind of humanity, whereby we are bound one to another'.[8] J. A.'s acknowledgement of the pity owed to our common humanity, however, did nothing to shake his conviction that it was the 'cause and quarrel' that determined the true value of a man's death. By that criterion, Cranmer's apparent courage was 'folly' and 'obstinate stubbornness', and the old man had deserved his terrible fate. This nuanced, humane but ultimately steely assessment should give us pause before reading twenty-first-century attitudes and values into the complexities of the remote past.

The burning of Joyce Lewes at Lichfield in September 1557 illustrates some of the wider ambiguities in assessing the balance of advantage in this battle for hearts and minds. At first glance, her execution provides a textbook example of spontaneous popular support for the victim of a cruel and politically inept regime. Members of the crowd – Foxe says 'the most part' – shouted 'Amen' to her prayer at the stake for deliverance of the realm from papistry, and 'a great number' of the women present drank a toast with her before her death. In fact, however, the crowd was far from unanimous in her support. Bystanders railed at and reviled her as she passed through the crowd and while she stood chained at the stake, though Foxe explained this hostility away as having been orchestrated by the authorities.

However that may be, there was certainly nothing spontaneous about the demonstrations in support of Mistress Lewes. Foxe tells us that the night before her death she had 'desired certaine of her frends to come to her, with whom when they came, shee consulted how shee might be haue her self, that her death might be more glorious to the name of God, comfortable to his people, and also most discomfortable vnto the enemies of God'. The authorities had evidently got wind of this, however, and a priest was stationed by the pyre to write down the names of those who offered encouragement or comfort. Foxe tells us that those of her supporters who came from Coventry and elsewhere managed to escape, because the priest did not know their names, but the list of those arrested and forced to recant for drinking with her suggests that the 'great number' of *local*, Lichfield-based supporters amounted in the end to just eleven people – nine women and two men. One of the men was Nicholas Bird, a former sheriff of Worcester, who had already managed to delay Mistress Lewes's execution for months by refusing to preside at it himself.[9] One of the women was Agnes Glover, wife of the gospeller John Glover, the man who had first instructed Mistress Lewes in her evangelical opinions.[10] The demonstration at the execution, therefore, should be seen not as a spontaneous outburst by a sympathetic crowd, but as a concerted display by Mistress Lewes's own circle of evangelical comrades. And, in the event, all these sympathisers subsequently recanted.[11]

The authorities were not always so successful, however, in suppressing such demonstrations. When, early in the campaign, the priest John Laurence was burned at Colchester in March 1555, so weak from imprisonment that he had to be carried to the stake in a chair, 'young children came about the fire, and cryed, (as wel as young children could speake) saying: Lorde strengthen thy seruaunt, and keepe thy promise, Lord strengthen they seruaunt, and keepe thy promise'.[12] The pattern set at this execution was replicated at subsequent Colchester burnings. When ten people were burned there in a single day in August 1557, six in the morning and four in the afternoon, Foxe tells us that the 'bystanders cryed generally all almost: The Lord strengthen them, the Lord comfort them, the Lord poure his mercies vpon them, with such like wordes, as was wonderfull to heare.'[13]

At Ipswich, in November 1558, supporters similarly gathered round Alexander Gouche and Alice Driver at the stake, taking them by the hand and comforting them, and when the sheriff, already irritated by the two victims' prolonged psalm-singing, ordered the arrest of the comforters, more ran out from the crowd to join them: wisely, he decided at this point to leave well alone.[14] At the last mass execution at Smithfield, on 27 June 1558, members of a conventicle arrested in the fields at Islington were burned in the presence of the usual large crowd. As the authorities expected, these spectators included large numbers of London gospellers, who, by pre-arrangement, staged a demonstration, surrounding and embracing the victims at the stake with words of comfort, in defiance of a proclamation that had just been read, expressly forbidding prayers or other signs of support. The demonstration was coordinated by the group's minister, Thomas Betham, and it would be naive to assume that the crowd as a whole was made up of sympathetic protestants or, indeed, that the majority were anything other than eager spectators at a macabre entertainment.

This is not to deny the volatility of public feeling about the burnings in London and, indeed, in other urban communities, prone to protect their own whether or not they approved of their opinions. Unruly

London apprentices, many of them keen evangelicals, were often key elements in the disturbances in the city. In January 1556, the Privy Council ordered the Mayor and aldermen of London not only to ensure a strong presence of officers at every execution 'to see suche as shall misuse themselfes either by comforting, aiding or praysing thoffenders', but also to see to it 'that no householder suffer any of his apprentices or other servants to be abrode' at the time of any burning.[15] In November 1557, the execution of three heretics at Smithfield was postponed for twenty-four hours, apparently in deference to city solidarities. One of the three, Richard Gibson, a former free-willer who had already renounced some of his more radical religious opinions, was the grandson of a one-time Lord Mayor and the son of the bailiff of Southwark. Abbot Feckenham used the day's delay for an unsuccessful last-ditch attempt to talk the young man into a full recantation. Like the Cardinal and other leading churchmen, Feckenham was genuinely committed to converting rather than killing protestants, and was regularly employed to persuade prisoners to conformity, but it seems probable that his eleventh-hour efforts on this occasion were also made in deference to civic sensibilities, and the likelihood of special ill-feeling about the execution of a member of a leading city family.[16]

By the summer of 1558, those managing the burnings in London had recognised that high-profile Smithfield executions were providing the London gospellers with too much of the oxygen of publicity, and John Story, one of the campaign's most unflinching strategists, suggested instead that they should be sent for execution 'into odde corners into the countrey'.[17] This is the conclusion that Bonner himself drew from the disturbances at Smithfield on 27 June 1558. A few days later he wrote to Cardinal Pole, suggesting that the remaining six members of the same conventicle, then imprisoned in his house, should be speedily and quietly burned elsewhere. They were duly executed at Brentford on 14 July, and nobody protested.[18]

In fact, by 1557 most of the victims were from outside London, especially the towns and villages of Essex, East Anglia and the Weald of Kent. But even in communities without any evidence of sympathy for protestantism, the ties of neighbourhood could make the execution of dissidents problematic. Even in the looser conglomerates of the towns, people might be reluctant to assist in the execution of a neighbour, as in the case of the weaver John Noyes at Laxfield in Suffolk in September

1556, when, famously, all but one of the town's households doused their kitchen fires, thereby depriving the sheriff's men of lit coals to start the pyre.[19] Such local solidarity, whatever its ideological base or lack of it, was something the authorities ignored at their peril. Even a single sympathiser calling out 'the Lord strengthen thee' at a burning could make an impression, and was unwelcome to those in charge.[20] John Jarvis was the solitary Laxfield serving-man convicted of calling the sheriff's men 'villain wretches' at the burning of John Noyes. He was set in the stocks and whipped round the marketplace for his temerity, and his father and master each bound over for £5 apiece to ensure his future good behaviour, despite his not very convincing protestations that all he had actually said was 'good Lord, how the sinnewes of hys armes shrinke vp'.[21]

When all such local loyalties have been taken into account, it seems clear that support for the victims at the pyre does indicate the presence throughout the reign of a significant and persistent protestant minority. That minority was relatively strong in places such as the city of London, the Weald of Kent and the towns of the Stour valley, and used the public but comparatively anonymous forum of the crowd to express religious solidarity with the condemned. Such demonstrations highlight the protective webs of neighbourhood and kinship that, even in conformist communities, might insulate deviant minorities against effective repressive action. But all this does not amount to evidence for the sort of progressive nationwide disenchantment with the burnings that some historians have assumed or asserted. Even in London, where protestants remained a significant minority with powerful backers among the city elites, the burnings took place against a background of growing conformity. The city churches were being lavishly re-equipped, the livery companies and parishes were returning to a full catholic ceremonial round, and the funerals of prominent citizens, always an opportunity for status-enhancing, conspicuous consumption, were increasingly marked by elaborate doles, ostentatious intercessory liturgy and preaching by fashionable catholic dignitaries.[22] Foxe himself provides telling examples of communal hostility to protestant dissidents in 1557 and 1558, such as the London crowd who set upon the prisoner John Lithal in St Paul's Cathedral when he publicly refused signs of catholic veneration there: 'Then when they coulde not make me to kneele before the roode, neither to see their Masse, there gathered a great company about vs, and all against me. Some spit on me, and sayd: Fie on thee hereticke, and other said it was pitie I was not burned already.'[23] Such hostility was not confined to the capital. In August 1558, the Hampshire evangelical Thomas Benbridge was heckled at the stake by bystanders, one of whom suggested that his tongue should be cut out to prevent him expressing blasphemous sentiments.[24] Gospellers with the courage and individuality to suffer death for their convictions were not always comfortable or conciliatory neighbours. The Munt family, brazenly jeering at their conformist fellow parishioners in Essex as 'Church owles' who worshipped a blind God;[25] or Elizabeth Cooper standing up in her parish church in Norwich to call on her neighbours not to be deceived, until one of them, arms wide in angry amazement, demanded 'Master Sheriff, will you suffer this';[26] or Thomas Hudson, half-crazed by months in hiding, walking openly in the town of Aylsham 'crying out continually against the Masse and all theyr trumpery', and singing psalms all night in his house till a neighbour fetched the constables[27] – none of these can have endeared themselves to their local communities. Many people would have seen the burnings of such dissidents as just retribution, too long delayed, and the conventiclers of Great Bentley were denounced to the authorities not only by their priest, but also by seven other parishioners.[28]

John Philpot in December 1555, and Cranmer in March 1556, were the last major clerical leaders to be burned. From then on, the attention of the authorities was turned on the rank and file, especially targeting illegal congregations, a campaign that would reach its first climax in June 1556 with the burning of thirteen Essex conventiclers in a single day at Stratford-le-Bow (see Plate 25). Beleaguered protestants comforted themselves with the conviction that the blood of the martyrs was the seed of the Gospel, and that zealous sustainer of the martyrs, Elizabeth Fane, told Bonner from hiding that 'the very papists themselves now begin to abhor your bloodthirstiness', so that every child who could lisp knew how to say that 'Bloudy Bonner is bishop of London'.[29] Nevertheless, the horrors of burning certainly induced many wavering evangelicals into a conformity that both the authorities and dismayed protestant leaders believed might in time, given familiarity, due instruction and the weight of social pressure, stabilise into something more than mere external acquiescence. This was certainly part of the regime's overall strategy, and it was a promising enough way of proceeding. So far as we know, for example, John and Elizabeth Warne were the only two of the thirty conventiclers arrested at a communion in Bow churchyard in January 1555 to be burned: the rest evidently conformed. Years later, John Story would recall his own involvement in securing another mass recantation of this kind in 1556.[30]

Whatever one may think about the reality or likely staying power of such 'conversions', the level of evangelical backsliding under pressure was alarming enough to galvanise the exiled protestant leadership through 1555 and 1556 to an increasingly urgent campaign of *samizdat* publication, designed to stiffen resolve and halt the haemorrhage of timid and half-hearted gospellers, who were known as 'Nicodemites'.[31] This literature, whose abundance is often seen as a mark of the strength of protestantism, was actually a symptom of extreme anxiety among the reformed leadership.[32] But clearly their attempts to staunch the haemorrhage bore some fruit: many of those executed from mid-1555 onwards had at some earlier point renounced their beliefs under pressure, because of the rigours of imprisonment, fear of the fire or the persuasions of the catholic authorities.[33] The 'hell of conscience' that might afflict backsliders in such cases was common enough to become a trope in the records of heresy trials, as in the case of Thomas Whittle, the London cleric who signed a recantation in 1555, but who subsequently 'with much adoe' informed the horrified and contemptuous Nicholas Harpsfield

> that Sathan had bene with him in the night, and tolde him that he was damned, and weeping he prayed . . . to see the bill whereunto he subscribed, and when he sawe it, he tare out his name *è libro scilicet viuentium* [and of course also out of the book of the living].[34]

The Bristol weaver Richard Sharpe, who had recanted publicly in March 1556, was afterwards so tormented in conscience that early the next year he returned to his parish church during High Mass, 'came to the queere doore & sayd with a loud voyce: Neighbors, beare me recorde that yonder Idoll (and poynted to the aultar) is the greatest and most abhominable that euer was: and I am sory that euer I denied my Lord GOD.'[35] Sharpe's fatal gesture had perhaps been prompted by the anti-Nicodemite literary campaign being waged from Emden and elsewhere in Europe, by the example of more resolute martyrs, or by a general crystallising of confessional identity among hard-core gospellers under persecution. But, on occasion, such gestures of compunction might actually be triggered by the eagerness of the authorities to reward and stabilise the conversion of former evangelicals. When James Abbes – a young day-labourer from Stoke Nayland forced by the campaign against heresy into 'wandring and going from place to place, to auoide the pearill of apprehendinge' – was arrested in the summer of 1555, he recanted. His examination was conducted by the bishop of Norwich, John Hopton, who, recognising his poverty, gave him on his release an alms of forty pence.[36] The gift festered in Abbes' conscience and, in a gesture designed to highlight the heinousness of his apostasy by evoking the action of Judas in the Passion narrative, he returned and cast the money at the feet of the bishop: resisting all further persuasions and threats, Abbes was burned in August 1555.[37]

The intransigence of many of the accused posed an acute problem for the clergy charged with administering the law against them, yet, whether from prudence or from pity, anxious to find ways of avoiding their condemnation. Some of the suspects remitted to them by magistrates were poor and ill-educated, such as the cluster of Essex women sent to Bonner by John Mordaunt and Edmund Tyrrell in March 1556, at the beginning of a new and vigorous phase in the campaign against conventiclers in the county. Examined on the number of the sacraments, Elizabeth Thackwel and Katherine Hut told Bonner that 'they could not tel what a sacrament is', but they thought that matrimony, baptism and the Lord's supper were sacraments. Another of the group, the teenager Margaret Ellis, 'as a young mayde, unskilled, in her simple ignorance', thought there might be just one sacrament, 'but what it was she could not tell'. The bishops and their officials were just as aware as John Foxe of the invidiousness of condemning what the martyrologist called the 'weake imbecilitie . . . of seely pore women' and struggled to persuade many of those before them to 'keepe their consciences to themselves'. All too often, however, the victims refused to oblige. These poor Essex women might have been uncertain of the precise number of the sacraments, but they were clear that they would have no truck with restored catholicism. The sacrament of the altar was nothing but 'a dumme God and made with men's hands' and, as for the bishop of Rome, in the words of Katherine Hut, echoing those of the reformed English Litany, 'I forsake all his abhominations, and from them good lord deliuer vs.' Unable to budge them from such convictions and under the baleful scrutiny of the Council, Bonner had little choice, as Foxe wrote, but to 'knock [them] downe wyth the butcherly axe of hys sentence'.[38]

Many officials were manifestly reluctant to wield the axe of sentence, especially when the accused was a woman. Cecily Ormes, wife of a Norwich worsted weaver, had been first arrested as a heretic in the summer of 1556: brought before the chancellor of the diocese, Michael Dunning, she recanted. But the intensification of the protestant campaign against Nicodemism, and perhaps especially the example of more stalwart fellow evangelicals, worked on her mind. Eventually, though illiterate herself, she managed to have a letter drafted to Dunning, 'to let hym know that she repented her recantation from the bottome of her hart, & would neuer do the like againe while she liued'. Before the letter could be delivered, however, Mrs Ormes was arrested on 5 July 1557, pledging a toast to Simon Miller and Elizabeth Cooper at their burning (see Plate 26). Elizabeth Cooper may well have been the direct cause of Mrs Ormes's change of heart, for Cooper in turn had provoked her own arrest and condemnation by standing up during Mass to repudiate her own earlier recantation. Confronted by yet another woman apparently suicidally determined to trumpet her convictions to the authorities, Dunning 'offred her if she would goe to the Church and keepe her tongue shee should bee at lybertie, and belewe as shee wuld'. Mistress Ormes refused and, despite his declared reluctance to condemn 'an ignoraunt, unlearned and foolysh woman', the chancellor was obliged to proceed to sentence.[39]

Despite the evidence of the comparatively large number of women burned under Mary (fifty-six in all), Dunning was far from alone in this hesitation to condemn women, especially the young, the poor or the otherwise vulnerable, and some of the same attitudes are on display in the process against the twenty-year-old Colchester servant-girl Elizabeth Folkes. Her judge was William Chedsey, archdeacon of Middlesex, normally an implacable scourge of Essex heresy, who had told Thomas Haukes 'it is pitie that thou shouldest liue, or any such as thou art'.[40] Yet Chedsey went to great lengths to try to release Folkes. At her first examination he asked her only whether she believed there was a catholic church or not. When she said that she did, he at once released her into the custody of her uncle in the town, thereby giving her the opportunity to flee Colchester. She refused to go and, questioned again on whether or not she believed in a substantial and real presence in the Sacrament, declared that she believed 'it was a substantiall lye, and a reall lye'. Chedsey had to proceed to judgement, but even Foxe noted that while he read the sentence 'he wept, that the tears trickled down his cheeks'. Chedsey's reluctance to condemn Folkes may well have sprung from the realisation that there were influential heretics in the town considerably more deserving of pursuit, but whose outward conformity and social position protected them from scrutiny. The release of Folkes to her uncle's custody had been suggested by another member of Bonner's staff, the scribe John Boswell. In the previous August, Boswell had written to the bishop to draw attention to exactly this issue:

> Yt may please your good lord ship to be aduertised that I do se by experience that the sworne inquest for heresies, do moste comenly induct the simple, ignorant, and wretched heretickes, & do let the archheretikes go, which is one greate cause that moueth the rude multitude to murmur, when they see the simple wretches (not knowing what heresy is) to burne. I wysh (if it may be) that this common disease might be cured emongest the iurates of Essex. But I feare mee it wil not bee, so longe as some of them be (as they are) infected with the like disease.[41]

Boswell's suspicions had particular point in the case of Elizabeth Folkes. After her condemnation, the girl denounced but did not name the 'halting gospellers' present in the court, warning them to beware of blood guilt. She almost certainly had in mind her own master, Alderman Nicholas Clere. A prominent gospeller in Edward's reign, Clere was one of the many members of the Essex elite now covering his tracks by zealous action against plebeian evangelicals, and he may well have been instrumental in arranging his own servant's arrest. At any rate, Clere was conspicuous when Folkes was burned together with five other humble victims outside the town walls, and he 'showed hymselfe very extreame' against them all, even preventing them from praying.[42]

Folkes was a poor, single woman: process against married women heretics posed different problems. When another woman suspect, Alice Benden, was brought before Richard Thornden, suffragan bishop of Dover, in October 1556, he too bent over backwards to avoid bringing her to trial and judgement. Her religiously conservative husband had asked the wealthy men of Staplehurst to write to the bishop on his wife's behalf, and Thornden was clearly eager to park the problem on Edward Benden's shoulders. He asked Alice Benden if she would give an undertaking to go home and go to church. When she refused, he asked her if she would agree to be shriven by the parish priest, and got the same answer. 'Well, said he, go thy waies home, and go to the Church when thou wilt. Wherunto she answered nothing.'[43] After her release, her husband duly attempted to persuade her to go to Mass, but his (perhaps unguarded) complaints to other parishioners about her disobedience, when she once again refused, led to her re-arrest, imprisonment in horrifying conditions and ultimate condemnation.[44]

Perhaps the most extraordinary demonstration of the lengths to which the authorities might go to avoid condemning a woman was the case of Elizabeth Young, which Foxe places sometime in 1558. Young, who was illiterate, was nevertheless not only a member of an underground London congregation and a vehement sacramentary, but a colporteur of books from Emden and other protestant presses abroad. Arrested in a sweep against the heretical book trade in London, she was examined thirteen times before a succession of officials and commissioners, including the lawyer Thomas Martin and the dean of St Paul's, Henry Cole. It emerged from these examinations that she was a relapsed heretic, having been convened with her husband before Martin several years earlier. Threatened with racking and other tortures to induce her to incriminate other members of the book-smuggling network, she was in fact not tortured (probably because the authorities had managed to track down the purchasers of her books by other means).

What is more notable, perhaps, is that, though undoubtedly guilty and a relapsed heretic, she was not condemned. Instead, Cole at first tried to persuade her simply to affirm her belief 'in the faith of Christes Church', adding 'But to aske of thee what Christes church is, or where it is, I let it passe'. Eventually, by patient Socratic questioning, he managed to guide her into an ambiguous admission that 'Christ was not absent from his sacrament', on the strength of which convoluted declaration he discharged her, apparently with Bonner's connivance.[45] Cole had a special commission to pursue heretical books, and was perfectly well aware that Young was unrepentant. Yet he seems to have viewed the situation not entirely without a sardonic sense of humour. Two women neighbours stood as sureties for Mistress Young, and he teased them that they too were probably as heterodox as their friend: 'do ye not smell a little of heresy also . . . Yes, a little of the frying pan, or els wherefore have ye twaine so earnestly sued for her?'[46] He let them all go nonetheless. Foxe thought that Young had been released because in these last months of the reign officials such as Cole were aware that the Queen was dying, and were belatedly seeking to forestall retribution by conciliating the enemy. But Cole was too close to the Cardinal, too deeply involved in the regime and its campaign against heresy and too consistent in his later recusancy under Elizabeth, for that hypothesis to be plausible in his case. The real reason for Cole's favour to Mistress Young was almost certainly humanitarian, indicated in a casual aside by bishop Bonner. At the beginning of her penultimate examination, in which Cole first appeared as a protagonist and advocate on her behalf, the bishop, encountering the accused woman for the first time, asked 'Is this the woman that hath the three children?', a revealing glimpse of the briefing he had been given and the grounds on which the case for mercy had been made to him.[47]

Cole's compassionate treatment of Elizabeth Young and her friends should not be taken as a sign of loss of nerve about enforcement as a means of combating heresy in the face of failure or the imminent demise of the Queen. It is true that fewer protestants were burned in the course of 1558 than in any year since the campaign began, after a peak of twenty-eight in the single month of June 1557. The decline in prosecutions is to be explained not as a loss of nerve, however, but at least in part by the disruption caused by the devastating mortality of 1557 and 1558, as a virulent strain of influenza ravaged the country and swept away large numbers of the elite, including justices of the peace and many of the higher clergy. But, in any case, the numbers of intransigents being burned were declining at least partly because there were fewer intransigents to burn. The executions had done some of their intended work, and none but the most determined now held out openly against the regime. In 1558, the parish constable of St Bride's, Fleet Street, notoriously a nest of evangelicals, was admonished by Thomas Darbyshire to counsel Juliana Living to conformity. 'So do I', replied the constable: 'I bid her go to Masse, and to say as you say. For by the Masse, if you say the Crowe is white, I will say so too.'[48] Such ignoble conformity was hardly the stuff of counter-reformation catholic zeal, but neither did it bode well for continuing protestant resistance. Nicodemism was a way of survival: it might also be the slippery slope to assimilation.

In London, nevertheless, the inspirational and propaganda value of the burnings to the dwindling core of evangelicals was prompting a rethink. One London informer told Elizabeth Young, 'You care not for burning . . . By God's bloud, there must be some other meanes founde for you.'[49] Such comments reflected second thoughts not about the wisdom of executing the obdurate, but about the best way of preventing such executions being turned to advantage by the victims and their co-religionists. There was certainly no sign that the Privy Council, which had all along driven the campaign forward, was looking for an exit strategy. On the contrary, in the spring of 1558 they were still urging on the Bishop of London to strong action against the 'devyllishe opinions' of Essex dissenters, and in August 1558 the Council hardened the policy of repression in the light of events surrounding the appallingly protracted execution of a Hampshire gentleman, Thomas Benbridge.[50] Benbridge had been condemned by John White, bishop of Winchester, for a series of denials of the sacraments and priestly authority, and for maintaining that the devil was the head of the catholic church. At his execution, amid a hostile crowd, the pyre was badly built. When the flames slowly scorched his legs he shouted out that he recanted, and his friends hastily dismantled the fire. Doctor Seaton, the priest attending to preach at the burning, cobbled together some articles of recantation, which the reluctant Benbridge, threatened with a return to the flames, signed on the spot, using the stooped back of a bystander as a writing desk. The sheriff, Sir Richard Pecksall, the Marquis of Winchester's son-in-law, thereupon called the execution off, on his own authority.

When the Privy Council were informed, however, not even Pecksall's exalted family connections could protect him from their fury. The sheriff was ordered to have Benbridge 'executed out of hande'. Even if he still continued in his recantation, 'as he outwardly pretendeth', he was not to be reprieved, but to be allowed instead 'some suche discrete and lerned man as the Bishop of Wynchester shall appointe' to confer with him 'for the better confirmation of him in the Catholyke faythe and to be present also with him at his death for the better ayding of him to dye Goddes servaunte'. The Council wrote to Bishop White in similar vein, Pecksall himself was summoned to London to explain his actions and Benbridge was duly executed, on another badly constructed pyre (Foxe thought it deliberate), 'which did rather broyle hym, than burne him'.[51]

The Council's zeal in 1558 was matched by that of many of the commissioners, clerical and lay, active as ever that year in the regions. In April 1558, Archdeacon Chedsey and others were busy in Colchester with the perennial search for hard-core Essex conventiclers, in the midst of examinations that were to result in three executions, one of them that of a woman, Christian [sic] George. Her case illustrates the tight networks of affinity within which many conventiclers operated, for she was the second wife of Richard George, whose first wife Agnes had been one of thirteen Essex gospellers burned at Stratford-le-Bow in 1556. George himself and his third wife (he must have remarried immediately after Agnes's death) were arrested later the same year, and would escape burning only because of the death of Queen Mary. In the midst of these proceedings, however, Chedsey was suddenly summoned to Greenwich by the Privy Council for a consultation on some unspecified matter. But Chedsey was convinced that to suspend proceedings and go to London would be disastrous.

Essex was still a centre of radicalism, 'so many obstinate heretics, Anabaptists and other unruly persons . . . as was never heard of', and it was vital to maintain momentum in the attack on dissent. 'We be now in the myddest of our examination and articulation. And if we should give it off in the midst, we should set the country in such a rore, that my estimation, and the residue of the commissioners, shall be for ever lost.' A summons away to the Privy Council would look bad, he told Bonner, and might convince the gospellers and their supporters that 'we have no commission, but came of your Lordship's commandment, without any other warrant from the honourable Council', to the disturbance of the peace of the county, which was 'now drawing to some conformity'. He therefore found excuses to delay his appearance before the Council, and the three heretics were duly burned in May.[52] Elsewhere, the same clerical concern to maintain the impetus of a campaign perceived now as bringing the regions 'to some conformity' is in evidence, in the execution of the sixteen Islington conventiclers in June and July 1558, in nine executions in Suffolk from August through to the first week in November and in the five executions in Canterbury on 10 November, the significavits 'relaxing' the offenders to the secular arm for execution signed for the first time by the Cardinal himself.[53] And, in some places, the pace of the campaign may even have been escalating, as systematic visitation turned up more suspects. According to Foxe, a barely credible *ninety* unfortunates in the Salisbury diocese, awaiting examination by the Cardinal's protégé, Chancellor William Geffrie, were spared the ordeal only by Geffrie's sudden death on 28 August.[54] The campaign may or may not have been in danger of running out of suspects in some places: there is no sign anywhere that it was running out of steam.

CHAPTER 8

The Defence of the Burnings and the Problem of Martyrdom

The Marian regime has often been criticised for its failure to provide an effective justification of its anti-heretical policies. Catholic polemicists were, according to A. G. Dickens, 'at best a group of devoted mediocrities', and their apologetic efforts, according to David Loades, were 'tedious' and lacked 'the cutting wit and humour which their opponents sometimes displayed'.[1] In particular, it has been suggested that the regime failed woefully to seize the opportunity for effective propaganda offered by the burnings and the trials that preceded them, and that it did not even notice, much less exploit publicly, the doctrinal differences between the warring factions among its protestant prisoners, 'a critical lost opportunity'.[2]

As I observed in chapter three, tediousness is to some extent in the eye of the beholder, and I argued there for the force and effectiveness of Marian apologetic. But the notion that the regime somehow failed to defend the burnings publicly, or to exploit for propaganda purposes the weakness and divisions of the new faith, is certainly mistaken. This mistake is based largely on the failure to grasp that the campaign was carried on principally through the pulpit, in sermons at the place of execution, in the parish churches of communities where protestants were prominent and at high-profile preaching venues such as Paul's Cross. As we saw in chapter three, the regime was well aware of the divisions within the beleaguered protestant communities in England. The fissiparousness of the new religion was a commonplace of Marian polemic, routinely deployed not merely in print, but also in dealings with accused prisoners, even by lay councillors and magistrates. As Richard, Lord Rich told John Philpot, 'Al heretickes do boaste of the spirit of God, and every one woulde have a churche by himselfe'.[3] Sermons against the beliefs and practices of convicted heretics were, as we have seen, a routine accompaniment of the burnings, often at the place of execution itself or in neighbouring cathedral or parish pulpits on the Sundays before or after the execution. In addition, the regime maintained a steady stream of anti-heretical preaching at Paul's Cross, so that the protestant activist Elizabeth Fane reproached Bonner not only for murdering the saints, but for causing 'lyinge preachers' to 'blaspheme and belye them with railynge sentences when they are deade'.[4] The anti-heretical preaching that accompanied the burnings in London and the regions has been largely ignored by historians because, in the nature of things, it has left few traces in the records, and the sermons themselves have survived only in a few hostile summaries by Foxe.[5] But the fact of such provision suggests a more coherent strategy and a greater awareness of public opinion than the regime has usually been credited with. It seems obvious, moreover, that the decision to concentrate persuasion at the point and place of execution was a sound one, reaching a far larger audience than the likely readership of polemical pamphlets.

But the campaign against heresy and the defence of the burnings was not of course *confined* to the pulpit. The official apologists in print for the regime also addressed this question, to considerable effect. We have already noted in chapter three the most formidable of the Marian defences of the burnings, the anonymous pamphlet, *A Plaine and Godlye Treatise Concerning the Masse, for the Instructyon of the Simple and Unlearned People*. Published in the summer of 1555, when the campaign against executions was intensifying, it was reprinted four times before the end of the year, more than any other controversial pamphlet of the period.

The Treatise on the Masse was a powerful and racy defence of the central catholic doctrine of the Mass, and a scathing attack on the persons and principles of the protestants. It was also an unabashed justification of the campaign of repression, and its five editions in six months must have carried it to a readership far beyond London. For that large readership, it mustered the usual sixteenth-century defence of the use of holy violence, with a raciness and acerbity that suggest no misgivings at all about the use of the death penalty in defence of true religion. The victims of the burnings, it insisted, were not martyrs but criminals, 'by iuste lawes cast and condemned to burne for their obstinate heresie'. Yet they deluded the gullible 'with a subtle sort of suffering of death, furnished and set forth with fayned holy charity, and paynted paciens'. In this way, they tried 'to perswade the ignorant and unstable people that it were the onlie veritie and truth for the which they se these sinful livers and wicked heretikes justly condemned'. The author rehearsed the usual early-modern case against false martyrdom: the true martyr will always have led a holy life, will always display charity even towards his tormenters; above all, the sign of a true martyr is not courage but fidelity to the truth − 'he dies well who dies in a good quarrel'.[6] The argument was more than merely conventional, however, for the writer was concerned to tackle directly the undoubted impact of the burnings on crowds in London and beyond in the miserable summer of 1555. Above all, he was keenly concerned about the impression that the courage of the victims at the stake might make. As he admitted, 'it is no small matter to daly with death earnestly without feare and to playe with hote burning fyre and to kepe patience'. So, 'if any of these heretikes the devils deare derlynges could craftily doe, then would he thynke, the game were hys'. Satan had therefore created a sub-culture of support for these deluded people, to hold them steady in their error. The prison communities of like-minded protestants, the network of godly ministers and other sustainers visiting them, the specially heightened language of protestant fortitude − these were all the work of the devil, designed to insulate the victims from the terrible reality of their apostasy, and to bring them unrepentant to the fire.

> Therefore he first sendeth to suche . . . some of the blessed brotherhed of his ministers and messengers unto the prison, where they, with high laude and commendations . . . extolle the folishe obstinate wretche of his stoutness and high grace and knowledge of gods trueth. . . . Then with other giftes, good chere, and cherishinges (for they wyl spare for no cost) he is sone animated and so encoraged that lyke a bedlem madman he feareth not to fry. For he is brought (by suche meanes) into such a folish paradise, that he thinkes verely himself so light, that he shal lepe out of the fyre into gods bosom: where in very dede dying an obstinate hereticke he lepeth like a flounder out of the frying pan of temporal death into the perpetual and unquenchable fier of god's justice.[7]

The author of the *Treatise* was familiar with the evolving theatrical conventions at the pyre, and was scornfully dismissive of them. Lest their courage should fail and 'thys forced pacyens should be spied in the middes of their game', he claimed, some of the victims stupefied themselves with strong drink 'in stede of the gostly wyne of charitie and the zeale of God'.[8]

Others 'get them gunpowder or such vehement matter to spede them sone oute of theyr paynes, lest the visures of their painted paciens might fal of'. But, under all the trappings of persecuted holiness, the fundamental lack of charity that is the root of heresy could not be concealed. The very language in which the condemned protestants defied and reviled the authorities of church and state, who had justly condemned them, revealed at the last what they truly were. 'And no marveile. For when the wolves arse is set on fyre and begynneth to smarte, then wyl he wolvishly barke and bawle against the shepherdes and shepe.'[9] And so the argument, directed at the 'simple and unlearned' who naively took these false martyrs at face value, turned round finally on the reader. All who comforted and supported heretics and traitors were heretics and traitors themselves. And such were all they 'as crieth out sediciously unto them, The Lord comfort the[m], the Lord strength[en] the[m] in his truth, with other sedicious exclamacions or secrete mutteringes.' In comforting these criminals and making them martyrs 'they make the princes under whose lawe these heretickes are worthelye burnt, to be playne tyrauntes, and their iustices and the executors of suche paynes, cruell tormenters'. Therefore, let all faithful subjects beware 'that they fall not to lyke daunger'.[10]

London was the epicentre of the burnings and of reaction to them. In the first half of 1556, evangelical outrage in and beyond the city was stoked by the mounting pace of the executions, and most notably by that of Archbishop Cranmer at Oxford at the end of March. There was also a steady stream of executions of humbler victims closer to home, burned now in groups as a warning to the recalcitrant and a mark of the determination of the regime – six Essex coventiclers at Smithfield on 24 April;[11] six more at Colchester four days later; two London artisans at Stratford-le-Bow on 15 May, the pathos of these latter deaths heightened by the fact that one was blind and the other a cripple;[12] three women at Smithfield on 16 May;[13] and thirteen of the sixteen Essex conventiclers at Stratford on 27 June, the men bound to stakes, the women set loose in the midst of the pyre.[14] This was the context for what has become in recent years the most celebrated of the Marian treatises against heresy, Miles Hogarde's *The Displaying of the Protestants*. This first appeared in June 1556 and was reissued in an expanded edition, drawing attention to the excesses of the wilder London conventiclers, the following month. Hogarde's book has been the focus of growing critical and historical attention,[15] and it is not my concern to analyse it here in detail, except to emphasise how very much it is a book addressed to Londoners at a moment of crisis, designed to discredit not merely protestantism in general, but the track record of the evangelical minority in the capital, in particular up to the summer of 1556. Hogarde wittily and tellingly rallies the usual arguments against protestant claims to martyrdom, along much the same lines as the author of the *Treatise on the Masse*, adding his own touches, such as the clever use of an extract from a sermon by 'the late Prophete ofte by the protestantes compared to the old prophetes, called Latymer', justifying the burning of anabaptists in Edward's reign.[16] Like the *Treatise on the Masse*, *The Displaying of the Protestants* insists on the criminal eagerness of the protestant martyrs to die for their own brainsick fantasies, and the complicity of the London crowds

> crying by the waie as they passe to death: 'Be constant dere brethren, be constant in the faith, sticke to it, it is not this temporall paine which you ought to regarde, your breakfast is sharpe, your supper shalbe merye. Therefore the lorde strengthen you'. With these and suche like vayne woordes, they brynge the poore men in such fooles paradise, that thei with suche vaine arrogance, and small Charitee, sticke not to adventure themselfes into the fiery flambes.

Hogarde also illustrated the 'small Charitee' of the victims by retailing examples of unrepentant defiance at the stake, such as that of 'the grosse martyrs' Joan Butcher and Anne Askew, railing and spitting against the preachers at the pyre and 'making the sygne of the gallowes towards them'.[17] Hogarde had clearly been an eyewitness of many of the London burnings, and he ridiculed the credulous excesses of the supporters and followers of the victims, who had imagined the alarmed flight of Smithfield pigeons at the burning of John Rogers to be a manifestation of the Holy Ghost, or the relic hunters 'wallowing like pygges in a stie to scrape in that hereticall dongehill for the sayde bones'.[18] He used the knowledge of the opinions of individual radical victims that he shared with his London readers as evidence of the infinite divisions of protestantism, in contrast to the unity of the catholic church, 'not lacerated, devided or torne, but whole and intier'. Hogarde seems to have had the run of Bonner's house: he had participated in the examination of heretics, and was intimately well informed about events in the city. He drew on that knowledge in his pamphlet to highlight the outrageous side of protestant propagandist efforts. He retailed most of those incidents that had also been noted by shocked London chroniclers, and presented them as proofs of the anarchic and destructive character of the new religion – the knife thrown at the preacher during the 1553 Paul's Cross riot, the shaving of dogs and hanging of cats dressed as priests in the city, outrages against the Sacrament, the 'abhominable facte' of William Flower's murderous attack on the Westminster priest at Easter 1554, the stoning of the Greenwich Franciscans, and so on. All these localised London outrages, he argued, were instances of the more general truth that protestantism was inherently destructive, 'provokyng the good to conspiracies, alluryng the evil to put the same in practise . . . the devil's darlings, infected with treason the handmaide of heresie'.[19] Hogarde did not spare the devout London women who helped sustain the protestant prisoners in the capital's gaols, dismissing them as wicked daughters of heresy, 'these London ladies' who talk of nothing but religion and the apostles Peter and Paul, and whose 'scripture mouthes are ready to allure their husbandes to dye in the lordes veritie, because they would fayne have newe'.[20]

In July, one month later, Hogarde issued an expanded edition of this inspired journalistic broadside. To alert his readers to the anarchic views of the conventiclers who were now the regime's main targets, he added a lengthy description of a visit in Lent 1555 to a conventicle in a 'typpling house, nexte the signe of the Mermayde' at Islington. Led by 'olde father Browne the Broker of Bedlam', this establishment was patronised by 'the marchant men of London with Pat peny ale, Symperyng Sysse, and other fleering flurtes', attracting also the inevitable 'Jack Prentices' with their English testaments at their belts. Hogarde's account of Browne's sermon was designed to highlight again the divisions and incoherence of protestantism, epitomised in Browne's declaration that there were in England three religions – 'my lorde Chancellors religion', 'Cranmers, Latymers and Ridleys' religion, and 'Goddes Religion'. 'My Lorde Chauncelors, he sayde, was nought, Cranmers and the others religion not good, but Goddes religion was the best.' In the aftermath of Cranmer's execution, the point was being made that, for the radical protestant underground, neither the former archbishop nor Ridley nor Latimer counted as martyrs.[21]

Hogarde's witty and formidable polemic did have a positive as well as a destructive dimension. He acknowledged the help of an anonymous friend in writing the *Displaying of the Protestants*, and the argument of the book drew on Cardinal Pole's distinctive analysis of the evils of the reformation. Hogarde highlighted the role of More, Fisher, the Carthusian fathers and the other Henrician martyrs, as witnesses in 'the quarrel of God and his churche'. This was a new emphasis in 1556, and one that can be traced directly to the Cardinal and his circle. But the real thrust of his book was deconstructive, a savagely entertaining dismissal of the 'deathes of our cranke Heretykes', whose memories, he claimed, already 'lye dead and are buryed in the grave of cankred oblivion, covered with perpetuall infamye, excepte they be enrolled in a fewe threehalfpennye bookes which steale out of Germany, replete as wel with treason . . . as with other abhominable lyes'.[22]

Telling as all this was, there was an element of wishful thinking in it, and something more was needed in the battle for hearts and minds than Hogarde's rough humour or the more structured polemic of the *Treatise on the Masse*. That 'something more', a positive theory and exemplification of catholic martyrdom to supplement the polemic against protestant 'pseudo-martyrs', was to emerge from the circle round the cardinal legate later the same year. It would focus on the catholic martyrs of Henry's reign, above all the figure of Sir Thomas More. The Henrician martyrs had been conspicuous by their absence from catholic polemic for the first two years of the regime, but More and Fisher were in the air in official and semi-official utterances in 1556, the year in which they were, for the first time, invoked by name as exemplars in Marian polemical works. James Cancellar's *The Pathe of Obedience*, which went through two editions in 1556, made much of them, contrasting the Henrician martyrs for the unity of the church with the recent victims of the Marian campaign:

> Maye it not be asked, howe many iust Ables in oure daies haue suffered, for the vnitye of Christes Catholicke Church in this Realme, the cruell deathe of Marterdome? I meane not here of those late Heretickes that latelye haue beene iustly burned for their heresies, as Hoper, Rogers, Ridlei, Latimer, & Cranmer, & such lyke: but I mene of those which haue suffered for the vnitie of the Catholycke churche of Christe, as dyd that holy father Docter Fysher sometyme Byshop of Rochester, and Sirre Thomas More sumetyme Chaunceler of thys Relme, Docter Powel, Fetherstone, Reinoldes, Rochester, Newdigat, wt many other notable lerned men after them.[23]

Hogarde had contrasted the immortal memories of More, Fisher and the other Henrician martyrs with what he thought the deserved oblivion of 'our cranke Heretkes . . . buryed in the grave of cankred oblivion' in *The Displaying of the Protestants*.[24] His list of the Henrician martyrs was the fullest of the reign, but he was specially circumstantial about the monks of the Charterhouse, naming all eighteen of them. The sequence in which Hogarde gave their names is almost exactly that in which they appear in a remarkable print published in Rome in 1555,[25] under the patronage of Juan Alvarez de Toledo, cardinal bishop of Frascati, Roman Inquisitor, and cardinal protector of the Carthusian order.

The print (see Plate 27) depicted the martyrdom of the English Carthusian in six vivid scenes, in which the victims themselves were vested in their habits but their tormenters were dressed as Roman soldiers, linking their sufferings to the martyrdoms of the early church and anticipating the iconography of English martyrdom that would emerge under Jesuit influence a generation later.[26] This print, whose text emphasised that the Carthusians had died for their fidelity to 'the Chair of Peter and our catholic faith' was undoubtedly another indication of the intense interest in the restoration of catholicism in England that was exciting Roman circles at this time, and the pictures drew on the latest Roman and, indeed, papal iconography. But the commission is unlikely to have originated in the Curia, and certainly not with Cardinal Alvarez who, as an associate of Papa Caraffa and a key figure in the Roman Inquisition, can have been no friend of Pole's. Alvarez was evidently acting specifically in his capacity as protector of the Carthusian order, so the project is most likely to have been instigated by the surviving English Carthusians, notably Maurice Chauncy, who had compiled the martyrological narrative on which the print was based.[27]

Chauncy and his English colleagues re-established the order in England in June 1555, and the print was almost certainly connected to this event.[28] At the end of January, Pole had been asked by Julius III's notorious favourite, the inappropriately named Cardinal Innocenzo del Monte, to provide an accurate list of the Carthusian martyrs.[29] Hogarde may have had a copy of whatever list Pole sent to Rome: but the likeliest explanation for his naming all eighteen Carthusian martyrs is that he had seen and been impressed by a copy of this very striking Roman print, which must therefore have been circulating in England. An English-language version of the Roman print would have been an asset to Pole's church, but no English artist in 1555, catholic or protestant, was capable of engraved work of this quality, and, after the Queen's demise, a developed catholic martyr iconography would take another generation to emerge. For much the same reasons, only a single protestant martyr picture appears to have been produced for Marian England, and it too was the work of a sophisticated foreign engraver working in continental Europe.[30]

It was was More and Fisher, however, who dominated catholic thinking about martyrdom in 1556 and 1557. They were invoked together early in 1556, bizarrely and horribly, in Henry Cole's sermon at Cranmer's burning, in which the deaths of Northumberland and the protestant bishops were presented as belated if inadequate compensation for the executions of More and Fisher.[31] In the weeks before his burning in March 1556, Cranmer was given a copy of More's *Dialogue of Comfort* to read, a heavily ironic choice in which one surely sees the hand of Pole. But the central documents here are the great folio edition of More's *English Works* edited by More's nephew William Rastell, which appeared at the end of April 1557, and Nicholas Harpsfield's biography of More, ostensibly commissioned by More's son-in-law William Roper, but clearly intended to accompany Rastell's edition of the *English Works*.[32] The editing of the *English Works* and the writing of Harpsfield's life have often been interpreted as private initiatives by More's family and friends.[33]

But Rastell and Roper's championship of the memory of More cannot so easily be separated from the wider restoration of catholicism under the Cardinal. Both men were prominent figures in Pole's diocese. Both served as MPs for Canterbury; Rastell was legal councillor for the city from 1555, and both were very actively involved in the campaign against heresy. Roper was among the handpicked group of catholic JPs named to the Canterbury heresy commission established in April 1556, soon after Pole's consecration as archbishop, and both he and Rastell were appointed to the national commission established, with even more sweeping powers and a wider mandate, in February 1557. Roper himself had functioned as an interrogator and witness in prosecutions well outside the Canterbury diocese as early as the summer of 1554.[34] As we have seen, More and Fisher had been at the centre of Pole's spiritual vision and understanding of the reformation since the writing of his treatise *De Unitate* against Henry VIII. The composition of Harpsfield's life of More and the issuing of More's English works formed an ambitious double project: to refashion More's image as a paradigm of lay orthodoxy and true martyrdom, and to make available his anti-heretical and martyrological writings in English. Rastell and Roper served the Cardinal in the legal battle against heresy, and Harpsfield was his most effective diocesan collaborator. It therefore seems inconceivable that such a double venture could have been launched by men so close to the Cardinal without Pole's knowledge, encouragement and help. Yet, the orientation of both books towards the specific circumstances of the fight against heresy in 1557 has been insufficiently appreciated.

The *English Works* of More appeared with a dedicatory epistle from Rastell to the Queen, signalling the project's official status and unerringly targeting the central preoccupation of the regime with heresy in the spring of 1557. The epistle denounced the 'obstinate and stubborn malice, and also . . . proud and arrogant presumption' of unrepentant protestants, while emphasising the utility of More's writings for 'confuting of all perverse opinions, false doctrines and devilishe heresies'.[35] The edition contained all More's vernacular controversial works, but it culminated with his devotional treatises, prayers and letters from the Tower of London. The letters in particular provided a powerful counterweight to the prison letters of the protestants then circulating. More's letters offered a moving picture of a noble and almost quietist catholic saint, following a very different road to martyrdom from what the regime saw as the arrogant and presumptuous self-immolation of the victims of the Marian burnings. In one of his Tower works, the Latin treatise *De Tristitia Christi* (Of the Sorrow of Christ), More had emphasised Christ's fear of death in Gethsemane, and he saw in that fear a reassurance about his own struggles to avoid the death sentence. Christ says 'Let the brave man have his high-spirited martyrs, let him rejoice in imitating a thousand of them. But you, my timorous and feeble little sheep . . . follow my leadership . . . See, I am walking ahead of you along this fearful road.'[36] How More applied this to his own condition was fleshed out in his last letters to his daughter Margaret. In one of these he reported that his accusers had reproached him for not 'speaking out plain' against the Act of Supremacy, so that

> it appeared well I was not content to dye though I sayd so. Whereto I answered as the trouth is, that I have not been a man of such holy living, as I myght be bold to offer myself to death, lest God for my presumpcion might suffer me to fall; and therefore I put not myself forward, but draw backe. Howbeit, if God draw me to it himself, then truste I in his great mercy, that he shall not fail to geve me grace and strength.[37]

Here was a carefully presented pattern of martyrdom radically different from the strident protestant heroics that the apologists for the regime felt were so beguiling the blind and foolish London crowds. And that pattern was developed even more explicitly and at length in Nicholas Harpsfield's *Life and Death of Sr Thomas Moore*, presented to William Roper as a New Year gift in January 1557. Harpsfield had been a refugee with the More family in Antonio Buonvisi's house in Louvain, and wrote the biography at Roper's request, drawing on Roper's own reminiscences as his main source. Buonvisi's role in linking many of the activists of the Marian restoration has yet to be explored: he was, for example, the 'fonde patron and second father' of the heresy-hunting Dr John Story.[38] He was also almost certainly responsible for introducing Harpsfield to Pole, the beginning of a very close working relationship. It has been almost universally assumed that Harpsfield did most or all of the work on his biography of More during his years of exile.[39] In fact, however, in three different places in the preparatory memoir of More compiled to provide Harpsfield with copy, Roper refers the reader to letters and other writings of More 'in the book of his works', making it clear that Roper's text, while predating Harpsfield's, was nevertheless written when the Folio edition of the works was being prepared for the press – that is, almost certainly in 1556.[40] Since Harpsfield's book (which also refers to the imminent publication of the Folio edition of More's *English Works*) was a New Year gift in 1557, we can be virtually certain that his life of More was written at the end of 1556.

This is in itself an astonishing fact, and makes a vast difference to how we should read the *Life of Moore*. Harpsfield was Pole's right-hand man, archdeacon of Canterbury and the principal agent both of the reimposition of catholicism in the dioceses of Canterbury and London, and of the campaign to root out heresy there. He had spent a good part of 1556 carrying out the visitation of Kent; he had heavy administrative and legal duties in the diocese of London and as a heresy commissioner for Canterbury; and, at Pole's request, he had already written that year a Latin account of Cranmer's recantations and burning, for circulation abroad, a text that closely reflected Pole's own attitudes to his unhappy predecessor.[41] It seems inconceivable that this hectically busy ecclesiastical administrator would have devoted so much time to so elaborate a literary work as More's biography without Pole's knowledge and support, indeed without Pole's commission.

However that may be, Pole's ideas and influence marked every page of Harpsfield's book, whose final sections in particular provided what amounted to a résumé of Pole's distinctive perspective on the history of the English reformation. The whole book was, in fact, designed to demonstrate the contention of Pole's treatise *De Unitate*, that More's 'speciall peerlesse prerogative' was that he was above everything 'our blessed protomartyr of all the laytie for the preservation of the unitie of Christ's Church'.[42] Harpsfield provided a very full account of More's arrest, trial and last days, and the understanding of martyrdom informing the narrative was drawn from More himself. In contrast to the eagerness of protestant self-incrimination and noisy public protest that marked some of the arrests, trials and executions of 1556–7, Harpsfield emphasised both More's determined attempts to avoid death, and his patient resignation and confidence in God when it became inescapable. He devoted an equal amount of space to More's career as a controversialist, insisting on the permanent value of More's writings against heresy, and, along the way, informing the reader of the imminent publication of Rastell's collected edition of all those writings. Revealingly, however, Harpsfield confined his account of More's opposition to heresy exclusively to his literary output. Though he treated other aspects of More's work as a lawyer, judge and public servant, he said not a word about More's very active involvement in the pursuit and prosecution of heretics in the 1520s and early 1530s.

Harpsfield drew heavily on the *English Works*, and discussed at length More's *Confutation of Tyndale's Answer*, his *Apology* and the *Debellation of Salem and Byzance*.[43] These were in fact the books in which More devoted most space to justifying his pursuit and treatment of heretics: they therefore contained many descriptions of his pursuit and examination of suspects.[44] Yet Harpsfield, himself a busy pursuivant of heretics, concentrated entirely on what these books had to say about More's *literary* activities. He explored and attempted to refute protestant accusations about More's rough *writing* against heresy. He was totally silent, however, about the accusations of torture and illegality, which John Foxe would reiterate, and which later recusant writers would contest by repeating Erasmus's mistaken claim that no one had been executed for heresy while More was Chancellor.[45]

Again, Harpsfield discussed More's notorious epitaph in Chelsea parish church, included in both Latin and English in the folio *Workes*,[46] and in which Sir Thomas had famously inserted the provocative phrase that, as Lord Chancellor, he had been 'grevous to thieves, murderers and heretics', '*furibus autem homicides haereticisque molestus*'.[47] Once again, however, Harpsfield discussed this epitaph in precisely the same way that he discussed More's *Apology* and *Debellation*, defending it from a charge of vaingloriousness, pointedly avoiding direct citation of the key word '*molestus*' (grievous), but tacitly glossing it as if it alluded only to his writings. 'In the endighting of this his Epitaphe', Harpsfield wrote, More 'had not so much regarde unto himselfe, or his owne estimation, as to God's cause and religion, which he had *by open bookes* against the Protestantes defended'. It would be impossible to guess from Harpsfield's book that More had used his office to pursue the heretics themselves, rather than merely writing to confute their works. At this critical point in the Marian pursuit of heresy, one of the most active and effective pursuivants of heretics chose to eliminate that entire dimension of More's career. More the heresy-hunter was quite simply edited out of Harpsfield's portrait. Harpsfield celebrated More's triumph over 'these pestilent and poisoned heretics', than whom there were 'no greater enemies in the world to a common wealth'. In his presentation, however, it was exclusively by 'his noble books' that More 'conquered' them.[48]

This remarkable silence about More's legal pursuit of heretics was clearly dictated by the bitterness and tensions of 1556–7 and the dangerous volatility of public hostility in London to the burnings. More was announced in the opening pages of Harpsfield's book as a model citizen of London, 'the chiefe and notable principall Citie of this our noble Realme'.[49] He could serve the regime at this point as an ideal layman, the pattern of true martyrdom, invalidating by counter-example false protestant claims to that status, and as a magazine of arguments and rhetoric against heresy. More the persecutor was best left undiscussed. Nevertheless, the preoccupations of those years and the distinctive emphases of the Cardinal and his circle manifested themselves in Harpsfield's book in a multitude of other small details. One of these was More's prophetic declaration to Roper, at the height of Henry's catholic crusade against the early reformation when he and his colleagues were 'treading heretikes under our feete like antes', that the day would come when 'we gladly would wishe to be at a league and composition with them, to lett them have their churches quietly to themselves, so that they would be content to lett us have ours quietly to our selves'.[50]

This did not, of course, represent an acceptance on Harpsfield's part of any possibility of religious coexistence between catholics and protestants.

On the contrary, the prophecy provided a divinely ratified condemnation of the Henrician schism, which, in the eyes of the Cardinal, Harpsfield and their associates, had led inexorably and inevitably to the triumph of heresy in Edward's reign. More's sanctity had gained him a forewarning of the calamity of reformation, 'a sure ayme of the lamentable world that followed, and that we have sithens full heavily felt'.[51] There was a similarly topical resonance to the well-known anecdote about the scandalised protest of the Duke of Norfolk on finding More singing in a surplice in his parish choir at Chelsea, since one of the ways in which Harpsfield and his colleagues detected suspected heretics in his Kentish visitations was by their refusal to sing in the parish choir.[52] Perhaps most notably, however, Harpsfield's preoccupations as the principle clerical activist in the Marian campaign against heresy, and the conscious relevance of his work to the moment of its composition, surfaced in the extraordinarily savage passage, deliberately inserted by Harpsfield,[53] describing the fall of the young William Roper into heresy and his recovery by More.

Harpsfield's portrait of his friend and patron Roper is a picture of heretical arrogance. The cocksure young convert to the new religion abandoned his prayers for bible-reading, 'thinking it for him suffficient to gett onely thereby knowledge to be able among ignorant people to bable and talke, as he thought, like a great doctour'. All this echoed the outlines and even the very terms of the Cardinal's condemnation, at St Mary Arches earlier that year, of the over-eager lay 'studier of scripture' who thinks it enough to acquire book knowledge and then 'of his own wytt and labour . . . maketh hymselfe . . . a master and teacher'.[54] In Harpsfield's savage vignette, Roper thus became a type of the ill-informed and overweening lay heretic, a surrogate for those with whom Harpsfield and his colleagues wrestled daily in prolonged examinations.

Like his Marian counterparts, the protestant Roper had not been content 'to whisper [his heresy] hugger mugger', but thirsted to preach his 'newe broached religion', 'and thought himselfe very able so to doo, and it were even at Paules Crosse'. Bewitched by his own error, he proved impervious to all More's learning, reasoned arguments and fatherly counsel. In this he was just like the gospellers with whom the authorities had to deal in 1556, 'who for the most part through ignorance doo beginne to walke in the ways of heresie and after in that wicked way doo stande, and finally through malice doo desperately fast sitt in the chair of all iniquitie'. And it was in the end the prayers of the saint, not the arguments of the most learned man in England, that had brought Roper to a sense of 'his owne ignoraunce, oversight, malice and folie, and turned him againe to the Catholike fayth'.[55]

Harpsfield's *Life of Moore*, rather than the *Treatise on the Masse* or Hogarde's *Displaying of the Protestants*, is the masterpiece of the Marian martyrdom controversies. Though rarely considered in the light of the specific conditions of Mary's reign, it was in fact a tract for the times, exactly tuned to the circumstances of 1556–7. In it, Harpsfield provided a sophisticated reply to protestant martyrological claims, not in ridicule and contempt, but by holding up the image of a 'true' catholic martyr, a paradigm of lay orthodoxy for Marian London.

And yet, though Harpsfield's work is arguably the only book written by a Marian cleric that can still be read with unnalloyed pleasure today, it nevertheless remained, like the rest of his English writings, unpublished till the twentieth century. If one were looking for an argument in support of the claim that the Marian regime failed to grasp the value of the printing press, the non-publication of Harpsfield's *Life of Moore* is about as good as it is likely to get. One can only speculate why. The surviving manuscripts are Elizabethan or later, and it may be that Harpsfield's frantically busy life left him insufficient leisure in 1557, when he conducted a major visitation of Kent, to prepare his text for the press.

This can hardly be the whole explanation, however, because then or soon after he went on to write a lengthy sequel to the *Life of Moore*, his *Treatise on the Pretended Divorce between Henry VIII and Catherine of Aragon*, which also remained unpublished. Since the *Life and Death of Sir Thomas Moore* was intended as a pendant to the Folio *English Works*, it is possible (if not altogether likely) that the publisher's syndicate that financed the *Works* was unwilling to issue the biography until they had recouped on their major investment.

Or, just possibly, divisions within the ranks of the Marian establishment played a part. Harpsfield's book was emphatically a product of the Cardinal's circle, refracting in the gentler form of biography Pole's stern view of the treason of the clerks, indeed of the entire Henrician establishment, despite the divine gift of the witness of More, Fisher and the other martyrs of the 1530s against the king's idolatrous claims. For the many surviving Henrician conformists from Bonner downwards, the *Life and Death of Sir Thomas Moore* must have seemed a standing reproach. It was certainly so for Richard, Lord Rich, who, as the book makes clear, had given the fatal and probably perjured evidence on which Sir Thomas had been convicted. Rich was now a key figure in the Marian establishment, above all in the campaign against heresy in the Essex badlands. He cannot have relished a narrative in which he played the role of Judas. He had taken steps to see that Thomas Wattes, with his uncomfortable recollections of Rich's unsavoury past as an evangelical fellow traveller, was hurried to the stake. Did he have the clout to secure the suppression or delay of Harpsfield's book? Perhaps not, but the fact remains that the book never saw the light of day.

But it may be that here, too, as in the larger matter of the burnings, we are mesmerised by hindsight. We know that time ran out for the Marian regime on 17 November 1558. No one in 1557 knew that that was going to happen, and there was so much else to do. With the renewal of the campaigns of arrest and examination, and a heightened push against heretical books to conduct, with a war with France, with disastrous weather, dearth, and a fresh wave of epidemic disease decimating the population, not least its elites, the publication of More's biography and Harpsfield's other remarkable writings of 1556–7, with all their atunement to the needs of the time, evidently did not seem the most urgent priority. The same dire conditions no doubt contributed to the drastic reduction we have already noted in the publication of books of all kinds in 1558, secular as well as religious.

The burnings themselves peaked at twenty-eight in June 1557, then dropped steeply thereafter. There were eight in September 1557, none the following month and they would not again reach double figures until November 1558, when there were eleven. Some historians have followed Foxe in seeing in this decline the collapse of morale in the Marian regime, but I have suggested that there are reasons to doubt any such collapse. Certainly the notion of a loss of direction and morale is not borne out by Pole's own perceptions. In the summer of 1558, he told Bartolomeo Carranza that the campaign to restore catholicism in England had turned the corner, and that religion in the country was at last 'beginning to recover its pure form'.[56] Nor is there any sign that Pole thought that the prosecution and burning of heretics should now be halted.

The Convocation that met in February 1558 enacted fresh measures to halt the circulation and possession of heretical books and to root out heretical teaching in the universities,[57] while Pole himself issued a new commission (on 28 March 1558) to a clerical team led by Robert Collins to pursue heresy and heretics in the diocese of Canterbury.[58] In July 1558, he himself seems to have signed the significavit condemning a group of five Kentish radicals, the first time that he had taken a direct hand in the campaign.[59] Even the realisation that the Queen's health was failing and Elizabeth likely to succeed did not slow the campaign, for Pole himself was seen as a powerful bulwark against any attempt to restore the religion of King Edward. If Foxe is to be relied on, the informers and constables were as busy as ever with arrests and house-searches in London during August and September 1558. As news of the Queen's sickness circulated, one of the London gospellers, Juliana Living, was remanded in custody in the house of Richard Cluney, Bonner's summoner and keeper of the Lollard's Tower. There she was confronted by an informer, 'Dale, the promoter'. 'Wel', declared Dale, 'you hope and you hope: but your hope shalbe a slope. For though the Queene faile, shee that you hope for, shall neuer come at it: For there is my lord Cardinals grace, and many more betweene her and it.' And certainly, had Pole been still alive and in office as Archbishop when Elizabeth succeeded, he would indeed have presented his protestant cousin with a formidable obstacle to any reversal of the catholic restoration. It was the wholly unexpected double demise of cardinal as well as Queen, and not any gradual loss of direction or waning of determination, that halted the Marian project, and the Marian burnings, in their tracks.[60]

CHAPTER 9

The Legacy:
Inventing the Counter-Reformation

Between six and seven o'clock on the morning of 17 November 1558, soon after the elevation of the Host at a Mass celebrated in her sickroom, Queen Mary died. When the news was broken to Pole, himself lying mortally ill at Lambeth, he wept, and told the friends round his bed how closely his and the Queen's lives had been bound together in God's providence. Both had suffered many years for their fidelity to the faith, both had been made instruments to restore catholicism to England, and in that collaboration the bond of their shared Plantagenet blood had been intensified by a 'great conformity of mind and spirit', and by the unfailing confidence that the Queen had always placed in him: in the words of his grief-stricken companion Alvise Priuli, 'aggiundosi all congiuntione del sangue gran conformita d'animo con soma confidentia che S. M. haveva sempre mostrato d'havere in lui'.[1] By seven o'clock that evening, Pole, fearful of the consequences of the Queen's death 'in questo ultimo grave caso', but consoling himself in abandonment to God's providence, was himself dead. The Marian project was over, apparently as dead as the unhappy Mary and her cousin the Cardinal. Contemplating her death and its likely consequences for religion, Cardinal Wolsey's biographer, George Cavendish, master of excruciating elegiac doggerel, was for once moved to real eloquence:

> Hyghe preste of Rome. / O Paule appostolike
> And College conscripte / of Caradynalles all
> And ye that confesse / the ffaythe catholyke
> Of Cristes chirche / in yerthe unyversall
> O claerkes and religious / to you I call
> Pray for your patrone / your frend and founder
> Mary our Mastres / our quene of honoure
>
> Whiche late restored / the right Religion
> And faythe of ffathers / observed of old.

Subdewed Sectes / and all dyvision
Reducyng the fflockke / to the former fold.
A piller moste ferme / the churche to uphold.
Look where she lyeth / true ffaythes defendoure
Mary our Mastres / our quene of honoure.

Whan Sacred aulters / were all defaced
Images of Sayntes / with outrage burned
In stede of prestes / apostataes placed
Holy sacramentes / with spight down sporned
When spoyle and Ravyn / hade all overtorned
This Chaos confuse / thys hepe of horroure
Dissolvethe Marie / as queen of honoure.[2]

What was it that had died with Cardinal and Queen – the incipient counter-reformation, English style, or the last gasp of the middle ages? To some historians, it has seemed that Marian catholicism had indeed a past but never a future, for it lacked the vitality to survive in the harder, fiercer religious world of the late sixteenth century, and certainly had no power to shape its outcomes. English catholicism did indeed survive Mary's death, but only as a new growth, something different. The most distinguished exponent of that view, John Bossy, claimed thirty years ago that the Marian church had contributed almost nothing to the recusant catholicism of Elizabeth's reign, and hence, by implication, to the wider counter-reformation. Mary's church, he suggested, should be seen as part of the posthumous history of medieval Christendom, 'a far different thing' from what came afterwards.[3] David Loades has consistently argued that Pole's and Mary's church lacked 'the fire of the counter-reformation', precisely because it was informed by the superseded values of the humanism of the 1520s, and owed more to Erasmus and even to Cranmer than to Ignatius Loyola.[4]

More recently, Dr Lucy Wooding has argued that Marian catholicism was founded on an essentially Henrician humanist framework, and that it had 'no particular place for the papacy', an institution that she thinks Marian churchmen viewed as an administrative convenience rather than an article of faith. The harder, starker values of counter-reformation catholicism would therefore be embraced by Elizabethan catholics only when they had completed a painful transition away from the moderate and insular humanism that they had, to some extent, shared with their protestant opponents, towards something more international, much sterner and less accommodating.[5] For all these historians, therefore, the religion of the Marian regime must be sharply distinguished from the ardent and militant catholicism of the later sixteenth century, whether at home or abroad.

It has been the contention of this book, by contrast, that the spirit of the counter-reformation was in fact alive and well in Marian England. But the debate is anyway bedevilled by unreal distinctions: much that we consider most characteristic of counter-reformation piety (its high sacramentalism or its systematic use of affective meditation, for example) was essentially the focusing and routinisation of familiar aspects of late medieval devotion also. Ignatius Loyola's spiritual exercises were a distillation of the affective piety that characterised a hundred late medieval meditational handbooks. The religious ethos of Marian catholicism did indeed have medieval and humanistic roots. Like the rest of European catholicism, however, it was evolving towards the same heightened interiority and more intense sacramentalism that we associate with post-Tridentine catholicism. And, as we have seen, the Marian church under Pole's influence was also absorbing the more ardent reverence for the papacy that would be one of the marks of European catholicism after Trent.

In this final chapter, I want to consider briefly some of the ways in which that growing papalism shaped the response of the Marian church to the Elizabethan religious settlement, and to sketch the implications of that response for the later counter-reformation. However, it is worth dwelling briefly first on just two of the less tangible but equally significant signs of the evolving counter-reformation spirit in Marian piety. The first of these might easily be mistaken for a piece of medieval archaism, even as evidence for the sort of views from which I have just distanced myself.

William Peto, a friend of Thomas More and one-time member of Pole's Italian circle, returned to England with the Observant Franciscan community re-established at Greenwich in 1555. In 1556, he published an English translation of Thomas à Kempis's *Imitation of Christ*, designed, as his preface explained, as an antidote to the many heretical books that had 'seduce[d] the simple people' and brought them 'from the unitie of the catholyke church into perverse and abominable errours'.[6] The translation that Peto used had in fact first been published in the early

1530s by Richard Whitford, and it would be easy to misread Peto's reissue of a humanist version of this medieval devotional classic as a naive and nostalgic gesture, inadequate to the urgency of the times and the need for tough and focused polemic. But there was nothing retrograde about Peto's enterprise. He was a man of the counter-reformation, had spent twenty years working in the Italian church and had even been an assistant in Caraffa's Roman Inquisition.

The religious superiority of devotional over controversial texts was an axiom of the counter-reformation, which valued devout heart above inquisitive head, and was inclined to distrust lay doctrinal curiosity. That emphasis on the Christianity of the heart would be one of the energies driving the great flowering of European catholic devotional writing in the later sixteenth century. And, in this context, *Imitation of Christ* itself was no medieval fossil, but quite simply the most popular of all catholic devotional books. It ran through countless editions in all the major European vernaculars, and was revered second only to the Gospels by Ignatius Loyola. In mid-century Cordoba, the price of a copy of the *Imitation* doubled because of Jesuit promotion of it, and by 1558 virtually every Jesuit owned a copy.[7] Peto's edition was read by key Marian catholics – the British Library copy is one of two presented by the editor to Lady Elizabeth Pope, wife of the founder of one of the new catholic institutions of Marian Oxford, Trinity College. Lady Pope would enjoy a long widowhood as a pillar of Elizabethan recusancy, and Mass was said regularly in her Clerkenwell house.[8] No doubt Peto's edition of the *Imitation* helped sustain her resistance, as it certainly did that of many other recusants: a clandestine press would reissue it for the beleaguered Elizabethan catholics in 1575.[9]

Nor were the Observant Franciscans the only religious order promoting counter-reformation piety for the laity in Marian England. The Dominican William Peryn's *Spirituall Exercyses and Goostly Meditacions*, published in 1557, was dedicated to two English nuns: Katherine Palmer, abbess of the nuns of Syon at Isleworth, and Dorothy Clement, a Poor Clare at Louvain, and the daughter of Thomas More's adopted daughter, Margaret Giggs.[10] But the book was also aimed at 'al other that desire to come to the perfect love of God'. It was an adaptation of a work by Nicholas Van Ess, a Flemish associate of the Jesuits Peter Canisius and Peter Faber, and it incorporated elements of Ignatius's own spiritual exercises. Like Peto's edition of the *Imitation*, Peryn's book was destined to have a long life in English recusant devotion. It was much valued by Margaret Clitheroe, and would be reissued by a clandestine catholic press in 1598.[11]

Peto's and Peryn's works were by no means the only Marian writings to have a long shelf life as a resource for catholicism under Elizabeth. When the antiquary John Stow's London house was raided for popish books in February 1569, the pursuivants found, alongside the latest controversial texts by Hosius, Stapleton and others from the Louvain presses, no fewer than fifteen key Marian doctrinal, devotional and polemical works – sermons by Abbot Feckenham, Leonard Pollard, James Brookes (who had presided at Cranmer's trial); Procter's translation of Vincent of Lérins; Standish's *Trial of the Supremacy* and his attack on the English Bible; Bonner's *A Profitable and Necessarye Doctryne*; Watson's *Holsome and Catholyke Doctryne*; and Hogarde's *Displaying of the Protestants*.[12]

The spirit of the counter-reformation was even more clearly at work in Marian sacramental piety. In a deliberate move to rekindle catholic devotion to the body of Christ after the sacrileges of Edward's reign, Bartolomé Carranza had mobilised the resources of Philip's splendid Chapel Royal to mount an elaborate musical procession with the Blessed Sacrament through Kingston upon Thames on Corpus Christi day, 1555. That first procession had been a largely Spanish affair but, the following year, Bishop Bonner staged a similar procession through Whitehall. An eyewitness commented on the joy of the English crowds who flocked to the spectacle, kneeling in the street and 'weeping, and giving thanks to God because they were seeing such a good thing'.[13] The Legatine Synod itself took a momentous step in the same direction. Its second decree stipulated that the Blessed Sacrament was henceforth to be reserved not in the hanging pyx customary until then in England but, wherever possible, in a locked stone tabernacle raised above the high altar.[14] The immediate context for this prescription was a desire to ensure greater security and honour for the reserved Sacrament, and to prevent the sort of sacrilegious attacks on it that had taken place under Edward.

The new arrangements were implemented first in the cathedrals: Bishop Tunstall gave instructions in July 1556 for the construction of 'a becoming tabernacle constructed on the upper part of the altar' at Durham, and the injunctions for the legatine visitation of Gloucester that year specified that every parish should construct a 'decent tabernacle

set in the middest of the hie altar to preserve the most blessed sacramente
. . . with a taper or lampe burning before the same . . . after the example
of the tabernacle in the cathedral chuche at Gloucester'.[15] The lamp
before the Sacrament on the altar alerts us to the wider devotional
implications of these essentially practical arrangements. Reservation on
the high altar, which Pole borrowed from Roman custom, was a rarity
not only in England but everywhere in Europe in 1556. It would become
normative after Trent, however, and the growing focus of the prayer life
of the clergy and laity on the eucharistic presence in the tabernacle was
to become one of the most distinctive marks of counter-reformation
piety, promoting a new sacramental intensity and the spread of eucharistic
observances such as the 'Forty Hours Devotion'.[16] Pole's England had
here sounded a note that would resonate throughout Europe and beyond
for centuries.

This new sacramental intensity was directly reflected in official Marian
instructions for the laity. As we have seen, Thomas Watson's *Holsome and
Catholyke Doctryne*, published in June 1558, was one of four volumes
specially commissioned by the synod, and the only one published,[17] but
it was rapidly disseminated to the parishes. In many ways the most
remarkable theological product of Mary's reign, it was soberly expressed
but pervaded by a devout interiority in approaching all the sacraments
that was quite new in English official utterances. In our present context,
the collection was noteworthy in anticipating another of the most
characteristic features of counter-reformation piety, more frequent
communion, which Watson urged on the laity – 'the oftner he commeth,
the better it is'.[18]

These devotional developments were all significant indicators of new
spiritual stirrings in Marian catholicism, the first shoots in a promising
spring. But the distance that the Marian church had travelled in five years
from the uneasy compromises of Henry's and Edward's reigns would be
revealed above all by the remarkable and costly loyalty of the bishops
and the higher clergy to the papacy. The news of Mary's death and the
accession of Ann Boleyn's daughter brought a flood of protestant exiles
hastening back to England. By the time of Mary's funeral on 14
December, it was plain that Elizabeth was intent on overturning Mary's
catholic settlement. Bishop White of Winchester used his sermon at
Mary's funeral in Westminster Abbey to threaten all who 'wilfully
departed out of the catholic church' with certain damnation. He warned

that 'the wolves be coming out of Geneva, and other parts of Germany, and hath sent their books before, ful of pestilent doctrines, blasphemy and heresy, to infect the people', and praised Mary for having purged the realm of heresy, dwelling pointedly on the fact that the dead queen, 'remembering herself to be a *member* of Christ's church, refused to write herself *head* thereof'.[19] The subtext of all this could hardly be lost on the living queen. White found himself at once under house arrest, a fate that had already befallen Christopherson of Chichester, for similar sentiments preached at Paul's Cross on 27 November. Led by Archbishop Heath of York, the remaining bishops and Abbot Feckenham made a determined stand in the House of Lords, in a series of speeches that formed a comprehensive and eloquent broadside against the doctrine of the Royal Supremacy and the novelty of protestant teaching, 'lately brought in, allowed no where, nor put in practice, but in this realme only'.[20]

Ever since Pole's arrival, the tone and even the very wording of his ardent papalism had been absorbed into the regime's official publications and preaching. The extent to which the higher clergy had internalised this unequivocally religious understanding of the papacy was revealed in their response to the reimposition of the Royal Supremacy at Elizabeth's accession. Archbishop Heath, a former Henrician and Edwardine conformist whose conscience had once been elastic enough to reject the pope and accept the first Edwardine Prayer Book, might have been expected to be lukewarm at best about papal authority. Instead, he placed it at the centre of his stand against the new regime. Obedience to the See of Peter transcended 'the pope's person', he told the House of Lords. Paul IV had indeed been 'a very austere stern father unto us, ever since his first entraunce into Peter's chayre', and, if it were a matter of mere liking or loyalty to the man, 'then the cause were not of such greate importaunce, as it is in very dede'. But the necessity of papal authority was rooted rather in the love of Christ, who had not 'lefte his churche, which he had dearly bought by th'effusyon of his most precyous bloode, without a head'. The unity of the church was founded on Peter's authority, and therefore 'by our leapinge out of Peter's shippe, we must nedes be overwhelmed by the waters of schism, sects and divisions'.

In a now familiar reference, borrowed from Pole, Heath emphasised that it was from Rome in the days of Pope Eleutherius and Pope Gregory that England had received her ancient faith.[21] If the claims of the reformers were true, therefore, 'we have byne deceyved all this while', and 'th'inhabitants of this realme shalbe forced to seke fourther for another gospel of Christe, another doctrine, faithe, and sacraments, then we hitherto have receyved. Whiche shall brede suche a schism and errour in faithe, as was never in any Christian realme.'[22]

Bishop Cuthbert Scott of Chester was equally impassioned. The pope, he told the Lords, was the instrument of that unity for which Christ had prayed on the night before his passion, the one shepherd of Christ's one sheepfold, Christ's 'vicar-generall in earthe, to governe and rule all his whole flock'. Peter had been given a new name by Christ, 'so that he shoulde have a new priviledge or preferment, to be the foundation, grounde and staye of Christe's churche . . . whiche thinge doth nowe appeare in the succession of Peter'. Without the pope, he asked, 'what certaintye can we have of our faithe? Or howe shall we staye our selves, waveringe in the same in this our tyme?' In all the bewildering divisions of contemporary Christendom, Peter and his successors were the God-given foundation 'whereunto men might safely cleave and leane, as unto a sure and unmovable rocke in matters of faithe, knowinge certeynly that in so doinge they shall not falle'.[23] Where the bishops led, the rest of the clergy followed. The Lower House of Convocation, whose prolocutor was Nicholas Harpsfield, rallied to the bishops with an affirmation of the doctrines of transubstantiation, of the sacrifice of the Mass and of papal supremacy: this declaration was duly endorsed by both universities.[24]

Yet all this clerical unanimity did precisely nothing to deflect the new regime. By midsummer 1559, the Acts of Supremacy and Uniformity were back in place, and Pole's most important reforms had been undone by legislation returning First Fruits and Tenths to the Crown, and brazenly allowing Elizabeth to asset-strip any diocese during episcopal vacancies. Within a year of Mary's death, all fourteen surviving catholic bishops had refused the Oath of Supremacy and had been deprived: Goldwell of St Asaph escaped abroad and made his way to Rome, and from there to the Council of Trent. Christopherson of Chichester, White of Winchester, Baynes of Lichfield and Coventry, Oglethorpe of Carlisle, Morgan of St David's and Tunstall of Durham were all dead of old age or influenza. Just one solitary Henrician survivor, Kitchin of Llandaff, caved in, accepted the Oath of Supremacy and was ignominiously restored to his bishopric.

The rest of the bishops stood their ground and were eventually gaoled, along with the leading catholic disputants and the key figures in Pole's administration – Henry Cole, John Boxall, the Harpsfield brothers, Archdeacon Chedsey, Anthony Draycot, the lay lawyers John Story and Thomas Martin, Seth Holland, dean of Worcester, and many more. All were imprisoned, and many would spend the rest of their lives in captivity.[25] On 4 December 1559, soon after their deprivation but before their confinement, five of them – Heath of York, Bonner of London, Bourne of Bath and Wells, Turberville of Exeter and David Pole of Peterborough – made a last stand. They wrote a joint letter to the Queen to warn her against schism and heresy, which she was embracing 'in lieu of the ancient catholic faith, which hath been long since planted within this realm, by the motherly care of the church of Rome'. They urged her to imitate her sister who, 'being troubled in conscience with what her father and her brother's advisers had caused them to do', had restored the catholic faith and acknowledged the pope's supremacy. Outraged, Elizabeth reminded them of their own schismatic past. Who had encouraged her father more than 'you, good Mr Hethe, when you were bishop of Rochester? And you, Mr Boner, when you were archdeacon? And you, Mr Turberville?'[26] The whole exchange, and especially the Queen's uncomprehending appeal to the bishops' conformist Henrician past, illustrates the intellectual and moral watershed that the Marian restoration represented.

The deprivation, imprisonment or exile of the entire episcopate and their key helpers was in one sense, of course, a godsend for Elizabeth, clearing the way for the installation of men committed to the new religion. At another level, such radical discontinuity was a defeat for the new regime, and a dramatic testimony to the achievement of Pole and Mary. It signalled the re-centring of English catholicism round the papacy. This startling realignment had taken place since Pole's arrival and would have been unimaginable even a decade before. But it was not confined to the episcopate: almost equally dramatic was the rejection of Elizabeth's settlement by a majority of the clerical elite of England. It had been Pole's intention, as it had been Cranmer's, to turn the cathedrals from sinecures into centres of reform. More than 170 canons of cathedrals, about a quarter of the total number, feature somewhere in Pole's correspondence, and 79% of his contacts in the cathedrals were graduates, almost half of them (44%) with degrees in theology, another indication of the weight that Pole put on the clergy as teachers and preachers. Pole's Legatine Synod had legislated to establish seminaries in the cathedral schools, and four such seminaries had been founded or were in the process of foundation when Mary died. The success of this ongoing transformation was now made clear, by the extraordinary exodus from 1559 onwards of cathedral prebendaries and office-holders conscientiously unable to conform to a protestant church.[27]

The high mortality among clergy in 1559 and 1560 makes precise counting difficult but, of the 261 English and Welsh prebendaries whose position I have been able to establish with some degree of confidence, 137 resigned or were deprived by Elizabeth for refusal to conform to the settlement, while 124 remained in post. The pattern is even more pronounced for office-holders: out of 77 dignitaries – deans, precentors, chancellors, archdeacons and the like – whose stance towards the settlement I have been able to identify, 43 resigned or were deprived, while 34 remained in post. So, fewer than half of Mary's cathedral dignitaries were willing to serve her sister. That bald statistic only begins to take on its truly remarkable significance if one compares it with the situation at Mary's accession. Then, more than two-thirds of all the prebendaries and higher dignitaries who had served in Edward's protestant church conformed and remained in post to serve in Mary's catholic church.

The dramatic stiffening of spine and principle among the higher clergy that that difference represents becomes even clearer when one looks more closely at the career patterns of the Elizabethan conformists and the dissidents. More than half of the cathedral dignitaries who accepted Elizabeth's settlement had already been in post before Mary's accession. Of the deans, chancellors and other higher officials refusing conformity, and hence deprived under Elizabeth, however, only one-fifth were pre-Marian appointments, while an amazing four-fifths had been newly promoted by Mary and Pole. The resisters, therefore, came overwhelmingly from among the Marian appointees. This is a remarkable testimony to the regime's ability to recognise or to inspire men with a principled commitment to catholicism. The same basic pattern holds for the much larger sample of prebendaries. Here, two-thirds of those refusing conformity had been promoted by Mary and Pole, and just one-third were pre-Marian appointments: once again, the resisters were overwhelmingly Pole's and Mary's men.[28]

This massive displacement of the cathedral clergy has been hurried past by far too many historians, for it was no mere negative gesture. Many of the ejected were scholars, immersed in the same combination of patristic learning and catholic humanism that had shaped Pole's own religious convictions.[29] Some of them were to become crucial contributors to the domestic counter-reformation as the fosterers and theorists of recusancy, and leaders in the construction of the Elizabethan catholic community. And many of the dissidents escaped to the continent, to become players in the European counter-reformation. Those who remained in England would provide catholic sacraments and teaching, stiffen lay resistance and, in general, become a thorn in the flesh for the new protestant establishment. Just a few examples must stand for all.

John Blaxton, the sub-dean of Exeter and commissary for heresy in that diocese, was also archdeacon of Brecon in his native diocese of Hereford, and had been one of the key figures in the battle against protestantism in the Exeter diocese. Deprived in 1559, Blaxton returned to Hereford, where he gathered round him a group of ejected clergy from Exeter and elsewhere. Fêted by the conservative local population, who at one point led Blaxton and his friends in a torchlit procession through the streets, their disruptive presence made the imposition of thoroughgoing protestantism in the area almost impossible. In 1564, Bishop Scory complained bitterly that his diocese was plagued by 'diverse fostered and mayntayned that be iudged and esteemed some of them to be learned, which in Queene Maryes daies had livings and officeis in the churche, which be mortall and deadly ennemys to this religion'. In addition to Blaxton, these included Thomas Ardern, a theologian and deprived prebendary of York and Hereford, and Gregory Basset, another theologian and preacher, formerly warden of the Exeter Greyfriars and, like Blaxton, active against heresy in Marian Exeter.[30] According to Scory, these troublesome papistical dissidents were openly supported by the remaining prebendaries of Hereford, who, the bishop complained, 'will neither preache, reade homilies nor minister the holy communion . . . so that this churche which shuld be the light of all the diocese ys very darkenes, and an ensample of contempt of true religion, whom the citei and countre aboughte folowe apase'.[31]

This pattern was repeated elsewhere: John Morwen was a young Oxford classicist who had served Bonner as secretary and chaplain, and had been rewarded with a prebend in St Paul's. Deprived in 1559, and for a time imprisoned in the Tower, he had returned to his native Cheshire by 1561. There, with one eye still on events in London, he greeted news of the burning of St Paul's steeple in June 1561 with a brilliantly opportunistic broadside scattered round the streets of Chester, in which the burning of the cathedral was presented as the judgement of God on the new bishops and their *ersatz* religion. Until his eventual arrest in 1583, Morwen was a tireless and effective catholic agitator, persuading the gentry of the north-west to boycott protestant worship and to sign pledges of loyalty to the pope.[32]

These deprivations were replicated all over England: at St Paul's, the dean, the treasurer, all six archdeacons and ten other prebendaries;[33] at York, the chancellor, both archdeacons and nine other prebendaries;[34] at Salisbury, the dean, one of two archdeacons and eleven prebendaries;[35] at Winchester, the dean, one of two archdeacons and seven other prebendaries;[36] at Lincoln, five of the six archdeacons (the sixth, Michael Dunning, was an ardent papist who would certainly have been deprived had he not died in 1559) and fourteen prebendaries; and so on.[37] The more prominent figures were gaoled. Seth Holland, deprived dean of Worcester, had shared Pole's Italian exile, was with him when he died and served as one of his executors: he himself would die a prisoner in the Marshalsea.[38] This astonishing conscientious exodus from the cushioned stalls of Barchester to gaol or the wilderness was something new in Tudor England, indeed in reformation Europe. Its drastic scale was a telling witness to the internalisation of the core convictions of the Marian counter-reformation by a clear majority of the higher clergy. The pope and the Mass had become touchstones of conscience for which these pillars of the establishment, like their bishops, were willing to sacrifice everything.

Far fewer of the lower clergy demonstrated this sort of resolution, and most conformed. But we lack detailed local studies to establish the real extent of the disruption at parish level. If the example of the diocese of Chichester is anything to go by, the combination of mortality from influenza and deprivation for popery posed a serious problem in the early years of the new settlement. For one reason or another, in Sussex almost half the livings in the diocese had been vacated between 1558 and 1561, and 'it was possible to walk from the Surrey border to the Sussex coast . . . crossing sixteen parishes in every one of which the incumbent had either been deprived or had died in the influenza epidemic'.[39]

The penetration of the Marian counter-reformation was, if anything, even more marked in the universities, where Pole's draconian visitations of 1556–7 had successfully reversed the protestant gains of Edward's reign. In Oxford especially, the influence of Spanish Dominicans such as Bartolomé Carranza, Pedro de Soto and Juan de Villagarcia had sparked a catholic resurgence that horrified Elizabeth's new men. 'Our Universities are so depressed and ruined', John Jewel told Heinrich Bullinger in May 1559,

> that at Oxford there are scarcely two individuals that think with us. . . . . That despicable friar, Soto, and another Spanish monk . . . have so torn up by the roots all that Peter Martyr had so prosperously planted that they have reduced the vineyard of the Lord to a wilderness.

So in both universities but especially in Oxford, the Royal Supremacy and the new Prayer Book were widely rejected. Robert Horne, protestant bishop of Winchester, conducted visitations of New College, Corpus and Trinity, Oxford in 1561 and told Cecil that he dared not press his enquiries too far because, had he done so, 'I should not scarcely have left twain in some one house'.[40] As it was, almost every Oxford head of house was deprived or induced to resign – Balliol, Lincoln, Merton, Christchurch, Trinity, University, Queen's and Magdalen all suffered religiously inspired changes of regime by 1561, and the new catholic foundation of St John's lost two presidents in quick succession. Only Dr Whyte of New College remained in post, and everyone knew that he was a crypto-papist. New College saw a purge of the fellowship in 1560, which dislodged Thomas Stapleton, Nicholas Sander and John Fowler, all to be key figures in the European counter-reformation, and eleven more fellows were expelled over the next couple of years. New College's catholicism would prove chronically persistent: a third of the fellowship refused the Oath of Supremacy immediately and, in the ten years after the imposition of the Elizabethan settlement, twenty-nine in all would be removed for popery, many of them elected after 1559.[41]

Cambridge was to prove more adaptable, with survivors such as Andrew Perne at Peterhouse or John Pory at Corpus making an effortless transition to the new regime. But even here the casualty rate was high. Trinity's master, Bishop Christopherson, died under house arrest in December 1558. John Young, the fire-eating master of Pembroke who had led the re-catholicisation of Marian Cambridge, was deprived and clapped in gaol. He was still a prisoner at the time of his death in Wisbech Castle, twenty-two years later. The masters of Magdalene, Jesus, Trinity Hall and Caius were also ousted, while Bailey of Clare fled abroad to Louvain and then to Douai. Of the Marian heads who remained, some were certainly crypto-papists, most famously Dr Caius but also Philip Baker at King's. Appointed in 1559 after Elizabeth's accession, he had already been deprived of his London livings for refusing the Oath of Supremacy and would be a notorious supporter of the old religion in reformed Cambridge. Our knowledge of the effects on college fellowships is hazier. Nicholas Sander, however, told Cardinal Morone in 1561 that sixteen fellows of Trinity had left the college for the sake of religion, several of whom had gone abroad. The election of twenty new fellows in Trinity in 1560, of fifteen at St John's in the same year and of thirteen more in 1561, speaks for itself about the upheavals that Elizabeth's accession entailed.[42]

As Sander's report indicated, many of the ousted cathedral dignitaries and academics sought refuge in the catholic universities of France and Flanders. In the early 1560s, well over a hundred made their way abroad, the bulk of them to Louvain or Douai. At Louvain, they clustered in two lodging houses nicknamed 'Oxford' and 'Cambridge'. The list of émigrés from New College alone reads like a roll call of the stars of Elizabethan recusancy. Thomas Stapleton, who would eventually succeed Michael Baius as professor of scripture at Louvain, earned a European reputation as a controversialist second only to that of Bellarmine – Gregory XIII had his *Antidota Apostolica* read aloud at meals. There were more than 140 individual editions of his various writings by 1640 and a four-volume folio *Opera Omnia* in Paris in 1620.[43]

John Fowler became the most important catholic printer of the Elizabethan period, responsible for more than fifty books, including the writings of William Allen, Thomas Stapleton, Richard Bristow and Nicholas Sander, Laurence Vaux's Catechism and translations of key devotional works such as *The Imitation of Christ* and *The Jesus Psalter*.[44] Owen Lewis would make a distinguished administrative and episcopal career in Italy, including a four-year spell as vicar-general of Borromeo's Milan: he was present at Borromeo's deathbed. He remained, however, deeply involved with England and helped secure the finances of Douai College and funding for the Douai-Rheims Bible.[45] And, perhaps most famously of all, Nicholas Sander, still only in his late twenties when ejected from New College, would combine a stream of pungent polemics against Elizabeth's church with an astonishing European career – theologian to the Polish Cardinal Hosius at the final sessions of the Council of Trent, advocate for the reception of the Council's decrees in Germany and Poland, Regius Professor of Theology at Louvain, candidate for the cardinalate, and political activist until his mysterious death in the early 1580s in Ireland, where he had gone to foment rebellion and a Spanish invasion. Sander's best book, *De Origine ac Progressu Schismatis Anglicani*, was a history of the English reformation, extending Pole's and Harpsfield's accounts of the Henrician schism down to the reigns of Edward and Elizabeth. It became one of the seminal texts of the European counter-reformation, running into eight Latin editions, translated into French and German, and, via its dozens of imitators, shaping both catholic and protestant histories of the reformation well into the eighteenth century.[46]

Although some of the exiles were senior figures – Thomas Harding, Morgan Phillips, Bishop Cuthbert Scott, who escaped to Louvain in 1563 – many were young men, like Sander. It has often been noted that the English reformation was, in its early stages at any rate, a youth movement: much the same can be said of the English counter-reformation. The expulsions from the universities after 1559 exiled a generation of ardent young intellectuals schooled in Pole's and Mary's church. Moving into the wider world of Tridentine reform, they encountered the blossoming counter-reformation, certainly, but they also brought it with them from Marian Oxford.

Along with Sander, the best known of these young men is probably William Allen, Lancashire man and fellow of Oriel, who had proceeded MA at the same degree congregation at which Thomas Harding and Nicholas Harpsfield took their doctorates. Two years younger than Sander and an altogether less flamboyant character, Allen nevertheless fully shared his ardent commitment to the restoration of catholicism in the university. Sander was the Latin orator chosen to welcome Pole's legatine commission for the momentous visitation of the university in 1556. As a junior head of house – he was principal of St Mary's Hall from that year – and, more importantly, as proctor in 1556 and 1557, Allen was one of those directly responsible for implementing the visitation. Both men eagerly befriended the Spanish theologians whom Pole placed in Oxford to renew catholic theology there, especially Juan de Villagarcia, the Regius Professor of Divinity, whom Sander reverentially called 'Pater Johannes'. Sander assisted Villagarcia very directly in the Oxford revival by offering courses of lectures in both the key restored disciplines of scholastic theology and canon law.[47] Elizabeth's accession drove Allen to Malines, and then to Douai where, in 1568, he founded the English College, which would pride itself on being the first full-blown Tridentine seminary anywhere in Europe, and it was certainly the single most important English counter-reformation institution.

Sander made his way to Rome in 1559. His rhapsodic account of his arrival and stay there in a letter to another young Oxford exile, the future Jesuit John Rastell, makes abundantly clear the ardent spirit in which these men travelled. Sander's letter is full of the wonders of catholic Italy: the relics of Padua and Milan, more glorious than any pagan antiquities; the Holy House of Loreto; above all, the spiritual splendour of Pius IV's Rome, its stupendous relics of Christ and his saints, its catacombs, the ardour of its sacramental life, the piety of its people and its priests. In a revealing glimpse of the ardent papalism encouraged in Marian Oxford, he reminded Rastell of their conversations there with 'Pater Johannes', how they had often talked 'about the glory and splendour' of Rome and how 'we all thought that Peter was the first in dignity on earth'. Now he had seen how true all that was, 'for not only is doctrine incorrupt here' but, despite its reputation for vice, Rome was in fact 'the one place above others in which the holiest life is led', which was no doubt why the Devil was now busily at work in England 'traducing the Supreme See'.[48]

Twenty years on, the themes of Sander's letter would be taken up and expanded in Gregory Martin's *Roma Sancta*, a paean of praise and gratitude to counter-reformation Rome by the translator of the Douai-Rheims Bible. It has rightly been called 'the first survey of the new piety of Rome' in the wake of the Council of Trent. Martin's book is very much fuller, more detailed and more eloquent than Sander's brief account, but the same ardent religious attitudes were already on display in the letter from the young exile from Marian Oxford.[49]

It was not only the fire-eating young who responded so eagerly to the spirit and institutions of counter-reformation Europe. While Sander, Allen and their colleagues in the early 1560s regrouped in the universities of continental Europe, one of the principal movers and shakers of the Marian church toiled on at his desk in a cell in the Fleet prison. In 1566, Nicholas Harpsfield smuggled abroad and published the massive thousand-page product of these labours. Harpsfield's *Dialogi Sex contra Summi Pontificatus . . . Oppugnatores* was a comprehensive anti-protestant Latin polemic in dialogue form. It particularly targeted the Lutheran Centuriators of Magdeburg, who had begun publication in 1560. It culminated in an all-out attack on the first edition of Foxe's *Acts and Monuments*, which had appeared in 1563. In the final, sixth dialogue, which occupied a quarter of his book, Harpsfield excoriated what he took to be Foxe's deliberate lies and incompetent errors about the Marian pursuit and punishment of heresy. In doing so, he was in effect defending the record and integrity of the whole Marian enterprise, in which he had been so central a figure. *Dialogi Sex* is emphatically a work of the 1560s, its primary focus on the *Magdeburg Centuries* natural enough given Harpsfield's historical interests and the provocative dedication of the later volumes of the *Centuries* to Queen Elizabeth. In his prison cell, Harpsfield had no direct access to the developing European counter-reformation. But, like all the other English catholic writers of the 1560s, he drew readily and unselfconsciously on European resources, quoting from and defending the recently concluded Council of Trent, whose decrees had at last been promulgated in January 1564. He also drew on the Jesuit *Annual Letters*, praising their missionary work in the Americas and the Far East, and celebrating the miracles that accompanied their mission preaching as signs of the truth of catholic Christianity.[50]

Harpsfield's use of such sources in composing his *Dialogi Sex* makes explicit the European context for the whole Marian project. Historians who argue for the essential insularity of Marian theology and apologetic sometimes write as if there had been no booksellers in England, and as if the defenders and strategists of Marian catholicism read only works published in England and in English. In fact, of course, they routinely drew on the writings of contemporary European theologians – Castro, Tapper, Pighius.[51] Bishop Watson cited the still unpromulgated decrees of Trent in his discussion of penance in the *Holsome and Catholyke Doctryne*. Bishop Scott acquired Stanislaus Hosius's *Christianae Catholicaeque Doctrinae Propugnatio*, with its preface by Peter Canisius, soon after its publication in 1558, and used material from it on the reformation in northern and central Europe in his speech on the Supremacy Bill in the House of Lords in the spring of 1559.[52]

But the Marian enterprise did not merely reflect developments in European catholicism. That enterprise itself became a crucial influence in the final stages of the Council of Trent and, through Trent, in the catholic church as a whole. Cardinal Hosius himself was impressed by the learning and eloquence of Nicholas Sander in 1560, and recruited him as theological adviser when he was appointed legate for the final sessions of Trent. At Trent, Hosius's residence became the centre for a group of exiled English theologians, including Bishop Thomas Goldwell of St Asaph, who had ordained Sander.[53] Hosius was not Sander's only important cardinalatial contact, however. A born networker, Sander had also sought the patronage of the Cardinal protector of England, Pole's friend and collaborator Giovanni Morone, now delivered from the Inquisition prison in which he had languished during the latter part of Caraffa's papacy, and once more high in papal favour. In May 1561, Sander prepared a long report for Morone on the heroic response of the Marian establishment to the Elizabethan settlement, highlighting the sufferings of the bishops and the other prisoners, not forgetting the displaced cathedral and university clergy now cast adrift in England or Europe because they had not 'bowed the knee to Baal'.[54]

Morone's intense interest in England was more than the conscientious discharge of the official protectorship of England that he had inherited from Pole. Pole's spiritual legacy had become a precious commodity, his reputation for sanctity and his reforming efforts in England a potential asset for the reforming party round Morone, now emerging from the fog of suspicion and hostility that had overshadowed them under Pope Paul IV. With the death in 1560 of Alvise Priuli, Pole's companion and literary executor, custodianship of Pole's reputation passed with his papers to Morone and to the Mantuan Cardinal Ercole Gonzaga. In consultation with Girolamo Seripando, they decided to launch the newly established Roman press of Paolo Manutio by publishing a selection of Pole's key writings. The book was to be a reform manifesto, designed not only as a posthumous vindication of the English Cardinal against Paul IV's suspicions, but, through Pole, to publicise and rehabilitate the ideals of his Italian reforming circle. With the final stages of the Council of Trent looming, the key item in this collection was to be Pole's *De Concilio*, the treatise he had composed while presiding legate at the Council's opening sessions. But, at Seripando's suggestion, an elaborated edition of the acts of Pole's Legatine Synod was also included, under the title *Reformatio Angliae*, providing an exemplar of what a truly catholic reform might look like in practice. With Manutio's dedication to Pope

Pius IV and Pole's short treatise on the baptism of Constantine added as a makeweight, the collection duly appeared in 1562, and 220 copies were hastily despatched to Trent for the edification of the Council fathers.[55] Other (pirated) editions of the *Reformatio Angliae* appeared the same year in Venice and at Dillengen, a testimony to the interest that Pole and his English activities had aroused.

In the run-up to Trent's final and, in terms of practical reform, most momentous sessions, therefore, the Marian restoration took on a new European significance. In particular, Pole's third synodal decree (on the residence of bishops) and his eleventh (on the establishment of seminaries) spoke directly to the most urgent concerns of the Council fathers, and would decisively shape their thought and action. The Council's most important long-term reform – its seminary legislation – was to be little more than an expansion of the arrangements that Pole and his colleagues had conceived and set in place for England. And, in a final irony, the catechism devised by Bartolomé Carranza for England, which Pole was having translated into English in the summer of 1558 and for which Carranza was languishing at that very moment in the cells of the Spanish Inquisition, would be taken as a framework for the drafting of the catechism of the Council of Trent.[56]

Nor was the influence of the Marian reforms at Trent and after confined to the circulation of the legatine decrees. Pole's immediate circle was scattered: some, like his chaplain and envoy to Elizabeth, Seth Holland, to end their lives in prison; others, such as Pate and Goldwell, in flight to the safety of catholic Europe. Among these was Pole's datary and legal adviser, Niccolo Ormanetto, a key member of the legatine team, who had coordinated the visitation of the universities in 1556. Ormanetto was doubly qualified as an activist for catholic reform, for he had served Gian Matteo Giberti in Verona before joining Pole's English staff. He now made his way via Rome to Milan, where Borromeo appointed him vicar-general, to publish and execute the decrees of Trent there.[57] Unsuprisingly, Borromeo's first Milan Synod of 1565 incorporated Pole's decree on pastoral visitation word for word into its chapter on the subject.[58] Borromeo clearly identified Pole's circle in general with the whole cause of catholic reform. Thomas Goldwell fled to Rome, where he became both *custos* of the English pilgrim hostel and superior of the Theatine community of San Silvestro in Rome. As we have seen, he was active in the last sessions of Trent, but, in 1565, he was sent by Borromeo to join Ormanetto in implementing Trent in Milan.[59] And, as we have already noted, the Oxford-trained canon lawyer Owen Lewis would also serve Borromeo as vicar-general.

Marian catholicism died with its Queen and its Cardinal. But, in one of history's customary ironies, it was at the very moment of its dissolution that the wider counter-reformation credentials of Pole's and Mary's project were most unequivocally declared. Its reform programme, embodied in the published acts of Pole's synod, would help shape Trent's most momentous innovation – the seminary. The revived papalism that was Pole's legacy was the inspiration for what can fairly be described as the heroic stand made by those most unexpected of heroes, the bishops and dignitaries of the English church. Marian catholicism inspired the generation of ardent activists who would provide Elizabethan catholicism with its core convictions, its best writers, its most characteristic institutions and its martyrs. It set adrift in mainland Europe a diaspora of talented academics and administrators whose interests and convictions merged seamlessly into those wider movements for reform that we call the counter-reformation, and who would themselves contribute to its creative ferment. The Latin term 'Inventio' is a very rich one: it carries the meanings to devise or create, as well as to find or discover. In both senses, the Marian church 'invented' the counter-reformation.

Notes

NOTES TO CHAPTER I

1. A. G. Dickens, *The English Reformation*, 2nd edn (London, 1989), p. 311, and ch. 12, *passim*.

2. John Bossy, *The English Catholic Community 1570–1850* (London, 1975), p. 4: I do not want here to enter into the problems surrounding the use of terms such as 'counter-reformation' and 'catholic reformation', for which see John O'Malley, *Trent and All That: Renaming Catholicism in the Early Modern Era* (Cambridge, MA, 2002).

3. Rex Pogson, 'Cardinal Pole: Papal Legate to England in Mary Tudor's Reign', unpublished PhD thesis, University of Cambridge, 1972.

4. David Loades, *The Reign of Mary Tudor*, 2nd edn (London, 1991), pp. 96–128.

5. For Loades's later, more favourable, but still qualified appraisal, see 'The Spirituality of the Restored Catholic Church' in T. M. McCoog (ed), *The Reckoned Expense* (Woodbridge, 1996), pp. 3–20, and his contributions to E. Duffy and D. Loades (eds), *The Church of Mary Tudor* (Aldershot, 2006).

6. J. Loach, 'The Marian Establishment and the Printing Press', *English Historical Review*, 100, 1986, pp. 138–51: contrast her earlier 'Pamphlets and Politics 1553–8', *Bulletin of the Institute of Historical Research*, 48, 1975, pp. 31–45.

7. Susan Brigden, *London and the Reformation* (Oxford, 1989), pp. 520–632.

8. E. Duffy, *The Stripping of the Altars: Traditional Religion in England 1400–1580* (New Haven and London, 1992), pp. 524–64.

9. Christopher Haigh, *English Reformations: Religion, Politics and Society under the Tudors* (Oxford, 1993), pp. 203–34.

10. John Foxe, *Acts and Monuments: The Variorum Edition* (hriOnline, Sheffield 2004), available at http://www.hrion-line.ac.uk/johnfoxe/. Except where stated otherwise, all quotations from Foxe are from the online edition of the 1583 *Acts and Monuments*.

11. Thomas F. Mayer, 'A Reluctant Author: Cardinal Pole and his Manuscripts', *Transactions of the American Philosophical Society*, NS, 89, 1999; *Reginald Pole: Prince and Prophet* (Cambridge, 2000); *Cardinal Pole in European Context* (collected papers, Aldershot, 2000); *The Correspondence of Reginald Pole* (Aldershot, 2002 (four volumes to date)).

12. John Edwards and Ronald Truman (eds), *Reforming Catholicism in the England of Mary Tudor* (Aldershot, 2005); Duffy and Loades, *Church of Mary Tudor*; Jonathan Dean, '*Catholicae Ecclesiae Unitatem*: Nicholas Harpsfield and English Reformation Catholicism', unpublished PhD thesis, University of Cambridge, 2004; William Wizeman, *The Theology and Spirituality of Mary Tudor's Church* (Aldershot, 2006); Lucy Wooding, *Rethinking Catholicism in Reformation England* (Oxford, 2000).

13. For the impact of all this in a single rural community, see E. Duffy, *The Voices of Morebath: Reformation and Rebellion in an English Village* (New Haven and London, 2001), pp. 111–51.

14. See below p. 73–5.

15. Diarmaid MacCulloch, 'Worcester: A Cathedral City in the Reformation', in Patrick Collinson and John Craig (eds), *The Reformation in English Towns, 1500–1640* (London, 1998), pp. 94–112, esp. pp. 106–7.

16. I have discussed this destruction and plunder in 'The End of it All: The Material

Culture of the Medieval English Parish Church and the 1552 Inventories of Church Goods', in C. Burgess and E. Duffy (eds), *The Parish Church in Late Medieval England* (Donington, 2006), pp. 381–99.

17. Duffy, *Stripping of the Altars*, pp. 543–64.

18. The process was surveyed by Ronald Hutton, 'The Local Impact of the Tudor Reformations', in Christopher Haigh (ed), *The English Reformation Revised* (Cambridge, 1987), pp. 114–37.

19. As happened at Stamford in Berkshire: see Duffy, *Stripping of the Altars*, pp. 547–8.

20. RSTC 16217, CUL Rit.a.155.1. The inscription on the title page reads 'Pray for the good prosperitie and welfare off Richard Perkin the elder who bowht this mass book and gave the same to the paryshe church of Sant Peters Tempsford the xxviij day off November Anno D 1557'. A second inscription in the same hand under the crucifix at the start of the Canon of the Mass requests prayers for Perkyn's soul, indicating that he had died in the interval between the two inscriptions, but still in the reign of Mary.

21. John Gough Nichols (ed), *The Diary of Henry Machyn* (Camden Society, 1848), p. 130.

22. MacCulloch, 'Worcester', p. 109.

23. Richard Marks, 'The Howard Tombs at Thetford and Framlingham: New Discoveries', *Archaeological Journal*, 141, 1984, pp. 252–68; Philip Lindley, 'Innovations, Tradition and Disruption in Tomb Sculpture', in D. Gaimster and P. Stamper (eds), *The Age of Transition: The Archaeology of English Culture 1400–1600* (Oxford, 1997), pp. 77–92.

24. M. Biddle, 'Early Renaissance at Winchester', in J. Crook (ed) *Winchester Cathedral* (Chichester, 1993), pp 257–304.

25. Below, pp. 168–70.

26. W. K. Jordan and M. R. Gleason, 'The Saying of John, Late Duke of Northumberland on the Scaffold 1553', *Harvard Library Bulletin*, 23, 1975, pp. 139–79, 324–55; Mayer, *Reginald Pole*, pp. 282–3. Subsequent Roman publications emanating from Pole's circle about the progress of the Marian restoration included *Il felicissimo ritorno del regno d'Inghilterra alla Catholica*

unione & obedientia della sede Apostolica (Rome, 1555), and *Copia delle lettere del sereniss. Re d'Inghilterra & del Reverendiss. Card. Polo . . . sopra . . . obedientia della sede apostolica* (Rome, 1554–5).

27. Below, pp. 197–200.

28. Pole's opening address at Trent was translated and edited by Vincent McNabb in the *Dublin Review*, 1936, pp. 152–9.

29. This is the subtitle to the second volume of Professor Mayer's calendar of Pole's correspondence, covering the years 1547–54: Mayer (ed), *Correspondence of Reginald Pole*.

30. Mayer, *Cardinal Pole in European Context*, chs 4 and 5 (separately paginated).

31. Edward Gee (ed), *The Jesuit's Memorial for the Reformation of England* (London, 1690), pp. 20–3.

32. For the scale, impact and significance of the deprivations of married clergy under Mary, see Helen L. Parish, *Clerical Marriage and the English Reformation* (Aldershot, 2000), pp. 186–224.

33. Foxe [1583], p. 1950.

34. Below, pp. 50–54.

35. Foxe [1583], p. 1588.

36. Christina Garrett, *The Marian Exiles* (Cambridge, 1938).

37. Ibid., pp. 11–12; *Calendar of State Papers Spanish*, vol XIII, p. 217.

38. Foxe [1583], p. 1564.

39. ODNB; Foxe [1583], p. 1420.

40. ODNB; Foxe [1583], p. 1499.

41. ODNB. Barlow's very circumstantial recantation, repudiating each of his protestant writings, was printed in Strype, *Ecclesiastical Memorials*, vol III, part 1, pp. 242–3. His early, anti-Lutheran treatise, *A Dyaloge Descrybyng the Orygynall Ground of these Lutheran Faccyons* (London, 1553), RSTC 1461 and 1462, was reissued by John Cawood, the Queen's printer, late in 1553, probably as part of Barlow's (temporary) rehabilitation.

42. Bale's comments are in *Scriptorum Illustrium Maioris Britanniae . . . Catalogus*, 2 vols (Basel, 1557–9), vol II, p. 112: '*Ioannes Baroetus, Linnae in Nordouolgia ex honesta familia prognatus, atque inter Carmelitas sodales illic & Cantabrigiae ad theologiae doctoratum usque nutritus, optimeque institutus, relucente tandem Dei ueritate, inter primos cum*

Simone quodam Euangelicum dogma suscepit. Nunc autem, quo uertiginis spiritu ductus nescio, tanquam uilissimus canis, ad uomitum est reuersus.' I owe this reference to my pupil Mr Oliver Wort.

43. Ralph Houlbrooke, 'The Clergy, the Church Courts, and the Marian Restoration in Norwich', in Duffy and Loades (eds), *Church of Mary Tudor*, pp. 124–46.

44. Wallace T. MacCaffrey, *Exeter, 1540–1640: The Growth of an English Country Town*, 2nd edn (Cambridge, MA, 1975), p. 189.

45. Foxe [1583], p. 1984.

46. *Original Letters Relative to the English Reformation, Written During the Reigns of King Henry VIII, King Edward VI, and Queen Mary: Chiefly from the Archives of Zurich* (Parker Society, 1847), p. 515.

47. Thomas Sampson, *A Letter to the Trew Professors of Christes Gospell Inhabitinge in the Parishe off Allhallows in Bredstrete in London* (Strasbourg, 1554), RSTC 21683, sig Aiii.

48. Thomas Becon, *A Comfortable Epistle, too Goddes Faythfull people in Englande* (Wesel, 1554), RSTC 1716, sigs Aii–Aii (v).

49. Foxe [1570], p. 1947.

50. Brett Usher, 'John Jewel Junked', *Journal of Ecclesiastical History*, 59, July 2008, p. 503.

51. Gina Alexander, 'Bonner and the Marian Persecutions' in Haigh, *English Reformation Revised*, p. 169; Brigden, *London and the Reformation*, p. 563. Brigden, whom I follow here, puts the numbers of convinced London protestants higher than Alexander.

52. Ash Wednesday fell on 27 February 1555.

53. *The Declaration of the Bishop of London*, RSTC 3280.3, held at the Parker Library, Corpus Christi College, Cambridge. This is the only surviving copy of the original printed broadsheet and has manuscript alterations by Thomas Thirlby, bishop of Ely, adapting Bonner's text for the Ely diocese: Thirlby left the date unaltered, which indicates that he was working from an early printing of Bonner's draft. Bonner's original is in Foxe [1583], p. 1531.

54. 'Instructions for the Curates', printed broadsheet, York Minster Library, RSTC 26098.7, articles iv–vi. The instructions assume the reconciliation with Rome as an accomplished fact and so the document dates from the beginning of Lent 1555: the

RSTC suggested date of 1554 is correct only if the Old Style dating of the New Year from 25 March is observed.

55. L. E. Whatmore (ed), *Archdeacon Harpsfield's Visitation Returns 1557* (Catholic Record Society, 1950, 1951), *passim*.

56. Vat Lat 5968, fol 379v.

57. Gerald Bray (ed), *The Anglican Canons 1529–1947*, Church of England Record Society, vol 6 (Woodbridge, 1998), pp. 102–5; David Wilkins, *Concilia Magnae Brittaniae et Hiberniae*, vol IV (London, 1737), pp. 123, 145–6.

58. On this subject, see my essay 'Cardinal Pole Preaching', in Duffy and Loades, *Church of Mary Tudor*, pp. 176–200.

59. Edmund Bonner, *Interrogatories upon which . . . Churchwardens shalbe Charged* (London, 1558), RSTC 10117, no. 47.

60. Nichols, *Diary of Henry Machyn*, pp. 49, 58, 66, 69, 73, 74, 75, 78, 79, 88, 97–8, 100, 131, 132, 139, 165, 168; Miles Hogarde, *The Displaying of the Protestants* (London, 1556), RSTC 13557, fol 119v.

61. Nichols, *Diary of Henry Machyn*, p. 131.

62. Order from Philip and Mary to JPs of Norfolk, 25 March 1555, in Gilbert Burnet, *The History of the Reformation of the Church of England* (London, 1850), vol II, p. cclxxi; APC, vol V, p. 148.

63. Foxe [1583], pp. 1616–17.

64. CRP, vol III, nos 1096, 1166.

65. Ibid., no. 243.

66. Foxe [1583], pp. 1998, 1716; the examinations of Wolsey and Pygot, in which Pecock took part, are documented in Cambridge University Library, Ely Diocesan Register G 1/8, fols 81–3v.

67. BL Harley Ms 416, fols 123–4v, quoted in Patrick Collinson, 'The Persecution in Kent', in Duffy and Loades, *Church of Mary Tudor*, pp. 327–8.

68. Foxe [1583], p. 1998.

69. John Olde, *The Acquital or Purgation of the Moost Catholyke Christen Prince Edward VI* ('Waterford' [Emden], 1555), RSTC 18797, sig A2.

70. Loades, *Reign of Mary Tudor*, pp. 292–3.

71. For which, see the essay by Claire Cross, 'The English Universities 1553–58', in Duffy and Loades, *Church of Mary Tudor*, pp. 57–76; Elizabeth Russell, 'Marian Oxford and the Counter-Reformation',

in C. M. Baron and C. Harper Bill (eds), *The Church in Pre-Reformation Society* (Woodbridge, 1998), pp. 212–27. The Marian visitation of the University of Cambridge is documented in John Lamb (ed), *A Collection of Letters, Statutes and Other Documents . . . Illustrative of the History of the University of Cambridge* (London, 1838), pp. 177–274.

72. J. Brodrick, *St Peter Canisius* (London, 1935), pp. 168–218, and esp. pp. 211–14, for a letter of St Ignatius to Canisius in August 1554, advocating very much the same kinds of measures against protestants in Austria as were being adopted in England. This notorious letter became a matter of intense controversy between catholics and protestants during the *Kulturkampf* in nineteenth-century Germany.

73. Thomas F. Mayer, 'The Success of Cardinal Pole's Final Legation', in Duffy and Loades, *Church of Mary Tudor*, pp. 149–75: he was correcting the conclusions of Rex Pogson, 'Cardinal Pole'.

74. The address was translated by Vincent McNabb as 'Cardinal Pole's Eirenikon', *Dublin Review*, 1936, pp. 149–60.

75. For debate about the demographic impact of the epidemics of 1556–9, see J. S. Moore, 'Jack Fisher's 'Flu: A Visitation Revisited', *Economic History Review*, 46, 1993, pp. 280–307; M Zell, 'Fisher's Flu and Moore's Probates: Quantifying the Mortality Crisis of 1556–60', *Economic History Review*, 47, 1994, pp. 354–8; J. S. Moore, 'Jack Fisher's 'Flu: A Virus Still Virulent', *Economic History Review*, 47, 1994, pp. 359–61.

76. David Loades, 'The Marian Episcopate', in Duffy and Loades, *Church of Mary Tudor*, pp. 33–56; Joseph Bergin, *The Making of the French Episcopate* (New Haven and London, 1996), *passim*; idem, 'The Counter-Reformation Church and its Bishops', *Past and Present*, 165, 1999, pp. 30–73.

77. Bray, *Anglican Canons*, pp. 156–9.

78. Haigh, *English Reformations*, p. 225; G. E. Aylmer and Reginald Cant (eds), *A History of York Minster* (Oxford, 1977), p. 203. For the slow implementation of seminary foundation elsewhere, see Kathleen M. Comerford, 'Italian Tridentine Diocesan Seminaries: A Historiographical Study', *Sixteenth Century Journal*, 29, Winter 1998, pp. 999–1022; Xenio Toscani, 'I seminari e il clero secolare in Lombardia nei secoli XVI–XIX', in A. Caprioli, A. Rimoldi and L. Vaccaro (eds), *Chiesa e società: appunti per una storia delle diocesi Lombarde* (Brescia, 1986), pp. 215–62, and the same author's 'Recenti studi sui seminari italiani in età moderna', *Annali di Storia dell'Educazione e delle Istituzione Scholastiche*, 7, 2000, pp. 281–307; P. T. Hoffman, *Church and Community in the Diocese of Lyon, 1500–1789* (New Haven, 1984), pp. 74–8.

79. John Feckenham was in trouble with the Privy Council on 29 November 1554 for a sermon on this theme. APC, vol IV, p. 85.

80. Rex Pogson, 'Revival and Reform in Mary Tudor's Church: A Question of Money', in Haigh, *English Reformation Revised*, p. 141.

81. Hugh Glasier, *A Notable and Very Fruitefull Sermon Made at Paules Cross, the XXV Day of August* (London, 1555), RSTC 11916.5, sigs Ev (v)–Evi.

82. Details of Pole's remission of First Fruits and the reallocations of surpluses are in Wilkins, *Concilia*, vol IV, pp. 175–6. For the financial measures in general, see Pogson, 'Revival and Reform', pp. 146–50; CRP, vol 3, nos 1337 (Pole to Morone, 9 August 1555) and 1344 (Pole to (Goldwell?), late summer 1555); Jennifer Loach, *Parliament and the Crown in the Reign of Mary Tudor* (Oxford, 1986), pp. 135–7.

83. PRO SP 69/11, fol 119, Sir Edward Carne to Mary, 11 December 1557, quoted in Pogson, 'Cardinal Pole', pp. 97–8, though Pogson does not make this connection.

Notes to Chapter 2

1. A main theme of Thomas F. Mayer's *Reginald Pole, Prince and Prophet* (Cambridge, 2000).

2. *Calendar of State Papers Spanish*, vol XIII, pp. 366, 370.

3. Thomas F. Mayer, *Cardinal Pole in European Context* (Aldershot, 2000), ch. 1, p. 116.

4. Thomas M. McCoog, 'Ignatius Loyola and Reginald Pole: A Reconsideration', *Journal of Ecclesiastical History*, 17, 1996, pp. 257–73; Thomas Mayer, 'A Test of Wills: Pole, Loyola and the Jesuits in England' in T. M. McCoog, *The Reckoned Expense* (Woodbridge, 1996), pp. 21–8.

5. Rex H. Pogson, 'Reginald Pole and the Priorities of Government in Mary Tudor's Church', *Historical Journal*, 18, 1975, p. 20.

6. Ibid., pp. 19, 18, 13, 16.

7. David Loades, *The Reign of Mary Tudor*, 2nd edn (London, 1991), pp. 272, 276, 293.

8. Christopher Haigh, *English Reformations: Religion, Politics and Society under the Tudors* (Oxford, 1993), p. 224.

9. Diarmaid MacCulloch, *The Later Reformation in England, 1547–1603*, 2nd edn (London, 2001), p. 20. But MacCulloch offers a much more positive account of Pole's regime in *Reformation: Europe's House Divided, 1490–1700* (Harmondsworth 2003), pp. 280–6.

10. For example, Mayer, 'A Test of Wills', pp. 21–37, esp. pp. 21, 27–8, 32.

11. CRP, vol III, nos 1036, 1266; W. J. Young (ed), *Letters of St Ignatius of Loyola* (Chicago, 1959), pp. 361–2; *Epistolarum*, vol V, pp. 117–18. For Ignatius's larger aspirations, see McCoog, 'Loyola and Pole', pp. 259–62. A generation later, Robert Parsons would see the reconversion of England in the same way as a launching pad for the recovery for the church of the rest of north-eastern Europe: Edward Gee, *The Jesuit's Memorial for the Reformation of England* (London, 1690) pp. 148–51.

12. Archivio Segreto Vaticano, Misc Arm. 11, fols 34r–35r, transcribed in John P. Marmion, 'The London Synod of Cardinal Pole', unpublished MA thesis, Keele University, 1974, pp. 100–2.

13. Reported by Nicholas Harpsfield, citing a letter of Pole's written after the conclave of 1550 – the letter itself has not been identified and occurs neither in *Epistolarum Reginaldi Poli* nor in Mayer's Calendar of the *Correspondence of Reginald Pole*: citation in Nicholas Pocock (ed), *A Treatise on the Pretended Divorce between Henry VIII and Catharine of Aragon, by Nicholas Harpsfield DD* (Camden Society, 1878), p. 296.

14. In thinking about Pole's intellectual priorities, I have benefited both from the Revd Dr Dermot Fenlon's seminal *Heresy and Obedience in Tridentine Italy: Cardinal Pole and the Counter Reformation* (Cambridge, 1972), and from a number of invaluable email exchanges.

15. CRP, vol II, no. 595, pp. 98–9; *Epistolarum*, vol IV, pp. 65–73.

16. For the manuscripts and publication history, see Thomas F. Mayer, 'A Reluctant Author: Cardinal Pole and his Manuscripts', *Transactions of the American Philosophical Society*, NS, 89, 1999, pp. 43–7; quotations are from the English translation by J. G. Dwyer, *Pole's Defence of the Unity of the Church* (Westminster, MD, 1965).

17. He told Henry Cole in 1537 that, when he began to write the *De Unitate*, he had considered 'the pope's authority for a human constitution and adiaphoron', but that as he wrote the Holy Spirit had shown him otherwise: CRP, vol I, no. 115, p. 113. For the account that Pole received from Antonio Buonvisi of Thomas More's similar conversion to belief in a *jure-divino* papal primacy, see Strype, *Ecclesiastical Memorials*, Vol III, part 2, pp. 492–3.

18. CRP, vol II, nos 601–4, pp. 102–20.

19. Matthew 16:18, 'Thou art Peter, and upon this rock I will build my church'; John 21:35, 'Feed my lambs, feed my sheep'; and Luke 22:32, 'But I have prayed for thee, that thy faith may not fail'.

20. Dwyer, *Pole's Defence of the Unity of the Church*, pp. 185, 237 and *passim*.

21. Ibid., p. 69.

22. Ibid., pp. 247, 287.

23. Ibid., pp. 95, 106n, 255: Pole was drawing here on accounts of the legendary British King Lucius alluded to in Bede and the *Liber Pontificalis*, and elaborated by Geoffrey of Monmouth: see Ernest Jones, 'Geoffrey of Monmouth's Account of the Establishment of Episcopacy in Britain', *Journal of English and German Philology*, 40, 1941, pp. 360–3; Shafer Williams, 'Geoffrey of Monmouth and Canon Law', *Speculum*, 27, 1952, pp. 184–90. Felicity Heal, 'What Can King Lucius Do for You? The Reformation and the Early British Church', *English Historical Review*, 120, 2005, pp.

593–614 deals with the use of the story in reformation polemic: Heal is aware of the later influence of Pole's use of the Lucius and Eleutherius legend in his speech to Parliament in 1554, but misses his earlier deployment of it in *De Unitate*.

24. Dwyer, *Pole's Defence of the Unity of the Church*, pp. 241, 245, 254–5; for the innovative character of Pole's thought here, see Brad S. Gregory, *Salvation at Stake* (Cambridge, MA, 1999), pp. 265–8.

25. Behind Pole's hostility to Henry's settlement lay a broader hostility to Machiavellianism: see Adriano Prosperi, 'Il principe, il cardinale, il papa: Reginald Pole lettore di Machiavelli', in *Cultura e scrittura di Machiavelli: Atti del Convegno di Firenze–Pisa 27–30 ottobre 1997* (Rome, 1998), pp. 241–62; Peter Donaldson, *Machiavelli and the Mystery of State* (Cambridge, 1988).

26. *Calendar of State Papers Spanish*, vol XI, p. 130. It should be noted, however, that Northumberland's speech traced the religious ills of England back into Henry's reign, and not merely Edward's.

27. Ibid., p. 216.

28. CRP, vol II, no. 634, p. 137 (Pole to Parpaglia, 7 August 1553).

29. I paraphrase the long Latin text as printed in M. A. Tierney (ed), *Dodd's Church History of England*, vol II (London, 1839), pp. xciv–xcvi; CRP, vol. II, no. 649, pp. 161–3.

30. CRP vol II, no. 759, p. 230.

31. Ibid., no. 664, pp. 171–2.

32. Vat Lat 5968, fol 171.

33. *Calendar of State Papers Spanish*, vol XI, pp. 419–22.

34. Latin text of Mary's letter of 15 November in Tierney, *Dodd's Church History*, vol II, pp. cii–civ; CRP, vol II, no. 757, pp. 228–9.

35. Tierney, *Dodd's Church History*, vol II, p. ciii.

36. Vat Lat 5968, fols 172–3.

37. TRP, vol II, no. 407, pp. 36, 37.

38. David Loades, *Mary Tudor: The Tragical History of the First Queen of England* (Kew, 2006), p. 107.

39. Foxe [1583], p. 1428.

40. The greatest protestant publicity coup of the reign was the swift production in the autumn of 1553 of a translation of Gardiner's 1535 tract *De Vera Obedientia*, in defence of the Royal Supremacy, with Edmund Bonner's preface, and with a commentary contrasting Gardiner and Bonner's present attitudes with their support for Henry's schism in the 1530s: the edition was probably the work of John Bale. This embarrassing ghost from the Henrician past ran through three editions by the end of the year: *De Vera Obediencia an Oration . . . Marke the Notes in the Margine* (London?, 1553), RSTC 11585–7.

41. James Arthur Muller (ed), *The Letters of Stephen Gardiner* (Cambridge, 1933), p. 352.

42. John Gough Nichols (ed), *Narratives of the Days of the Reformation* (Camden Society, 1869), p. 182.

43. J. A. Muller, *Stephen Gardiner and the Tudor Reaction* (London, 1926), p. 223.

44. *Calendar of State Papers Spanish*, vol XII, p. 170.

45. Foxe [1583], p. 1425.

46. Muller, *Stephen Gardiner and the Tudor Reaction*, p. 60.

47. Pole was making a scriptural allusion here to the Song of Songs, in a passage that identified the Queen as God's chosen instrument: Song of Songs 6:8–9: 'My perfect one is but one. She is the only one of her mother, the chosen of her that bore her . . . who is she that cometh forth as the morning rising, *fair as the moon*, bright as the sun, terrible as an army set in array?'

48. *Letters of Stephen Gardiner*, pp. 496–501; for the publication history of Pole's treatise, see Mayer, *Reluctant Author*, pp. 75–80.

49. *Letters of Stephen Gardiner*, pp. 464–7; Pole's reply, rejecting '*moderatione alcuna*' where the unity of the church was at stake, is in CRP, vol II, no. 867, pp. 292–3.

50. CRP, vol II, no. 778, pp. 244–7. The editor does not discuss whether it was used, but notes Jennifer Loach's description of it as a 'draft of a speech made to parliament at the absolution' (Loach, *Parliament and the Crown in the Reign of Mary Tudor* (Oxford, 1986), p. 175): full text in Vat Lat 5968, fols 107–27, quotation in text from fol 120. This version is much more forceful than the final address to Parliament: Loach considered that the intransigence about church property reflected in it may have delayed agreement over the reconciliation.

51. Foxe [1583], pp. 1472–3; John Gough Nichols (ed), *The Chronicle of Queen Jane* (Camden Society, 1850), pp. 78–9.

52. I have used the expanded text, probably prepared for publication, in Vat Lat 5968, fols 305–59. Versions of the speech circulated widely and it was eagerly reported: for other versions, see the editorial matter in CPR, vol II, no. 991, pp. 366–8.

53. Vat Lat 5968, fols 309–11.

54. Ibid., fols 322v–6v.

55. Ibid., fols 335v–45.

56. Ibid., fols 352–3.

57. Ibid., fols 354–5. Pole's reference here to the need for Englishmen to show the same signs of their reconversion as the converts in the earlier church had done is a coded reference to the need for them to re-endow the church with wealth stolen from the monasteries: compare Vat Lat 5968, fol 119: 'And what rigorousness is this to persuade yow to do the lyke in goodes unlawfully gotten that the primitive multitude of the churche dyd with their goodes lawfully possessed . . . which the vereye lawes do bynd you unto, as it were for the fruycte of renovation of the churche in the realme that might followe hereof, and as I doubt not should follow, whereby yow shuld be a light and a myrrour to the rest of all Christendom.'

58. George Marshall, *A Compendious Treatise in Metre Declaring the Firste Originall of Sacrifice, and of the Building of Aultares and Churches, and of the Firste Receavinge of the Christen Fayth in England by GM* (London, 1554), RSTC 17469, sig Biii.

59. See, for example, the description of the effects of the schism in the homily on the authority of the church (by Henry Pendleton): *Homilies Sette Forth by the Right Reverende Father in God, Edmunde Byshop of London* (London, 1555), RSTC 3285.7, fols 41v–42.

60. Ibid., fols 53v–54.

61. Foxe [1583], p. 1531.

62. Richard Rex, 'Morley and the Papacy: Rome, Regime and Religion', in Marie Axton and James P. Carley (eds), '*Triumphs of English*': *Henry Parker, Lord Morley, Translator to the Tudor Court* (London, 2000), pp. 87–105, though the connection to Pole, however, is not made. Morley's 'Treatise

on the Miracles of the Sacrament' is printed on pp. 253–69.

63. Quotation at p. 255, King Lucius at p. 257, though Pope Eleutherius is not mentioned by name.

64. For Morley's motivation, see Rex's comments in 'Morley and the Papacy', pp. 87–9.

65. Thomas Martin, *A Traictise Declaring and Plainly Proving, that the Pretensed Marriage of Priestes, and Professed Persons, is no Marriage* (London, 1554), RSTC 17517, sigs Aiiii–Aiiii (v).

66. A response came in John Ponet, *An Apologie Fully Aunsweringe . . . a Blasphemous Book* (Emden, 1556), RSTC 20175, pp. 166–74. Ponet pointedly asked why, if Henry was a originator of schism and a heretic, his body had not been exhumed but remained undisturbed in the royal chapel at Windsor.

67. *Chronicle of Queen Jane*, p. 82.

68. Foxe [1583], p. 1520.

69. Ibid., p. 1708.

70. Ibid., p. 1589.

71. Ibid., p. 1828.

72. Pocock, *A Treatise on the Pretended Divorce* was written as a pendant to Harpsfield's *Life of More*, putting in all the invective that had been deliberately excluded from the *Life*, and was completed in 1557 or 1558 (clear from references to the completed *Life* and to Mary as still reigning). It proclaimed its closeness to Pole himself by discussion of the conclave in which he was offered the papacy, and by quotation from his unpublished correspondence (pp. 295–6). For the story of Ahab, see 1 Kings 16:29–22:38 (the reference to dogs licking his blood is at 1 Kings 22:37); the reference to dogs licking Henry's blood is in the *Treatise*, p. 203. Like the rest of Harpsfield's extraordinary Marian writings, the *Treatise* had not reached print by the time of the Queen's death, and remained in manuscript form until the nineteenth century. Its language and ideas gained currency in counter-reformation Europe, however, as one of the major sources for Nicholas Sander's enormously influential *De Origine ac Progressio Schismatis Anglicani*. See Christopher Highley, 'A Pestilent and Seditious Book: Nicholas Sander's *Schis-*

matis Anglicani and Catholic Histories of the Reformation', *Huntington Library Quarterly*, 68, 2005, pp. 151–71.

73. W. H. Frere and W. M. Kennedy, *Visitation Articles and Injunctions of the Period of the Reformation*, Alcuin Club collections, vols 14–16 (London, 1908–10), vol II, p. 401.

74. The exception is Mayer, *Reginald Pole*, pp. 246–50.

75. See my 'Cardinal Pole Preaching' in E. Duffy and D. Loades, *The Church of Mary Tudor* (Aldershot, 2006), pp. 176–200.

76. *Epistolarum*, vol V, pp. 72–3. [*Ego vero qui quotidie magis experientia disco, qui sit infecti atque infirmi hujus corporis status, hoc reperio, ubi major est verbi copia, ibi minus homines proficere, ea abutentes; quod nusquam magis videmus accidere, quam Londini; nec tamen nego necessarium esse verbi praedicationem, sed nisi vel ante sit, vel simul constituta Ecclesiastica disciplina, dico potius obesse verbum, quam prodesse, quia hoc carnales homines ad inanem aurium delectationem, non ad salutarem animi disciplinam, et alimentum transferunt.*]

77. Mayer, *Reginald Pole*, p. 250.

78. Vat Lat 5968, fols 277r–303v.

79. No manuscript now survives, but Strype printed it (in a copious but incomplete state) from Foxe's papers: *Ecclesiastical Memorials*, vol III, part 2, pp. 482–510.

80. Vat Lat 5968, fols 379–99 (scribal copy; for other drafts, see Mayer, *Reluctant Author*, p. 70, item a).

81. Vat Lat 5968, fols 277r–303v.

82. Ibid., fols 419–41 ('Secunda Omelia') and 446–82v ('Homilia Tertia Angliae [*sic*]'.

83. Vat Lat 5968, fols 444–5.

84. Ibid., fol 449.

85. Eg ibid., fols 230–1v.

86. '*Parvuli petierunt panem, et non erat qui frangeret illis*' (Lamentations 4:4).

87. Vat Lat 5968, fols 379r–v.

88. Ibid., fols 396v–7.

89. Ibid., fols 398v–9.

90. Ibid., fols 420v–1.

91. Ibid., fols 421, 427v, 432v.

92. Ibid., fol 429.

93. Deuteronomy 32:7.

94. Vat Lat 5968, fols 421r–v.

95. Ibid., fols 459–78v.

96. Ibid., fols 467r–v.

97. See below, chs 3 and 4.

98. Vat Lat 5968, fols 444r–v.

NOTES TO CHAPTER 3

1. Edward J. Baskerville, *A Chronological Bibliography of Propaganda and Polemic Published in English between 1553 and 1558* (Philadelphia, 1979).

2. Jennifer Loach, 'The Marian Establishment and the Printing Press', *English Historical Review*, 100, 1986, pp. 138–51; J. W. Martin, 'The Marian Regime's Failure to Understand the Importance of Printing', *Huntington Library Quarterly*, 154, 1980–1, pp. 231–47.

3. But see D. M. Loades, 'The Theory and Practice of Censorship in Sixteenth-century England', *Transactions of the Royal Historical Society*, 5th series, 24, 1974, pp. 141–57.

4. TRP, vol II, no. 390, pp. 5–8.

5. TRP, vol II, no. 407, p. 36.

6. P. M. Took, 'Government and the Printing Trade, 1540–1560', unpublished PhD thesis, University of London, 1978, pp. 271–99.

7. Ibid., pp. 225–8.

8. RSTC 16079–16086, 17629, 17629.5.

9. I am indebted to Peter Blayney for permission to cite these figures from his unpublished paper, 'The English Book Trade under Edward VI and Mary I'.

10. Baskerville, *Chronological Bibliography*, pp. 34, 40, 85.

11. RSTC 16215–9; and see Plates 12 and 13.

12. RSTC 16244–50, 16252 (Use of York).

13. RSTC 16151–6.

14. RSTC 15836–47, 15860 (Use of York).

15. RSTC nos 16058–16086.

16. E. Duffy, *The Voices of Morebath: Reformation and Rebellion in an English Village* (New Haven and London, 2001), pp. 167–8.

17. I have in mind such works as RSTC 5160.3, J. Hooper (?), *Whether Christian Faith Maye be Kept Secret*; RSTC 10016, *A Letter Sent from a Banished Minister*; RSTC 15059, John Knox, *An Admonition or Warning*; RSTC 1730, Thomas Becon, *A Comfortable Epistle*; RSTC 21683, Thomas Sampson, *A Letter to the Trew Professors of Christes Gospell*.

18. *The Saying of John, Late Duke of Northumberlande upon the Scaffolde* (London, 1553), RSTC 7283.

19. RSTC 13557–8 (Hogarde) and RSTC 24754 (Proctor).

20. *The Workes of Sir T More . . . Written by Him in the Englysh Tonge* (London, 1557), RSTC 18076.

21. A. G. Dickens, *The English Reformation*, 2nd edn (London, 1989), p. 312.

22. David Loades, *The Reign of Mary Tudor*, 2nd edn (London, 1991), p. 286.

23. Alison Shell, *Catholicism, Controversy and the English Literary Imagination, 1558–1660* (Cambridge, 1999).

24. Baskerville, *Chronological Bibliography*, pp. 9–10.

25. Foxe [1583], p. 1708.

26. Neither Lucy Wooding, *Rethinking Catholicism in Reformation England* (Oxford, 2000) nor William Wizeman, *The Theology and Spirituality of Mary Tudor's Church* (Aldershot, 2006) draw on the evidence of the heresy trials.

27. RSTC 24754–5, John Proctor (translator and editor), *The Waie Home to Christ and Truth Leadinge from Antichrist and Errour, Made and Set Furth in the Latine Tongue by that Famous and Great Clarke, Vincent . . . Above XI Hundred Yeres Paste* (London, 1554), sig Aiii (v). Vincent of Lerin's appeal to the universal assent of the ages and of the whole of Christendom – 'quod semper, quod ubique, quod ab omnes' – was fundamental for the Marian church's apologetic. Another translation was published by Tottel in the same year as Proctor's first edition: *A Boke Written by one Vincentius Leriniensis* (London, 1554), RSTC 24747.

28. John Standish, *A Discourse Wherein is Debated Whether the Scripture Should be in English* (London, 1554), RSTC 23207, 2nd edn 23208.

29. *The Triall of the Supremacy Wherein is Set Fourth the Unitie of Christes Church* (London, 1556), RSTC 23211.

30. I base this deduction on the list of Marshe's titles given in RSTC, vol III, p. 115. Marshe was in trouble with the Privy Council for what appears to have been opportunistic pirating of Thomas Watson's *Holsome and Catholike Doctrine* in the summer of 1558: see below, p. 69.

31. The most reliable guide to the contents and main contentions of this Marian catholic writing is Wizeman, *Theology and Spirituality of Mary Tudor's Church*, though its otherwise helpful thematic treatment of the material inevitably militates somewhat against a contextualised reading of individual texts.

32. *A Necessary Doctrine and Erudicion for any Chrysten Man Set Furth by the Kynges Maiestye* (London, 1543), RSTC 5176.

33. Ibid., sigs Fiv (v)–Gii(v).

34. Edmund Bonner, *A Profitable and Necessarye Doctryne with Certayne Homelies Adioyned Therevnto* (London, 1555), RSTC 3283.3, sigs Siv (v)–Aaii (v).

35. Ronald B. Bond (ed), *Certain Sermons or Homilies (1547)* (Toronto, 1987), p. 79.

36. Edmund Bonner, *Homelies Sette Forth by the Righte Reuerende Father in God, Edmund Byshop of London* (London, 1555), RSTC 3285.7, fols 13v–16v.

37. *An Honest Godlye Instruction, and Information for the Tradynge, and Bringinge vp of Children* (London, 1556), RSTC 3281.

38. *The Prymer in Englyshe for Children, After the Use of Salisburye* (London, 1556), RSTC 16075, 16075.5.

39. Bartolomé Carranza de Miranda, *Commentarios sobre el catechismo christiano*, ed. José Ignacio Tellechea Idígoras, 2 vols (Madrid, 1972); *Epistolarum*, vol V, p. 74.

40. Legatine Constitutions of Cardinal Pole, printed in Gerald Bray (ed), *The Anglican Canons 1529–1947*, Church of England Record Society, vol 6 (Woodbridge, 1998), pp. 104–5; CRP, vol III, p. 545; *Epistolarum*, vol V, p. 74.

41. Thomas Watson, *Holsome and Catholyke Doctryne Concernynge the Seven Sacraments of Chrystes Churche* (London, 1558), RSTC 25112, 25112.5, 25114 (official eds); 25112.5 (pirated edition by Kingston and Walsh – see APC, vol V, p. 346. For a discussion of Watson's sermons, see the essay by William Wizeman in E. Duffy and D. Loades (eds), *The Church of Mary Tudor* (Aldershot, 2006) pp. 258–80.

42. Watson, *Holsome and Catholyke Doctryne*, fols 61v–62.

43. John Dudley, *The Sayinge of John Late Duke of Northumberlande* RSTC 7283 (unpaginated).

44. John Christopherson, *An Exhortation to All Menne to Take Hede and Beware of Rebellion* (London, 1554), RSTC 5207, sigs

Tiii–iii (v), Tvi (v)–Tvii (v).

45. As in John Proctor's fighting preface to Vincent of Lerin's *Commonitary*, a key text for the Marian church, which Proctor translated as *The Waie Home to Christ and Truth from Antichrist and Errour* (London, 1554), RSTC 24754–5. 'But in Englande I am perfecte and none of you can sai nay and saie truth: but that ye have growen in wickeddnes as ye have growen in this newe religion, in somuch that there was never such unthriftines in servauntes, suche unnaturalness in childen, suche unruliness in subiectes, suche fierceness in enemies, suche unfaithfulness in frendes... Have thei not broken many good and godlye ordenaunces, and set uppe none? Have they not caused for greate concorde and unitie, great tumulte and rebellious sedition? For godly fasting, riotous feasting? For devoute praiying, pevishe prating? For peace, God's plenty and inough: warre, dearth and famine more than inough? I write and wepe in my harte to considre, what may be written of the wretched condition and state that our countrie hath been in of late yeres' (sigs Bv–Bvi).

46. Foxe [1583], p. 1876.

47. See the king's arms in Christopherson, *An Exhortation*, sig Vi (v); for the beards and wives, see John Proctor, *The Waie Home to Christ and Truth*, sig Biii (v), and the anonymous conservative narrative of the reformation in Worcester, cited in Diarmaid MacCulloch, 'Worcester: A Cathedral City in the Reformation', in Patrick Collinson and John Craig (eds), *The Reformation in English Towns, 1500–1640* (London, 1998), p. 106.

48. Foxe [1583], p. 1765.

49. James Brookes, *A Sermon Very Notable, Fruitefull and Godlie* (London, 1553), RSTC 3838, sig Dvi (v).

50. Proctor, *Waie Home to Christ*, sig Biii.

51. *Displaying of the Protestantes with a Description of Divers of their Abuses* (London, 1556), RSTC 13557, fols 72v–75.

52. James Cancellar, *The Pathe of Obedience* (London, 1556), RSTC 4564, sig Ciii (v).

53. *An Exclamation upon the Erroneous and Fantasticall Sprite of Heresy* [O Heresy with Frenzy], RSTC 10615, in Hyder

E. Rollins (ed), *Old English Ballads, 1553–1625* (Cambridge, 1920), no. 6, quotation at pp. 30–1.

54. A. G. Dickens, 'Robert Parkyn's Narrative of the Reformation', in *Reformation Studies* (London, 1982), p. 304.

55. Jane Wilson (ed), *Sermons very Fruitfull, Godly and Learned by Roger Edgeworth* (Cambridge, 1993), p. 365.

56. J. W. Martin, 'Miles Hogarde: Artisan and Aspiring Author in Sixteenth-century England', *Renaissance Quarterly*, 34, 1981, pp. 359–83.

57. For a discussion of this Wayland Primer, see E. Duffy, *The Stripping of the Altars: Traditional Religion in England 1400–1570* (New Haven and London, 1992), pp. 537–43.

58. *A Plaine and Godlye Treatise Concernynge the Masse* (London, 1555), RSTC 17629 and 17629.5 (separate printings); *The Primer in Englishe (After the Use of Sarum) Whereunto is Added a Treatise Concerning the Masse* (London, 1555), RSTC 16063–5.

59. RSTC 16064, sig Riii.

60. Below, pp. 166–8.

NOTES TO CHAPTER 4

1. In calculating the numbers, I have relied on the list prepared for the John Foxe Project by Dr Tom Freeman, to whom I am indebted for access to that list.

2. Gina Alexander, 'Bonner and the Marian Persecutions', in Christopher Haigh (ed), *The English Reformation Revised*, Cambridge 1987, p. 175.

3. John Christopherson, *An Exhortation to All Menne to Take Hede and Beware of Rebellion* (London, 1554), RSTC 5207, sig ciij.

4. Foxe [1583], p. 1528.

5. Andrew Pettegree, *Marian Protestantism: Six Studies* (Aldershot, 1996), p. 162 (my emphasis – the adverb is as tendentious as it is revealing).

6. Ibid.

7. Ibid., p. 161.

8. Ibid., p. 164.

9. Figures from Professor William Monter: see Augustino Borromeo (ed), *L'Inquisizione: Atti del Simposio Internazionale 1998* (Vatican City, 2003), p. 454.

10. ODNB. *Alfonso a Castro Zamorensis, Adversus Omnes Haereses, Libri XIIII* (Antwerp, 1556), sigs Aii–Aiii (v): *De Iusta Haereticorum Punitione Libri III* (Lyon, 1556). Castro believed that only incorrigible heretics should be killed, after every other means of persuasion had been tried and failed, and his sermon may have been influenced by the apparently summary process against the six Essex heretics examined and sentenced by Bonner on 8–9 February 1555.

11. This calculation, based on the cases related in Foxe, would have been almost impossible without the help of the analytical list of martyrs prepared for the Foxe project by Dr Tom Freeman, who generously allowed me access to the list.

12. R. W. Dixon, *History of the Church of England from the Abolition of the Roman Jurisdiction*, vol IV (London, 1891), p. 5; John Bradford, *A Sermon of Repentance* (London, 1553), RSTC 3496, sigs Aii–Aiii.

13. [John Bale], *De Vera Obedientia: An Oration made in Latine by the Right Reverende father in God Stephan Bishop of Winchestre* ('Rome', 1553), RSTC 11587, sig Aii (v).

14. Foxe [1583], p. 1484.

15. TRP, vol II, no. 390, p. 5.

16. APC, vol IV, p. 317.

17. For the soldier and the dagger, see Dixon, *History of the Church of England*, vol IV, p. 17n; John Gough Nichols (ed), *The Diary of Henry Machyn* (Camden Society, 1848), p. 41; Foxe [1583], pp. 1604–5.

18. 1 Mary I, cap 3.

19. Foxe [1583], pp. 1983–4.

20. APC, vol IV, pp. 317–19.

21. Ibid., pp. 322, 327–8, 330, 333, 335–6, 338, 340, 345.

22. Diarmaid MacCulloch, *Thomas Cranmer: A Life* (New Haven and London, 1996), pp. 547–53.

23. Letter of John Newman to the bishop of Dover, in Foxe [1583], p. 1686; for Haukes, see p. 1588; for Bradford, see pp. 1608–9.

24. J. F. Mozley, *John Foxe and his Book* (London, 1940), pp. 35–6, translating Foxe, *Rerum in Ecclesiae Gestarum* (Basel, 1559), p. 202.

25. Strype, *Ecclesiastical Memorials*, vol III, part 2, p. 369.

26. See below, p. 169.

27. Thomas Cranmer, *Miscellaneous Writings and Letters*, (Cambridge, 1846), p. 127.

28. *Calendar of State Papers Venetian*, vol V, p. 392; *Calendar of State Papers Spanish*, vol XI, p. 421.

29. *The Saying of John Late Duke of Northumberlande upon the Scaffolde* (London, 1553), RSTC 7283; John Gough Nichols (ed), *The Chronicle of Queen Jane and of Two Years of Queen Mary* (Camden Society, 1850), pp. 18–19, 21; Richard Garnett (ed), *The Accession of Queen Mary, Being the Contemporary Narrative of Antonio de Guaras, a Spanish Merchant Resident in London* (London, 1892), pp. 105–9.

30. Thomas F. Mayer, *Reginald Pole: Prince and Prophet* (Cambridge, 2000), pp. 282–3; *Chronicle of Queen Jane*, pp. 18–20. The impact of Northumberland's confession and the extent of European protestant dismay can be gauged from the fact that Theodore Beza wrote a treatise to offset the damage – A. H. Chaubard (ed), *Une oeuvre inconnue de Theodore de Beze: Réponse à la confession du feu Jean de Northumberlande, n'agueres decapité en Angleterre* (Lyon, 1959 [edited facsimile]). Other protestant accounts were also quickly in circulation in Germany and caught Lutherans there between dismay at the return of England to catholicism and disapproval of Northumberland's attempted overthrow of a legitimate ruler: Denis Hay, 'The "Narratio Historica" of P. Vincentius, 1553', *English Historical Review*, 63, 1948, pp. 350–6.

31. See above, pp. 11–14.

32. This is the menage of Christopherson's, *An Exhortacion to . . . beware of rebellion* and of Proctor's *Historie of Wyatt's rebellion*.

33. David Wilkins, *Concilia Magnae Brittaniae et Hiberniae* (London, 1737), vol IV, pp. 95–6.

34. *Chronicle of Queen Jane*, p. 54.

35. *Calendar of State Papers Spanish*, vol XII, p. 200.

36. Christopherson, *An Exhortacion to . . . beware of rebellion*, sig Jiii.

37. APC, vol IV, pp. 387, 395.

38. Foxe [1583], p. 1579.

39. Woodman's remark in Foxe [1583], p. 1987; *Certein Godly, Learned and Comfortable Conferences, Between the Two*

*Reuerende Fathers, and Holy Martyrs of
Christe, D. Nicolas Rydley Late Bisshopfe of
London, and M Hughe Latimer, Sometyme
Bisshop of Worcester, During the Tyme of their
Emprisonmentes* (Emden, 1556), RSTC
21047.3; [Myles Coverdale] (ed), *Certain
Most Godly, Fruitful and Comfortable Letters
of Such True Saintes and Holy Martyrs as in
the Late Bloody Persecution Gave their Lyves*
(London, 1564), RSTC 5885. Dr Thomas
Freeman is editing a new collection of
these prison letters as *Letters of the Martyrs*
for the Church of England Record Society.

40. 1 and 2 Philip and Mary, cap 6, printed in
H. Gee and W. H. Hardy, *Documents Illus-
trative of the History of the English Church*
(London, 1896), p. 384.

41. *Calendar of Patent Rolls, Philip and Mary*,
vol III, 1555–7, p. 81.

42. Foxe [1583], pp. 1689, 1805.

43. For the February 1557 Commission, see
Foxe [1583], pp. 1970–1; for the Canter-
bury Commission of 1556, see APC, vol.
III, pp. 24–5, and CRP, vol III, p. 1549b.

44. Printed in Gilbert Burnet, *The History of
the Reformation of the Church of England*
(London, 1850), vol II, p. cclxxiv.

45. David Loades, *The Reign of Mary Tudor*,
2nd edn (London, 1991), pp. 271–2.
Loades is consistent in minimising Pole's
influence over Mary: cf Loades, *Mary
Tudor: The Tragical History of the First Queen
of England* (Kew, 2006), pp. 184–5.

46. For Mary's acceptance of Pole's authority
in relation to her father's reputation, see
above, pp. 39–40. For Pole's letter to the
bishops in September 1555, endorsing
Mary's instructions, see CRP, vol III, no.
1363; *Epistolarum*, vol V, pp. 86–8; and
below, pp. 144–5. For the Venetian ambassador on Mary's dependence on Pole's advice, see *Calendar of State Papers Venetian*,
vol VI, part 1, pp. 391–2. For Pole's account
of his close collaboration with Mary, see
CRP, vol III no. 2252; *Epistolarum*, vol V,
pp. 71–2; and see the discussion of this letter (to Carranza) in my essay, 'Cardinal
Pole Preaching', in E. Duffy and D.
Loades, *The Church of Mary Tudor* (Aldershot, 2006), pp. 176–200, esp. p. 180.

47. APC, vol IV, pp. 322, 327–8, 330, 333, 338,
349, 387, 394, 395, 403; vol V, pp. 17, 61, 88.

48. Strype, *Ecclesiastical Memorials*, vol III, part
1, pp. 338–9; Burnet, *History of the Reformation*, vol II, p. cclxxi.

49. Foxe [1583], p. 1683.

50. Ibid., pp. 1895, 1896, 1912, 1917, 2006.

51. Ibid., pp. 2027, 2072.

52. Ibid., pp. 2089–90.

53. Foxe [1583], p. 1942.

54. Ibid., p. 1486.

55. Ibid., p. 1767.

56. Ibid., pp. 1605–6.

57. Ibid., pp. 1494–9; ODNB.

58. ODNB.

59. Ibid.; John Craig, 'Rowland Taylor's Mar-
ginalia', *Historical Research*, 64, 1991, pp.
411–20.

60. Notably Robert Ferrar, bishop of St
David's at the end of March; in April,
George Marsh, formerly curate to
Lawrence Saunders and conspicuous as
one of the few evangelical activists in Lan-
cashire; and, at the end of May, John
Cardmaker, vicar of St Bride's, Fleet
Street.

61. Foxe [1583], p. 1558.

62. Ibid., p. 1533.

63. Ibid., pp. 1533–4.

64. Ibid., p. 1536.

NOTES TO CHAPTER 5

1. Gilbert Burnet, *The History of the Reformation of the Church of England* (London,
1850), vol II, p. cclxxi.

2. There were, of course, Lollard precedents:
see Anne Hudson (ed), *Two Wycliffite Texts:
The Sermon of William Taylor 1406: The Testimony of William Thorpe 1407* (Oxford,
1993).

3. David Loades, *The Oxford Martyrs* (Lon-
don, 1970), pp. 192–233; Diarmaid Mac-
Culloch, *Thomas Cranmer: A Life* (New
Haven and London, 1996), pp. 554–605.

4. *De Iusta Haereticorum Punitione Libri III. F.
Alfonso a Castro Zamorensis . . . Nunc Recens Accurate Recogniti* (Lyon, 1556),
p. 180: '*secreto . . . et non publicae coram pop-
ulo*' and '*popularem et inanem gloriam cap-
tant, cupiuntque ab omnibus laudari, et pro
doctissimis habere*'.

5. British Library, Harley Ms 421, fols 96r–
98v.

6. Foxe [1583], pp. 2092–3.
7. Ibid., pp. 1539, 1542, 1595, 1602, 1681, 1844.
8. Foxe [1563], p. 1111; Foxe [1583], p. 1539.
9. Foxe [1583], p. 1535, and see the very similar article offered to Pygott, Knight and Lawrence in February 1555 (ibid., p. 1542), which adds the detail that they had been 'a good space in [Bonner's] house, having freely meate and drinke, and also divers times instructed and informed'.
10. Ibid., p. 1595.
11. Foxe was embarrassed by these beliefs, and concealed them: Patrick Collinson, 'The Persecution in Kent', in E. Duffy and D. Loades, *The Church of Mary Tudor* (Aldershot, 2006), pp. 326–31; Harley Ms 421, fols 94v, 95r, 101r–103r; Strype, *Ecclesiastical Memorials*, vol III, part 1, pp. 541–2.
12. Foxe [1583], p. 1588.
13. Ibid., p. 1620.
14. Ibid., p. 1812.
15. Ibid., p. 1821.
16. Foxe [1576], pp. 1770–1, quoted more fully above, p. 72.
17. Foxe [1583], p. 2000.
18. Ibid., p. 1996.
19. Ibid., p. 1578.
20. Ibid., p. 1539.
21. Ibid., pp. 1537–8.
22. Ibid., p. 1912.
23. Ibid., p. 1616.
24. Ibid., p. 1716.
25. Ibid., p. 1895.
26. Ibid., pp. 1911–12.
27. *Calendar of State Papers Spanish*, vol XIII, p. 138.
28. Foxe [1583], p. 1529.
29. *Alfonso a Castro Zamorensis, Adversus Omnes Haereses, Libri XIIII* (Antwerp, 1556).
30. *De Iusta Haereticorum Punitione Libri III*, pp. 180, 356.
31. Burnet, *History of the Reformation*, vol II, p. cclxxiv.
32. Rowena J. Smith, 'The Lambe Speaketh . . . : An English Protestant Satire', *Journal of the Warburg and Courtauld Institutes*, 61, 1998, pp. 261–7; Malcolm Jones, 'The Lambe Speaketh . . . : An Addendum', *Journal of the Warburg and Courtauld Institutes*, 63, 2000, pp. 287–94; *The Huntyng of*

the *Romyshe Vuolfe, Made by Wylliam Turner Doctour of Phisik* (Emden, 1555?), RSTC 24356; and see Plates 28 and 29. The print, in its original Latin-text format, survives *in situ* only in the Bodleian library copy of Turner's book.
33. Foxe [1583], pp. 1526–7.
34. Ibid., p. 1508.
35. APC, vol V, p. 104.
36. Foxe [1583], pp. 1679–80.
37. APC, vol V, pp. 139, 141, 147, 150, 153, 154.
38. Burnet, *History of the Reformation*, vol II, p. ccccxx.
39. Foxe [1583], pp. 1914–17.
40. Ibid., p. 1690.
41. Ibid., pp. 1679–70.
42. Andrew Pettegree, *Marian Protestantism: Six Studies* (Aldershot, 1996), p. 157.
43. Foxe [1583], p. 1509.
44. Ibid., p. 1510.
45. Peter Lake and Michael Questier, 'Agency, Appropriation and Rhetoric under the Gallows', *Past and Present*, 153, 1996, pp. 64–107.
46. *Calendar of State Papers Spanish*, vol XIII, p. 147.
47. *Calendar of State Papers Venetian*, vol VI, part 1, pp. 43–5; APC, vol V, p. 120.
48. Foxe [1563], pp. 1144–5.
49. Foxe [1583], pp. 1573–7; C. L. Kingsford (ed), *Two London Chronicles* (London, 1910), pp. 42–3; Charles Wriothesley, *A Chronicle of England During the Reigns of the Tudors, from A.D. 1485 to 1559*, ed. W. D. Hamilton (London, 1875–7), vol I, pp. 127–8; John Gough Nichols (ed), *The Diary of Henry Machyn* (Camden Society, 1848), pp. 84–5.
50. APC, vol V, p. 115; Foxe [1583], pp. 1576–7.
51. Foxe [1583], p. 1574.
52. Ibid., pp. 1594–6; Brett Usher, 'Essex Evangelicals under Edward VI: Richard Lord Rich, Richard Alvey and their Circle', in David Loades (ed), *John Foxe at Home and Abroad* (Aldershot, 2004), pp. 51–61.
53. Foxe [1563], p. 1171.
54. Foxe [1583], p. 1583.
55. Foxe [1563], p. 1217.
56. Foxe [1583], pp. 1579–80.
57. APC, vol V, pp. 139, 141, 145, 147, 148, 150, 154, 158.
58. The tally of multiple burnings in the city

of Canterbury is very striking: six victims on 23 August 1555, five on 6 September, three on 30 November, five on 27 January 1556. No other place in England had a comparable series of multiple executions at this time and, though Pole was not yet archbishop, those in charge were his appointees, and it is hard to believe that he had not at least authorised this concentrated push against heresy in the diocese.

59. Foxe [1583], p. 1623.
60. Burnet, *History of the Reformation*, vol II, p. ccccxxi.
61. Foxe [1583], pp. 1558, 1682.
62. For this connection, see the letters of John Denley printed in Foxe [1563], p. 1246, of Richard Rothe in Foxe [1583], p. 2019, and of William Tyms in Foxe [1583], p. 2141.
63. Foxe [1583], pp. 1623, 1686.
64. Foxe [1570], p. 1867.
65. *A Declaration of the Lyfe and Death of J. Story* (London, 1571), RSTC 23297, sigs Ci (r)–Cii (v), and epilogue, sigs Diii (r), Diii (v).

NOTES TO CHAPTER 6

1. See the list in Susan Brigden, *London and the Reformation* (Oxford, 1989), pp. 608–12, but the numbers there are inflated in that she includes under 'London' executions in Westminster and Southwark, and clergy with London livings who were in fact based elsewhere, such as George Marsh (a point I owe to Dr Tom Freeman).
2. Strype, *Ecclesiastical Memorials*, vol III, part 2, p. 490 (Pole's St Andrew's day sermon, 1557).
3. See the article on Gilpin by David Marcombe in ODNB.
4. L. E. Whatmore (ed), *Archdeacon Harpsfield's Visitation Returns* (Catholic Record Society, 1950, 1951).
5. Thomas F. Mayer, *Reginald Pole: Prince and Prophet* (Cambridge, 2000), pp. 289–90; CRP, vol III, nos 1493, 1494, 1540, 1541, 1542, 1545, 1546, 1550, 1551.
6. Summarised from Bishop James Brookes's articles for the legatine visitation of Gloucester, in W. H. Frere and W. M.

Kennedy, *Visitation Articles and Injunctions of the Period of the Reformation*, Alcuin Club Collections, vols 14–16 (London, 1908–10), vol II, pp. 401–8; but the same concerns are evident in the London, Lincoln and Canterbury vistations, *pace* Professor Mayer's comment (*Reginald Pole*, p. 290) that 'overt worry' about heresy was 'absent' from Harpsfield's visitation of 1556. The arrests, abjurations and executions that flowed from the visitation (see above, pp. 127–8) are a sufficient indication that this judgement is too sweeping. The Lincoln articles are in Strype, *Ecclesiastical Memorials*, vol III, part 2, pp. 411–12.
7. Foxe [1583], pp. 2111–12: in Elizabeth's reign, Drayner would seek to exonerate himself from the charge of persecution by claiming that he had not worried about 'who adored the sacrament, or who not . . . for I set as litle by it, as the best of you all', but did it 'rather to looke vpon fayre wenches, then otherwise'.
8. Ibid., p. 1949; Strype, *Ecclesiastical Memorials*, vol III, part 2, p. 390.
9. See above, pp. 127–8, 145–8.
10. Foxe [1583], p. 1970; for the articles detecting irreverence used by Harpsfield, see British Library Harley Ms 421, fols 96–97v; for the examinations and confessions of some of the suspects, see ibid. 92r–95r and Strype, *Ecclesiastical Memorials*, vol III, part 1, pp. 540–2.
11. *Harpsfield's Visitation Returns*.
12. Ibid., p. 118; similar examples, pp. 207–8, 244.
13. Ibid., pp. 53, 99, 179, 183, 185, 188.
14. Ibid., p. 179.
15. Patrick Collinson, 'The Persecution in Kent', in E. Duffy and D. Loades, *The Church of Mary Tudor* (Aldershot, 2006), p. 322.
16. Foxe [1583], pp. 1594, 1905, 1909, 1919, 1972, 2089–90.
17. Ibid., pp. 1942, 2089–90.
18. Foxe [1563], pp. 1617–18.
19. Foxe [1583], pp. 1940, 2090.
20. Ibid., pp. 1940–1. Agnes Wardle's husband and son were also religious fugitives.
21. Ibid., p. 1683.
22. Ibid., p. 2023.
23. Ibid., pp. 1895–6.
24. Ibid., p. 1910.

25. Ibid., pp. 1971–3.
26. Ibid., pp. 1916–17.
27. Ibid., p. 1916.
28. According to Foxe, they devised the form of words themselves: ibid., p. 1974.
29. Foxe [1563], pp. 1616–18 (online edition, corrected page numbers).
30. Foxe [1583], p. 2006.
31. Foxe [1563], p. 1616.
32. Foxe [1583], pp. 2006–9. During the raid on the Munt household, Tyrrell notoriously tortured Rose Allin by burning her arm with a candle, an incident gruesomely illustrated in *Acts and Monuments*.
33. Ibid., pp. 2013–18.
34. Ibid., pp. 1970–1.
35. The whole saga, one of the most vivid in *Acts and Monuments*, is in Foxe [1583], pp. 1983–2002.
36. Ibid., p. 1998.
37. Ibid., p. 1996.
38. Ibid., p. 1988.
39. *Calendar of State Papers Venetian*, vol VI, part 1, pp. 110–11.
40. John Feckenham, *A Notable Sermon . . . at the Celebration of the Exequies of the . . . Quene of Spayne* (London, 1555), RSTC 10744, sigs Cvii (v)–Cviii (r).
41. APC, vol V, p. 169.
42. This is the view, for example, maintained by Pole's most recent biographer: Mayer, *Reginald Pole*, pp. 272–83. It is followed also by Anne Overell in her treatment of Pole in *Italian Reform and English Reformation c.1535–c.1585* (Aldershot, 2008), pp. 145–66; a similar view informs Lucy Beckett's fictional treatment of Pole in the novel, *The Time Before You Die* (San Francisco, 1999).
43. John Strype, *Memorials of Archbishop Cranmer* (Oxford, 1840), vol II, p. 972.
44. John Strype, *The Life of the Learned Sir John Cheke* (London, 1705), p. 150; *Calendar of State Papers Venetian*, vol VI, part 1, pp. 510, 526, 536, 668.
45. R. W. Dixon, *History of the Church of England from the Abolition of the Roman Jurisdiction* vol IV (London, 1891), pp. 608–16; Priuli in *Epistolarum*, vol V, pp. 346–7; *Calendar of State Papers Venetian*, vol VI, part 2, p. 769.
46. Foxe [1583], pp. 1914–16, 1972–3; for the dispensation by Pole, explaining the circumstances of the pardon, see Foxe [1563], pp. 1525–6.
47. *Calendar of State Papers Spanish*, vol VI, part 1, p. 226.
48. Gilbert Burnet, *The History of the Reformation of the Church of England* (London, 1850) vol II, p. cclxxiv.
49. *Epistolarum*, vol V, p. 88. Dated after 3rd Sept. 1555 in CRP III, p. 160, no. 1363. The passage is so crucial for understanding Pole's position that it demands quotation in full: '*hoc tantum quo ad coercendos haereticos pertinet scribendum curavimus, de quo cum multi pii hominess mecum egerunt, tum vero in primis Serennisima Regina, ut ad unumquemque vestrum scriberem, admonuit, ut quia rudi atque imperitae multitudini nonulli eorum non minus morientes obsunt, quam dum vivunt, huic rei sic provideatur, ut cum ii ad supplicium ducuntur concionator adsit, qui causam mortis qui eorum male actam vitam ac pertinaciam, qui indulgentiam et diligentiam adhibitam ut resipiscerent, et a morte liberarentur exponat. Ipsi autem haeretici etiam in extremo spiritu diligenter admonendi erunt, et ad suos errors cognoscendos, atque at poenitentiam omni ratione invitandi, ut divini judicii terrorem ante oculos habentes, Dei misericordiam implorent, quae poenitentibus a divina benignitate nunquam nimis sero implorare potest, neque ulli unquam vere, atque ex animo eam postulanti denegatur. Ita et hoc misericordiae opus usque ad extremum erga haereticos praestabitur, et populos eo scandalo liberabitur, in quod facile solet incidere, cum sine concionatore, qui haec exponat, miseri hominis in cruciatibus perferendis tolerantiam tantum videt, nec diaboli vim aut dolos sub falsa pietatis ac fortitudinis specie animadvertit*'.
50. For a daunting revelation of Pole's negative views on the schismatic episcopate, see Vat Lat Ms 5968, fols 10r–12r, a text for use at the Legatine Synod.
51. Ibid. fols 227–8.
52. Ibid. fols 228–228v.
53. Ibid. fols 256–256v.
54. British Library Harley Ms 421, fols 101r–103r; printed in Duffy and Loades, *Church of Mary Tudor*, p. 330.
55. Strype, *Ecclesiastical Memorials*, vol III, part 1, p. 542.
56. For what follows, see the discussion of

Pole's appointments in Thomas F. Mayer, 'The Success of Cardinal Pole's Final Legation', in E. Duffy and D. Loades (eds), *The Church of Mary Tudor* (Aldershot, 2006), pp. 171–4; on Harpsfield, in addition to ODNB, see CRP, vol IV, pp. 251–3.

57. CRP, vol IV, pp. 141–2.
58. Foxe [1583], p. 1667.
59. CRP, vol IV, pp. 166–7.
60. Ibid., pp. 214–16.
61. ODNB and CRP, vol IV, pp. 466–7.
62. *Epistolarum*, vol V, pp. 81–2; for the commencement of Geffrie's activities the same day, see Thomas Mayer in CRP, vol III, no. 1306, p. 132n.

NOTES TO CHAPTER 7

1. Foxe [1583], p. 1770; for Polycarp's words, see ibid., p. 42. The trials and executions of Latimer, Ridley and Cranmer are studied in David Loades, *The Oxford Martyrs* (London, 1970).
2. *Calendar of State Papers Venetian*, vol VI, part 1, p. 226.
3. Foxe [1583], p. 1935.
4. Ibid.
5. Ibid., p. 1888.
6. Diarmaid MacCulloch, *Thomas Cranmer: A Life* (New Haven and London, 1996), p. 600.
7. John Strype, *Memorials of Archbishop Cranmer* (Oxford, 1840), vol I, p. 552. The original is in British Library Harley Ms 422, fols 48r–52r.
8. Ibid., p. 559, my emphasis.
9. Foxe [1583], pp. 2012–13, 2023. I am grateful to Dr Tom Freeman for clarification of Nicholas Bird's role.
10. Ibid., pp. 2012–13. I am grateful to Dr Tom Freeman for drawing the connection to my attention.
11. For the abjuration of Agnes Glover, see British Library Harley Ms 421, fols 85v–86r.
12. Foxe [1583], p. 1543.
13. Ibid., p. 2009.
14. Ibid., p. 2049.
15. APC, vol V, p. 224.
16. See Eamon Duffy, 'Cardinal Pole Preaching', in E. Duffy and D. Loades (eds), *The Church of Mary Tudor* (Aldershot, 2006), p. 196.
17. *A Declaration of The Lyfe and Death of Iohn Story* (London, 1571), sig Di (v).
18. Inner Temple Library Petyt Ms 538/47, fol 3r, a reference I owe to Dr Tom Freeman.
19. Foxe [1583], pp. 2021–2.
20. As at the burning of John Hullier in Cambridge: ibid., p. 2004, 'Wherat a Sergeant named Brisley, stayed & bad him hold his toung or els he should repent it'.
21. Ibid., p. 2022.
22. A point that emerges clearly from Henry Machyn's diary – see the essay by Gary Gibbs, 'Marking the Days: Henry Machyn's Manuscript and the Mid-Tudor Era', in Duffy and Loades, *Church of Mary Tudor*, pp. 281–308. For Smyth's city preaching, see John Gough Nichols (ed), *The Diary of Henry Machyn* (Camden Society, 1848), pp. 59, 68, 70, 71.
23. Foxe [1583], pp. 2064–5.
24. Ibid., pp. 2046–7.
25. Ibid., p. 1616.
26. Ibid., p. 2005.
27. Ibid., p. 2035.
28. Foxe [1563], p. 1616.
29. Foxe [1583], pp. 1842–3.
30. *Lyfe and Death of John Story*, sigs Di (r)–Di (v): there is no record of such a large number (twenty-eight) condemned at one time, so it is possible that Story was talking about the Bow conventicle and that the exception, an 'elde woman that dwelt aboute Pawles Church' might be Elizabeth Warne, burned on 23 August 1555. But she did not live near St Paul's, was fifty-five years of age and was a relative of Story's, for whom he had, in fact, initially interceded.
31. Carlo Ginzburg, *Il Nicodemismo: simulazione e dissimulazione religiosa nell Europa del '500* (Turino, 1970); Carlos Eire, 'Calvin and Nicodemism: A Reappraisal', *Sixteenth Century Journal*, vol 10, 1979, pp. 45–69; Andrew Pettegree, *Marian Protestantism: Six Studies* (Aldershot, 1996), pp. 86–117.
32. *The Temporysour* (Wesel?, 1555), RSTC 18312; *An Epistle Wrytten by Iohn Scory* (Emden, 1555), RSTC 21854; *A Treatise of the Cohabitacyon of the Faithfull with the Vnfaithfull, Whereunto is Added. A Sermon Made of the Confessing of Christe and his*

Gospell, and of the Denyinge of the Same (Strasbourg, 1555), RSTC 24673.5; John Olde, *A Confession of the Most Auncient and True Christe[n] Catholike Old Belefe* (Emden, 1555), RSTC 18798; *A Spiritual and Most Precious Perle, Teachynge All Men to Loue [and] Imbrace the Crosse* (Wesel?, 1555), RSTC 25256; John Knox, *An Exposition upon the Syxt Psalme of Dauid, Wherein is Declared Hys Crosse, Complayntes and Prayers* (Wesel, 1556), RSTC 15074.6; *Certein Workes of Blessed Cypriane the Martyr* (Emden, 1556), RSTC 6152; *A Most Pythye and Excellent Epistell to Anymate All Trew Christians unto the Crosse of Chryste* (Wesel?, 1556), RSTC 10432; *The Examinacion of the Constaunt Martir of Christ, Iohn Philpot* (Emden, 1556), RSTC 19892.

33. See Emmanuel College Library Manuscript 260, fols 20r–24v, for a letter from the Essex martyr Ralph Allerton to fellow parishioners at Great Bentley, to whom he had formerly read and expounded scripture, rebuking them for attending Mass and deploring his own earlier recantation at Paul's Cross: 'now are ye bake a gayne unto that double horedome of the antichristian sinagoge'; 'I doo not go about to clothe myne own wicked dissimulacion in concentyng to the councell of England and to the bishop of London the which as you knowe I stode interdyted of treason, unlawful assembles/tumults and such lyke/ the which you/ your selves knowe right well/that I was never gyltye of anye of them.' I owe this reference to Dr Tom Freeman of the John Foxe project.

34. Foxe [1583], p. 1846.

35. Ibid., p. 2052; for similar examples, see pp. 1999, 2008, 2023.

36. I have opted for this figure though, in fact, Foxe was unsure whether the sum involved was 20*d*. or 40*d*. Perhaps surprisingly in the circumstances, he did not settle on 30*d*.

37. Foxe [1583], p. 1683.

38. Ibid., pp. 1910–1, 1980.

39. Ibid., pp. 2005, 2023.

40. Ibid., p. 1589.

41. Foxe [1563], p. 1619.

42. Foxe [1583], pp. 2007–8. After her first release, Folkes provoked her own re-arrest:

fearing that she would be suspected of having renounced her evangelical beliefs, she 'was in suche anguishe of minde and terrour of conscience, that (no remedye) shee woulde to the Papistes agayne, for any perswasions that could bee, and commyng before them at Cosins house at the white Harte in Colchester [the informal catholic headquarters in Colchester], she was at vtter defiaunce with them and their doctrine'.

43. Ibid., p. 1980.

44. Ibid., pp. 1980–1.

45. Ibid., p. 2065–6.

46. Ibid., p. 2070.

47. Ibid., p. 2069.

48. Ibid., p. 2064.

49. Ibid., p. 2063.

50. For Benbridge, see R. H. Fritze, ' "A Rare Example of Godlyness Amongst Gentleman": The Role of the Kingsmill and Gifford Families in Promoting the Reformation in Hampshire', in Peter Lake and Maria Dowling (eds), *Protestantism and the National Church* (London, 1987), pp. 154–5.

51. APC, vol VI, p. 361; Foxe [1583], pp. 2246–7.

52. Foxe [1583], p. 2037; British Library Harley Ms 416, fols 74r–v; Strype, *Ecclesiastical Memorials*, vol III, part 2, pp. 125–6.

53. Information from Dr Tom Freeman.

54. Foxe [1583], p. 2100.

NOTES TO CHAPTER 8

1. A. G. Dickens, *The English Reformation*, 2nd edn (London, 1989), p. 312; David Loades, *The Reign of Mary Tudor*, 2nd edn (London, 1991), p. 286.

2. Andrew Pettegree, *Marian Protestantism: Six Studies* (Aldershot, 1996), pp. 158–9.

3. Foxe [1583], p. 1807.

4. Ibid., p. 1843, and cf pp. 1567, 1952.

5. The sermon written for the boy bishop at Gloucester in 1558 by one of the prebendaries, Dr Richard Ramsey, joined in the 'pseudo-martyr' debate, attacking those who 'suffryd violence of fyre, hanging, headyng, banyssheng, or other just executions, for many and divers enormities in

their faith and manners, all though in the opinion of their favourers, they are taken for very holy martyrs only for their pretensed good quarrel and for their patient suffryng'. Ramsey perhaps had lingering memories of Hooper's execution at Gloucester in mind: unsurprisingly, he was one of the prebendaries ejected in 1559. See J. Gough Nichols (ed), *Two Sermons by the Boy Bishop* (Camden Society, 1875).

6. *A Plaine and Godlye Treatise Concernynge the Masse* (London, 1555), RSTC 16064 sig Ziv; for a thorough analysis of the standard sixteenth-century case against 'false' martyrdom, see Brad S. Gregory, *Salvation at Stake* (Cambridge, MA, 1999).

7. Ibid., (RSTC 16064), sig Yiii (v).

8. cf. Foxe [1583], p. 1690.

9. *A Plaine and Godly Treatise* (RSTC 16064), sigs Yiv–Zii.

10. Ibid., sigs Ziv–iv (v).

11. Foxe [1583], pp. 1895–8.

12. Ibid., pp. 1909–10.

13. Ibid., pp. 1910–11.

14. Ibid., pp. 1914–17.

15. J. W. Martin, 'Miles Hogarde: Artisan and Aspiring Author *in Sixteenth-Century England*', in *Religious Radicals in Tudor England* (London, 1989), pp. 83–105; Tom Betteridge, *Literature and Politics in the English Reformation* (Manchester, 2004), pp. 152–6.

16. *The Displaying of the Protestants* (London, 1556), RSTC 13558, fol 44v–45.

17. Ibid., fols 43, 47r–v.

18. Ibid., fol 62v.

19. Ibid., fol 102.

20. Ibid., fol 77.

21. Ibid., fols 121–4v.

22. Ibid., fol 69v.

23. James Cancellar, *The Pathe of Obedience, Compiled by Iames Cancellar, one of the Quenes Maiesties Moste Honourable Chapell* (London, 1556), RSTC 4565, sig Bvii. Like the *Treatise on the Masse*, Cancellar's book was published by John Wayland.

24. *Displaying of the Protestants*, fols 66v–9v.

25. Hogarde reverses the final two names.

26. Ann Dillon, *The Construction of Martyrdom in the English Catholic Community, 1535–1603* (Aldershot, 2002), pp. 52–62. Dr Dillon is preparing a book-length study of the print.

27. Its various recensions are discussed in the introduction by E. M. Thompson to G. W. S. Curtis (ed and trans), *The Passion and Martyrdom of the Holy English Carthusian Fathers: The Short Narration by Dom Maurice Chauncy* (London, 1935), and in Thompson's own *The Carthusian Order in England* (London, 1930), pp. 343–52.

28. David Knowles, *The Religious Orders in England, Vol III: The Tudor Age* (Cambridge, 1961), p. 439.

29. CRP, vol 3, no. 1024 (Cardinal Innocenzo del Monte to Pole, 9 January 1555).

30. See Plates 27–9.

31. Foxe [1583], p. 1885.

32. Thomas More, *The Workes of Sir Thomas More Knyght, Sometyme Lord Chancellour of England, Wrytten by Him in the Englysh Tonge* (London, 1557); E. V. Hitchcock (ed), *The Life and Death of Sr Thomas Moore, Knight, Sometymes Lord High Chancellor of England . . . by Nicholas Harpsfield . . . with an Introduction . . . by R. W. Chambers*, Early English Texts Society 186 (London, 1932).

33. Loades, *Reign of Mary Tudor*, p. 288.

34. CRP, vol 3, p. 252 For Roper's activities against heresy in Canterbury, see Foxe [1583], p. 1668 (against John Bland), 1970; and outside Canterbury, see ibid., pp. 1975–9 (against Philpot), 1852 (Bartlett Green), 2000–1 (Richard Woodman).

35. More, *Workes*, sig Cii.

36. Thomas More, *De Tristitia Christi*, ed. Clarence Miller, in Louis A. Schuster, Richard C. Marius et al. (eds), *Complete Works of St Thomas More* (New Haven, 1976), vol 14, pp. 101–5.

37. More, *Workes*, p. 1454.

38. *Calendar of State Papers Venetian*, vol VI, part 1, p. 111.

39. This is the position taken, for example, by Dr Tom Freeman in the ODNB article on Harpsfield.

40. William Roper, *The Life of Sir Thomas More*, in Richard S. Sylvester and Davis P. Harding (eds), *Two Early Tudor Lives* (New Haven and London, 1962), pp. 238, 244, 252.

41. Richard Monckton Milnes and James Gairdner (eds), *Bishop Cranmer's Recantacyons*, Miscellanies of the Philobiblon Society, 15 (London, 1877–84).

42. Harpsfield, *The Life and Death of Sr Thomas Moore*, pp. 209, 213.

43. Ibid., pp. 116–32.
44. Representative example in *The Confutation of Tyndale's Answer*, in Louis A. Schuster, Richard C. Marius et al. (eds), *Complete Works of St. Thomas More* vol 8, part 2 (New Haven and London, 1973), pp. 813–16.
45. John Guy, *Thomas More* (London, 2000), pp. 106–9; Philip E. Hallett (ed), *The Life and Illustrious Martyrdom of Sir Thomas More by Thomas Stapleton* (London, 1928), p. 29.
46. More, *Workes*, pp. 1419–22.
47. Harpsfield, *Life and Death of Sr Thomas Moore*, pp. 60–1.
48. Ibid., p. 207.
49. Ibid., p. 9.
50. Ibid., p. 69.
51. Ibid., p. 67.
52. Harpsfield, *Life and Death of Sr Thomas Moore,* p. 64; E. Duffy, *The Stripping of the Altars: Traditional Religion in England 1400–1750* (New Haven and London, 1992), p. 559.
53. There is no equivalent in Roper's memoir.
54. Vat Lat 5968, fol 396.
55. Harpsfield, *Life and Death of Sr Thomas Moore*, pp. 84–7.
56. E. Duffy, 'Cardinal Pole Preaching', in E. Duffy and D. Loades (eds), *The Church of Mary Tudor* (Aldershot, 2006), p. 184.
57. David Wilkins, *Concilia Magnae Brittaniae et Hiberniae* (London, 1737), vol IV, pp. 163, 166–7.
58. Ibid., pp. 173–4. CPR vol 3, p. 519, no. 2207
59. They were executed under Harpsfield's supervision on 10 November, one week before Pole's own death, and that of the Queen, the last executions of the reign: Foxe [1583], p. 2053. For the significavit, and some uncertainty as to whether Pole himself signed it, see CPR, vol 3, no. 2262.
60. Foxe [1583], p. 2063.

NOTES TO CHAPTER 9

1. 'Together with their shared blood was a great conformity of spirit and the supreme confidence that her Majesty always showed she had in him': CRP, vol. 5 no. 2311, p. 5804 (Priuli to his brother Antonio, Doge of Venice).

2. George Cavendish, *Metrical Visions*, ed. A. S. G. Edwards (Columbia, SC, 1980), pp. 135–41.
3. John Bossy, *The English Catholic Community* (London, 1975), p. 4.
4. David Loades, 'The Spirituality of the Restored Catholic Church', in Thomas M. McCoog, *The Reckoned Expense* (Woodbridge, 1996), pp. 3–19, esp. pp. 14–15.
5. Lucy Wooding, *Rethinking Catholicism in Reformation England* (Oxford, 2000), pp. 120, 129–30, 198, and *passim*.
6. For More's recommendation in *The Confutacyon of Tyndale's Answere* (London, 1532), RSTC 18079, sig Eeiiii (r); Peto's edition of the *Imitation, The Folowynge of Chryste Translated Oute of Latyn into Englysh, Newly Corrected and Amended* (London, 1556), RSTC 23966, 'A preface to the boke folowynge'.
7. John W. O'Malley, *The First Jesuits* (Carmbridge, MA, 1993), pp. 264–6.
8. I am indebted here to Professor James Carley for allowing me to see a copy of his unpublished paper 'William Peto, O.F.M.Obs., and the 1556 Edition of "The Folowinge of Chryste"'.
9. RSTC 23967 (false imprint of Cawood, 1556 on titlepage, but actually W. Carter, 1575).
10. RSTC 19784.
11. RSTC 19785; see A. F. Allison and D. M. Rogers, *The Contemporary Printed Literature of the English Counter-Reformation between 1558 and 1640*, vol 2 (Aldershot, 1994), no. 641.
12. Janet Wilson, 'A Catalogue of the "Unlawful" Books Found in John Stow's Study', *Recusant History*, 1990, pp. 1–30.
13. John Edwards, 'Corpus Christi at Kingston upon Thames', in Edwards and Truman, *Reforming Catholicism*, pp. 139–51.
14. David Wilkins, *Concilia Magnae Brittaniae et Hiberniae* (London, 1737), vol IV, p. 121.
15. Ibid., p. 48.
16. For the 'Forty Hours Devotion', see Mark S. Weil, 'The Devotion of the Forty Hours and Roman Baroque Illusions', *Journal of the Warburg and Courtauld Institutes*, 37, 1974, pp. 218–48.
17. See above, pp. 17–18, 68–9.
18. Thomas Watson, *Holsome and Catholyke Doctryne* (London, 1558), RSTC 25114, fol

lxi (v); and see William Wizeman, *The Theology and Spirituality of Mary Tudor's Church* (Aldershot, 2006), pp. 175–80.

19. Strype, *Ecclesiastical Memorials*, vol 3, part 2, pp. 536–50.

20. Their speeches are printed in John Strype, *Annals of the Reformation and Establishment of Religion . . . during . . . Queen Elizabeth's Happy Reign* (Oxford, 1824), vol I, part 2, pp. 399–407, 408–23, 431–50.

21. See above, pp. 35–7, 46–8.

22. Strype, *Annals*, vol I, part 2, pp. 399–407.

23. Ibid., pp. 408–23.

24. Wilkins, *Concilia*, vol IV, p. 179, translated in Philip Hughes, *Rome and the Counter-Reformation in England* (London, 1942), pp. 138–9.

25. T. E. Bridgett and T. F. Knox, *The True Story of the Catholic Hierarchy Deposed by Queen Elizabeth* (London, 1889); G. E. Phillips, *The Extinction of the Ancient Hierarchy* (London, 1905).

26. Strype, *Annals*, vol I, part 1, pp. 217, 218.

27. The count that follows is based on an analysis of the volumes of the magnificent revision of J. Le Neve, *Fasti Ecclesiae Anglicanae 1541–1857*, (London, 1969–), rev. edn by Joyce Horn et al.

28. Professor Thomas Mayer's unpublished conference paper 'Pole and the Cathedrals' makes many of these points, based on analysis of the biographical entries of cathedral clergy collected in CRP, vol IV.

29 The library catalogues of two of these exiled cathedral dignitaries – John Ramridge, dean of Lichfield, and Henry Joliffe, dean of Bristol – survive and throw a flood of light on the intellectual and religious formation of this new Marian clerical elite: see Christian Coppens, *Reading in Exile: The Libraries of John Ramridge, Thomas Harding and Henry Joliffe* (Cambridge, 1993). Joliffe had been an active disputant against Hooper in Edward's reign; Ramridge had a much lower polemical profile, but his stupendous library of over 450 volumes included editions of the major Greek and Latin Fathers and an abundance of writings by Erasmus, More and other humanists, as well as more pointed and polemical works by Contarini, Guitmand, Hosius and Alfonso de Castro. Ramridge's library, the

bulk of it almost certainly acquired before his exile, but steadily augmented until his murder while distributing alms in the street in Louvain in 1568, served as an important resource for the polemical writers of the Louvain English community.

30. CRP vol IV, pp. 61–6.

31. M. Bateson (ed), *Original Letters from the Bishops to the Privy Council* (Camden Society, 1896), pp. 19–21.

32. *The Works of James Pilkington* (Cambridge, 1842), pp. 481–6; ODNB.

33. J. Le Neve, *Fasti Ecclesiae Anglicanae 1541–1857, vol I: St Paul's London*, compiled by Joyce M. Horn (London, 1969), pp. 5, 7, 9, 10, 12–13, 14, 15, 20, 21, 28, 29, 34, 35, 41, 43, 47, 50, 53, 57, 58, 60, 61, 63.

34. J. Le Neve, *Fasti Ecclesiae Anglicanae 1541–1857, vol IV: York Diocese*, compiled by Joyce M. Horn and David M. Smith (London, 1975), pp. 6, 13, 18, 20, 22, 26, 28–9, 34, 36, 44, 48, 54, 60, 63, 65, 67.

35. J. Le Neve, *Fasti Ecclesiae Anglicanae 1541–1857, vol VI: Salisbury Diocese*, compiled by Joyce M. Horn (London, 1986), pp. 6–92.

36. J. Le Neve, *Fasti Ecclesiae Anglicanae 1541–1857, vol III: Canterbury, Rochester and Winchester Dioceses*, compiled by Joyce M. Horn (London, 1974), pp. 84. 86, 90, 91–3, 99, 103, 105.

37. J. Le Neve, *Fasti Ecclesiae Anglicanae 1541–1857, vol IV: York Diocese*, pp. 6, 7, 13, 18, 20, 22, 26, 28–9, 34, 36, 44, 48, 54, 60, 63, 65, 67.

38. ODNB.

39. Timothy J. McCann, 'The Clergy and the Elizabethan Settlement in the Diocese of Chichester', in M. Kitsh (ed), *Studies in Sussex Church History* (London, 1981), p. 114.

40. H. N. Birt, *The Elizabethan Religious Settlement: A Study of Contemporary Documents* (London, 1907), pp. 257, 274.

41. On the impact of the Elizabethan Settlement in Oxford, see Penry Williams, 'Elizabethan Oxford: State, Church and University', in James McConica (ed), *History of the University of Oxford Vol 3: The Collegiate University*, pp. 406 ff; James McConica, 'The Catholic Experience in Tudor Oxford', in T. M. McCoog, *The Reckoned Expense* (Woodbridge, 1996), pp. 39–63; Claire Cross, 'The English Uni-

versities, 1553–58', in E. Duffy and D. Loades, *The Church of Mary Tudor* (Aldershot, 2006), pp. 57–76.

42. H. C. Porter, *Reformation and Reaction in Tudor Cambridge* (Cambridge, 1958), pp. 101–7; Birt, *Elizabethan Settlement*, pp. 260–70; Cross, 'English Universities', pp. 57–76.

43. Marvin R. O'Connell, *Thomas Stapleton and the Counter-Reformation* (New Haven and London, 1964); Richard Stewart, 'Thomas Stapleton's Call to Rome', *Clergy Review*, 70, 1985, pp. 311–17; A. F. Allison and D. M. Rogers, *The Contemporary Printed Literature of the English Counter-Reformation between 1558 and 1640, Vol 1: Works in Languages Other than English* (Aldershot, 1989), pp. 154–64.

44. ODNB.

45. Ibid.

46. T. M. Veech, *Dr Nicholas Sanders and the English Reformation, 1530–1581* (Louvain, 1935); ODNB; Allison and Rogers *Contemporary Printed Literature of the English Counter-Reformation*, vol I, pp. 135–40, vol II, pp. 138–9; Peter Milward, *Religious Controversies of the Elizabethan Age* (London, 1978), pp. 13–15; Christopher Highley, '"A Pestilent and Seditious Book": Nicholas Sander's *Schismatis Anglicani* and Catholic Histories of the Reformation', *Huntington Library Quarterly* vol 68 (2005), pp. 151–71.

47. For Allen's early career and Spanish affiliations, see E. Duffy in ODNB; for Sander at Oxford, see Veech, *Nicholas Sanders*, pp. 8–22; his oration for the legatine visitation of the university is printed in Strype, *Ecclesiastical Memorials*, vol III, part 2, pp. 472–4; for his friendship with the Spaniards, see Andrew Hegarty, 'Carranza and the English Universities', in John Edwards and Ronald Truman (eds), *Reforming Catholicism in Mary Tudor's England* (Aldershot, 2005), pp. 169–70.

48. Sander's undated letter (probably written some time in 1561) is edited and translated by John B. Wainewright in *Catholic Record Society Miscellanea XIII* (London, 1926), pp. 1–5.

49. Gregory Martin, *Roma Sancta* [1581], ed. by George Bruner Parks (Rome, 1969), quotation from editor's introduction, p. xi.

50. Nicholas Harpsfield, *Dialogi Sex contra Summi Pontificatus, Monasticae Vitae, Sanctorum, Sacrarum Imaginum Oppugnatores . . . Nunc Primum . . . ab Alano Copo Anglo Editi* (Antwerp, 1566), pp. 323, 556–7, 707–10, 783–5; Alison and Rogers, *Contemporary Printed Literature of the English Counter-Reformation*, vol I, nos 636–8. See the important discussion of the *Dialogi Sex* in Jonathan Dean, 'Catholicae Ecclesiae Unitatem, Nicholas Harspfield and English Reformation Catholicism', unpublished PhD thesis, University of Cambridge, 2004, esp. pp. 77–101. The *Centuries* was an inevitable target for counter-reformation polemicists after 1560: Nicholas Sander's *De Visibilia Monarchia*, much indebted both to Pole and to Harpsfield, was also directed against the *Centuries*, and, when Sander's Oxford friend John Rastell joined the Jesuits in 1568, he was posted to Dillengen to act as research assistant to Peter Canisius for his reply to the Centuriators.

51. See the booklists given for Henry Cole and Thomas Paynell in A. B. Emden, *A Biographical Register of the University of Oxford* (Oxford, 1974), vol II.

52. Strype, *Annals*, vol I, part 2, pp. 417–18.

53. H. T. Wojtyska, *Cardinal Hosius: Legate to the Council of Trent* (Rome, 1967), pp. 211–16.

54. J. H. Pollen (ed), 'Dr Nicholas Sanders' Report to Cardinal Morone', *Catholic Record Society Miscellanea I* (London, 1905), pp. 1–47.

55. *De Concilio Liber Reginaldi Poli Cardinalis* (Rome, 1562); *Reformatio Angliae ex Decretis Reginaldi Poli Cardinalis, Sedis Apostolicae Legati Anno MDLVI* (Rome, 1562); Allison and Rogers, *Contemporary Printed Literature of the English Counter-Reformation*, vol I, nos 911–14; Thomas F. Mayer, *A Reluctant Author: Cardinal Pole and his Manuscripts* (Philadelphia, 1999), pp. 25–9; idem, *Reginald Pole: Prince and Prophet* (Cambridge, 2000), pp. 356–8; H. Jedin, *Papal Legate at the Council of Trent: Girolamo Seripando* (St Louis and London, 1947), pp. 557–61; Adam Patrick Robinson, 'A Reassessment of the Career of Cardinal Giovanni Morone (1509–1580)', unpublished PhD thesis, University of

London, 2008, pp. 130–3. For the importance of these publications in the longer struggle between the *zelanti* and the *spirituali*, see Paolo Simoncelli, *Il caso Reginald Pole: eresia e santita nelle polemiche religiose del cinquecento* (Rome, 1977), esp. pp. 201–16.

56. J. O'Donohoe, *Tridentine Seminary Legislation: Its Sources and its Formation* (Louvain, 1957); idem, 'The Seminary Legislation of the Council of Trent', in I. Rogger (ed), *Il Concilio di Trento e la Riforma Tridentina*, 2 vols (Rome, 1965), vol I, pp. 157–72.

57. J. M. Hedley and J. B. Tomaro (eds), *San Carlo Borromeo: Catholic Reform and Ecclesiastical Politics in the Second Half of the Sixteenth Century* (Washington, DC, 1988), p. 69; on Ormanetto's career more generally, see C. Robinson, *Nicolo Ormanetto: A Papal Envoy in the Sixteenth Century* (London, 1920).

58. José Ignacio Tellechea Idígoras, *Fray Bartholomi Carranza y el cardenal Pole* (Pamplona, 1977), p. 307.

59. ODNB.

Select Bibliography

This bibliography is neither a comprehensive listing of works on religion in the reign of Mary Tudor nor even a list of everything consulted in the preparation of this book. It includes only works cited in the footnotes and is designed to make identification of such items easier.

MANUSCRIPTS

British Library, Harley Ms 416
British Library, Harley Ms 421
Cambridge University Library, Ely Diocesan Register G 1/8
Corpus Christi College, Cambridge, Ms 111
Emmanuel College Library, Manuscript 260
Vatican Library, Vat Lat 5968. This large volume of manuscript sermons, speeches and letters of Reginald Pole was conserved in the 1950s by glueing tissue paper across many pages. The tissue has darkened and large parts of the manuscript are now unreadable. I have worked from the Bodleian Library's copy of the microfilm, which was fortunately made at the same time, when the tissue was transparent.

UNPUBLISHED THESES AND PAPERS

Peter Blayney, unpublished paper, 'The English Book Trade under Edward VI and Mary I'
James Carley, unpublished paper, 'William Peto, O.F.M.Obs., and the 1556 Edition of "The Folowinge of Chryste"'
Jonathan Dean, 'Catholicae Ecclesiae Unitatem: Nicholas Harpsfield and English Reformation Catholicism', unpublished PhD thesis, University of Cambridge, 2004
John P. Marmion, 'The London Synod of Cardinal Pole', unpublished MA thesis, Keele University, 1974
Rex Pogson, 'Reginald Pole: Papal Legate to England in Mary Tudor's Reign', unpublished thesis, PhD University of Cambridge, 1972
Adam Patrick Robinson, 'A Reassessment of the Career of Cardinal Giovanni Morone (1509–1580)', unpublished PhD thesis, University of London, 2008
Margaret Took, 'Government and the Printing Trade 1540–1560', unpublished PhD thesis, University of London, 1978

PRINTED BOOKS AND ARTICLES

Gina Alexander, 'Bonner and the Marian Persecutions', in C. Haigh (ed), *The English Reformation Revised* (Cambridge, 1987), pp. 157–75
A. F. Allison and D. M. Rogers, *The Contemporary Printed Literature of the English Counter-Reformation between 1558 and 1640*, 2 vols (Aldershot, 1989, 1994)
G. E. Aylmer and Reginald Cant (eds), *A History of York Minster* (Oxford, 1977)
(John Bale), *De Vera Obedientia: An Oration Made in Latine by the Right Reverende Father in God Stephan Bishop of Winchestre* ('Rome', 1553), RSTC 11587
William Barlow, *A Dyaloge Descrybyng the Orygynall Ground of these Lutheran Faccyons* (London, 1553), RSTC 1461 and 1462
C. M. Baron and C. Harper Bill (eds), *The Church in Pre-Reformation Society* (Woodbridge, 1998)
Edward J. Baskerville, *A Chronological Bibliography of Propaganda and Polemic Published in*

English between 1553 and 1558 (Philadelphia, 1979)

M. Bateson (ed), *Original Letters from the Bishops to the Privy Council* (Camden Society, 1896)

Thomas Becon, *A Comfortable Epistle, too Goddes Faythfull People in Englande* (Wesel?, 1554), RSTC 1716

Lucy Beckett, *The Time Before You Die: a novel of the Reformation* (San Francisco, 1999)

G. A. Bergenroth, Pascual de Gayangos, Martin A. S. Hume and Royall Tyler (ed), *Calendar of Letters, Despatches and State Papers Relating to the Negotiations between England and Spain*, 13 vols (London, 1862–1954)

Joseph Bergin, *The Making of the French Episcopate* (New Haven and London, 1996)

——, 'The Counter-Reformation Church and its Bishops', *Past and Present*, 165, 1999, pp. 30–73

Tom Betteridge, *Literature and Politics in the English Reformation* (Manchester, 2004)

M. Biddle, 'Early Renaissance at Winchester', in J. Crook (ed), *Winchester Cathedral* (Chichester, 1993), pp. 257–304

H. N. Birt, *The Elizabethan Religious Settlement: A Study of Contemporary Documents* (London, 1907)

Ronald B. Bond (ed), *Certain Sermons or Homilies (1547)* (Toronto, 1987)

Edmund Bonner, *The Declaration of the Bishop of London*, 1555, RSTC 3280.3

——, *Homelies Sette Forth by the Right Reverende Father in God, Edmunde Byshop of London* (London, 1555), RSTC 3285.7

——, *A Profitable and Necessarye Doctrine with Certayne Homelyes Adioyned Thereunto* (London, 1555), RSTC 3283.3

——, *An Honest Godlye Instruction and Information for the Tradynge, and Bringinge vp of Children* (London, 1556), RSTC 3281

——, *Interrogatories upon which . . . Churchwardens Shalbe Charged*, 1558, RSTC 10117

Augustino Borromeo (ed), *L'Inquisizione: Atti del Simposio Internazionale 1998* (Vatican City, 2003)

John Bossy, *The English Catholic Community, 1570–1850* (London, 1975)

John Bradford, *A Sermon of Repentance* (London, 1553), RSTC 3496

Gerald Bray (ed), *The Anglican Canons 1529–1947*, Church of England Record Society, vol 6 (Woodbridge, 1998)

T. E. Bridgett and T. F. Knox, *The True Story of the Catholic Hierarchy Deposed by Queen Elizabeth* (London, 1889)

Susan Brigden, *London and the Reformation* (Oxford, 1989)

J. Brodrick, *St Peter Canisius* (London, 1935)

James Brookes, *A Sermon Very Notable, Fruitefull and Godlie* (London, 1553) RSTC 3838

Rawdon Brown, G. C. Bentinck, H. F. Brown and Allen B. Hinds (eds), *Calendar of State Papers and Manuscripts Relating to English Affairs, existing in the Archives and Collections of Venice*, 14 vols (London, 1864–1908)

C. Burgess and E. Duffy (eds), *The Parish Church in Late Medieval England* (Donington, 2006)

Calendar of the Patent Rolls Preserved in the Public Record Office (London, 1891–)

James Cancellar, *The Pathe of Obedience* (London, 1556), RSTC 4564 and 4565

A. Caprioli, A. Rimoldi and L. Vaccaro (eds), *Chiesa e società: appunti per una storia delle diocesi Lombarde* (Brescia, 1986)

Bartolomé Carranza de Miranda, *Commentarios sobre el catechismo christiano*, ed. José Ignacio Tellechea Idígoras, 2 vols (Madrid, 1972)

Alfonso di Castro, *Alfonso a Castro Zamorensis, Adversus Omnes Haereses, Libri XIIII* (Antwerp, 1556)

——, *De Iusta Haereticorum Punitione Libri III. F. Alfonso a Castro Zamorensis . . . Nunc Recens Accurate Recogniti* (Lyon, 1556)

Catholic Record Society Miscellanea XIII (London, 1926)

George Cavendish, *Metrical Visions*, ed. A. S. G. Edwards (Columbia, NC 1980)

Certein Godly, Learned and Comfortable Conferences, Between the Two Reuerende Fathers, and Holy Martyrs of Christe, D. Nicolas Rydley Late Bisshoppe of London, and M Hughe Latimer, Sometyme Bisshop of Worcester, During the Tyme of their Emprisonmentes (Emden, 1556), RSTC 21047.3

Certein Workes of Blessed Cypriane the Martyr (Emden, 1556), RSTC 6152

A. H. Chaubard (ed), *Une oeuvre inconnue de Theodore de Beze: Réponse à la confession du feu Jean de Northumberlande, n'agueres décapité en Angleterre* (Lyon, 1959)

John Christopherson, *An Exhortation to All Menne to Take Hede and Beware of Rebellion* (London, 1554), RSTC 5207

Patrick Collinson, 'The Persecution in Kent',

in Duffy and Loades, *Church of Mary Tudor*, pp. 309–33

—— and John Craig (eds), *The Reformation in English Towns, 1500–1640* (London, 1998)

Kathleen M. Comerford, 'Italian Tridentine Diocesan Seminaries: A Historiographical Study', *Sixteenth Century Journal*, 29, Winter 1998, pp. 999–1022

Copia delle lettere del sereniss. Re d'Inghilterra & del Reverendiss. Card. Polo . . . spora . . . obedientia della sede apostolica (Rome, 1554–5)

Myles Coverdale (ed), *Certain Most Godly, Fruitful and Comfortable Letters of Such True Saintes and Holy Martyrs as in the Late Bloody Persecution Gave Their Lyves* (London, 1564), RSTC 5885

Thomas Cranmer, *Miscellaneous Writings and Letters* (Cambridge, 1846)

Claire Cross, 'The English Universities, 1553–58', in Duffy and Loades, *Church of Mary Tudor*, pp. 57–76

G. W. S. Curtis (ed and trans), *The Passion and Martyrdom of the Holy English Carthusian Fathers: The Short Narration by Dom Maurice Chauncy* (London, 1935)

J. R. Dasent (ed), *Acts of the Privy Council of England*, New series, 32 vols, (London, 1890–1907)

A Declaration of the Lyfe and Death of Iohn Story (London, 1571), RSTC 23297

A. G. Dickens, *The English Reformation*, 2nd edn (London, 1989)

——, 'Robert Parkyn's Narrative of the Reformation', in *Reformation Studies* (London, 1982), pp. 287–312

Ann Dillon, *The Construction of Martyrdom in the English Catholic Community, 1535–1603* (Aldershot, 2002)

R. W. Dixon, *History of the Church of England from the Abolition of the Roman Jurisdiction*, 6 vols (London, 1878–1902)

Peter Donaldson, *Machiavelli and the Mystery of State* (Cambridge, 1988)

John Dudley, *The Saying of John, Late Duke of Northumberlande upon the Scaffolde*, London 1553, RSTC 7283

E. Duffy, *The Stripping of the Altars: Traditional Religion in England 1400–1580*, (New Haven and London, 1992)

——, *The Voices of Morebath: Reformation and Rebellion in an English Village* (New Haven and London, 2001)

——, 'Cardinal Pole Preaching', in Duffy and Loades, *Church of Mary Tudor*, pp. 176–200

——, 'The End of it All: The Material Culture of the Medieval English Parish Church and the 1552 Inventories of Church Goods', in Burgess and Duffy, *The Parish Church in Late Medieval England*

—— and D. Loades (eds), *The Church of Mary Tudor* (Aldershot, 2006)

J. G. Dwyer (ed and trans), *Pole's Defence of the Unity of the Church* (Westminster, MD, 1965)

John Edwards, 'Corpus Christi at Kingston upon Thames', in Edwards and Truman, *Reforming Catholicism*, pp. 139–51

Carlos Eire, 'Calvin and Nicodemism: A Reappraisal', *Sixteenth Century Journal*, 10, 1979, pp. 45–69

—— and Ronald Truman (eds), *Reforming Catholicism in the England of Mary Tudor* (Aldershot, 2005)

A. B. Emden, *A Biographical Register of the University of Oxford* (Oxford, 1974)

The Examinacion of the Constaunt Martir of Christ, John Philpot (Emden, 1556), RSTC 19892

An Exclamation upon the Erroneous and Fantasticall Sprite of Heresy [O Heresy with Frenzy], RSTC 10615, in Rollins, 'Old English Ballads', no. 6

John Feckenham, *A Notable Sermon . . . at the Celebration of the Exequies of the … Quene of Spayne* (London, 1555), RSTC 10744

Il felicissimo ritorno del regno d'Inghilterra alla Catholica unione & obedientia della sede Apostolica (Rome, 1555)

Dermot Fenlon, *Heresy and Obedience in Tridentine Italy: Cardinal Pole and the Counter-Reformation* (Cambridge, 1972)

John Foxe, *Acts and Monuments: The Variorum Edition* (hriOnline, Sheffield, 2004), available at: http://www.hrionline.ac.uk/johnfoxe/

W. H. Frere and W. M. Kennedy, *Visitation Articles and Injunctions of the Period of the Reformation*, Alcuin Club Collections, vols 14–16 (London, 1908–10)

R. H. Fritze, ' "A Rare Example of Godlyness Amongst Gentleman": The Role of the Kingsmill and Gifford Families in Promoting the Reformation in Hampshire', in Peter Lake and Maria Dowling (eds), *Protestantism and the National Church* (London, 1987)

Stephen Gardiner, *De Vera Obediencia an Ora-*

tion . . . *Marke the Notes in the Margine* (London?, 1553), RSTC 11585–7

Richard Garnett (ed), *The Accession of Queen Mary, Being the Contemporary Narrative of Antonio de Guaras, a Spanish Merchant Resident in London* (London, 1892)

Christina Garrett, *The Marian Exiles* (Cambridge, 1938)

Edward Gee (ed), *The Jesuit's Memorial for the Reformation of England* (London, 1690)

H. Gee and W. H. Hardy, *Documents Illustrative of the History of the English Church* (London, 1896)

Gary Gibbs, 'Marking the Days: Henry Machyn's Manuscript and the Mid-Tudor Era', in Duffy and Loades, *Church of Mary Tudor*, pp. 281–308

Carlo Ginzburg, *Il Nicodemismo: simulazione e dissimulazione religiosa nell Europa del '500* (Turino, 1970)

Hugh Glasier, *A Notable and Very Fruitefull Sermon Made at Paules Cross, the XXV Day of August* (London, 1555), RSTC 11916.5

Brad S. Gregory, *Salvation at Stake* (Cambridge MA, 1999)

John Guy, *Thomas More* (London, 2000)

Christopher Haigh, (ed), *The English Reformation Revised* (Cambridge, 1987)

——, *English Reformations: Religion, Politics and Society under the Tudors* (Oxford, 1993)

Philip E. Hallett (ed), *The Life and Illustrious Martyrdom of Sir Thomas More by Thomas Stapleton* (London, 1928)

Nicholas Harpsfield, *Dialogi Sex contra Summi Pontificatus, Monasticae Vitae, Sanctorum, Sacrarum Imaginum Oppugnatores . . . Nunc Primum . . . ab Alano Copo Anglo Editi* (Antwerp, 1566)

Denis Hay, 'The "Narratio Historica" of P. Vincentius, 1553', *English Historical Review*, 63, 1948, pp. 350–6

Felicity Heal, 'What Can King Lucius Do for You? The Reformation and the Early British Church', *English Historical Review*, 120, 2005, pp. 593–614

J. M. Hedley and J. B. Tomaro (eds), *San Carlo Borromeo: Catholic Reform and Ecclesiastical Politics in the Second Half of the Sixteenth Century* (Washington, DC, 1988)

Andrew Hegarty, 'Carranza and the English Universities', in Edwards and Truman, *Reforming Catholicism*, pp. 153–72

Christopher Highley, '"A Pestilent and Seditious Book": Nicholas Sander's *Schismatis Anglicani* and Catholic Histories of the Reformation', *Huntington Library Quarterly* vol 68 (2005), pp. 151–71

E. V. Hitchcock (ed), *The Life and Death of Sr Thomas Moore, Knight, Sometymes Lord High Chancellor of England . . . by Nicholas Harpsfield . . . with an Introduction . . . by R. W. Chambers*, Early English Texts Society 186 (London, 1932)

P. T. Hoffman, *Church and Community in the Diocese of Lyon, 1500–1789* (New Haven, 1984)

Miles Hogarde, *Displaying of the Protestants with a Description of Divers of their Abuses* (London, 1556), RSTC 13557

Ralph Houlbrooke, 'The Clergy, the Church Courts, and the Marian Restoration in Norwich', in Duffy and Loades, *Church of Mary Tudor*, pp. 124–46

Ann Hudson (ed), *Two Wycliffite Texts: The Sermon of William Taylor 1406: The Testimony of William Thorpe 1407* (Oxford, 1993)

Paul L. Hughes and James F. Larkin (eds), *Tudor Royal Proclamations* 3 vols, (New Haven, 1964–9)

Phillip Hughes, *Rome and the Counter-Reformation in England* (London, 1942)

Ronald Hutton, 'The Local Impact of the Tudor Reformations', in Haigh, *English Reformation Revised*, pp. 114–37

José Ignacio Tellechea Idígoras, *Fray Bartholomi Carranza y el cardenal Pole* (Pamplona, 1977)

Instructions for the Curates, printed broadsheet, 1555, York Minster Library, RSTC 26098.7

H. Jedin, *Papal Legate at the Council of Trent: Girolamo Seripando* (St Louis and London, 1947)

Ernest Jones, 'Geoffrey of Monmouth's Account of the Establishment of Episcopacy in Britain', *Journal of English and German Philology*, 40, 1941, pp. 360–3

Malcolm Jones, 'The Lambe Speaketh . . . an Addendum', *Journal of the Warburg and Courtauld Institutes*, 63, 2000, pp. 287–94

W. K. Jordan and M. R. Gleason, 'The Saying of John, Late Duke of Northumberland on the Scaffold 1553', *Harvard Library Bulletin*, 23, 1975, pp. 139–79, 324–55

C. L. Kingsford (ed), *Two London Chronicles*, Camden Society 3rd Series 18 (London, 1910)

David Knowles, *The Religious Orders in England,*

Vol III: The Tudor Age (Cambridge, 1961)

John Knox, *An Exposition upon the Syxt Psalme of David, Wherein is Declared Hys Crosse, Complayntes and Prayers* (Wesel, 1556), RSTC 15074.5

Peter Lake and Michael Questier, 'Agency, Appropriation and Rhetoric under the Gallows', *Past and Present*, 153, 1996, pp. 64–107

John Lamb (ed), *A Collection of Letters, Statutes and Other Documents . . . Illustrative of the History of the University of Cambridge* (London, 1838)

J. Le Neve, *Fasti Ecclesiae Anglicanae 1541–1857* (London, 1969–, rev. edn by Joyce Horn et al).

Phillip Lindley, 'Innovations, Tradition and Disruption in Tomb Sculpture', in D. Gaimster and P. Stamper (eds), *The Age of Transition: The Archaeology of English Culture 1400–1600* (Oxford, 1997), pp. 77–92

Jennifer Loach, 'Pamphlets and Politics 1553–8', *Bulletin of the Institute of Historical Research*, 48, 1975, pp. 31–45

——, 'The Marian Establishment and the Printing Press', *English Historical Review*, 100, 1986, pp. 138–51

——, *Parliament and the Crown in the Reign of Mary Tudor* (Oxford, 1986)

David Loades, *The Oxford Martyrs* (London, 1970)

——, 'The Theory and Practice of Censorship in Sixteenth-Century England', *Transactions of the Royal Historical Society*, 5th Series, 24, 1974, pp. 141–57

——, *The Reign of Mary Tudor*, 2nd edn (London, 1991)

——, 'The Spirituality of the Restored Catholic Church', in McCoog, *The Reckoned Expense*, pp. 3–20

——, 'The Marian Episcopate', in Duffy and Loades, *Church of Mary Tudor*, pp. 33–56

——, *Mary Tudor: The Tragical History of the First Queen of England* (Kew, 2006)

Wallace T. MacCaffrey, *Exeter 1540–1640* (Cambridge, MA, 1975)

Timothy J. McCann, 'The Clergy and the Elizabethan Settlement in the Diocese of Chichester', in M. Kitsh (ed), *Studies in Sussex Church History* (London, 1981), pp. 99–122

James McConica, 'The Catholic Experience in Tudor Oxford', in McCoog, *The Reckoned Expense*, pp. 39–63

T. M. McCoog, 'Ignatius Loyola and Reginald Pole: A Reconsideration', *Journal of Ecclesiastical History*, 17, 1996, pp. 257–73

—— (ed), *The Reckoned Expense* (Woodbridge, 1996)

Diarmaid MacCulloch, *Thomas Cranmer: A Life* (New Haven and London, 1996)

——, 'Worcester: A Cathedral City in the Reformation', in Collinson and Craig, *The Reformation in English Towns*, pp. 94–112

——, *The Later Reformation in England, 1547–1603*, 2nd edn (London, 2001)

——, *Reformation: Europe's House Divided, 1490–1700* (Harmondsworth, 2003)

Vincent McNabb (ed), 'Cardinal Pole's Eirenikon', *Dublin Review*, 1936, pp. 149–60

Richard Marks, 'The Howard Tombs at Thetford and Framlingham: New Discoveries', *Archaeological Journal*, 141, 1984, pp. 252–68

George Marshall, *A Compendious Treatise in Metre Declaring the Firste Originall of Sacrifice, and of the Building of Aultares and Churches, and of the Firste Receavinge of the Christen Fayth in England by GM* (London, 1554), RSTC 17469

Gregory Martin, *Roma Sancta* [1581], ed. George Bruner Parks (Rome, 1969)

J. W. Martin, 'The Marian Regime's Failure to Understand the Importance of Printing', *Huntington Library Quarterly*, 154, 1980–1, pp. 231–47

——, 'Miles Hogarde: Artisan and Aspiring Author in Sixteenth-century England', *Renaissance Quarterly*, 34, 1981, pp. 359–83

——, 'Miles Hogarde: Artisan and Aspiring Author *in Sixteenth-century England*', in *Religious Radicals in Tudor England*, 1989, pp. 83–105

Thomas F. Mayer, 'A Test of Wills: Pole, Loyola and the Jesuits in England', in McCoog, *The Reckoned Expense*, pp. 21–8

——, *A Reluctant Author: Cardinal Pole and his Manuscripts*, Transactions of the American Philosophical Society, 89 (Philadelphia, 1999)

——, *Cardinal Pole in European Context* (Aldershot, 2000)

——, *Reginald Pole: Prince and Prophet* (Cambridge, 2000)

—— (ed), *The Correspondence of Reginald Pole* (Aldershot, 2002 (in progress, 4 volumes to date))

——, 'The Success of Cardinal Pole's Final

Legation', in Duffy and Loades, *Church of Mary Tudor*, pp. 149–75

Peter Milward, *Religious Controversies of the Elizabethan Age* (London, 1978)

Missale ad Usum Insignis Ecclesie Sarisburiensis, (Paris, 1555), RSTC 16217, CUL Rit.a.155.1

Sir Thomas More, *The Confutacyon of Tyndale's Answere* (London, 1532), RSTC 18079

——, *The Workes of Sir T More . . . Written by Him in the Englysh Tonge* (London, 1557), RSTC 18076

——, *The Confutation of Tyndale's Answer*, in Louis A. Schuster, Richard C. Marius et al (eds), *Complete Works of St Thomas More*, vol 8 (New Haven and London, 1973)

——, *De Tristitia Christi*, ed. Clarence Miller, in Louis A. Schuster, Richard C. Marius et al (eds), *Complete Works of St Thomas More*, vol 14 (New Haven, 1976)

J. S. Moore, 'Jack Fisher's' Flu: A Visitation Revisited', *Economic History Review* 46, 1993, pp. 280–307

——, 'Jack Fisher's' Flu: A Virus Still Virulent' *Economic History Review*, 47, 1994, pp. 359–361

A Most Pythye and Excellent Epistell to Anymate All Trew Christians unto the Crosse of Chryste (Wesel?, 1556), RSTC 10432

J. F. Mozley, *John Foxe and his Book* (London, 1940)

James Arthur Muller, *Stephen Gardiner and the Tudor Reaction* (London, 1926)

—— (ed), *The Letters of Stephen Gardiner* (Cambridge, 1933)

A Necessary Doctrine and Erudicion for any Chrysten Man Set Furth by the Kynges Maiestye (London, 1543), RSTC 5176

John Gough Nichols (ed), *The Diary of Henry Machyn* (Camden Society, 1848)

——, *The Chronicle of Queen Jane and of Two Years of Queen Mary* (Camden Society, 1850)

——, *Narratives of the Days of the Reformation* (Camden Society, 1869)

——, *Two Sermons by the Boy Bishop* (Camden Society, 1875)

Marvin R. O'Connell, *Thomas Stapleton and the Counter-Reformation* (New Haven and London, 1964)

John Olde, *The Acquital or Purgation of the Moost Catholyke Christen Prince Edward VI* ('Waterford' [Emden], 1555), RSTC 18797

——, *A Confession of the Most Auncient and True Christe[n] Catholike Old Belefe* (Emden, 1555), RSTC 18798

John W. O'Malley, *The First Jesuits* (Cambridge, MA, 1993)

——, *Trent and All That: Renaming Catholicism in the Early Modern Era* (Cambridge, MA, 2002)

Original Letters Relative to the English Reformation, Written During the Reigns of King Henry VIII, King Edward VI, and Queen Mary: Chiefly from the Archives of Zurich (Parker Society, 1847)

Anne Overell, *Italian Reform and English Reformation c. 1535–c. 1585* (Aldershot, 2008)

Helen L. Parish, *Clerical Marriage and the English Reformation* (Aldershot, 2000)

William Peto, *The Folowinge of Chryste, Translated oute of Latyn into Englysh, Newly Corrected and Amended. Wherevnto Also is Added the Golden Epystell of Saynt Barnarde* (London, 1556), RSTC 23966

G. E. Phillips, *The Extinction of the Ancient Hierarchy* (London, 1905)

James Pilkington, *The Works of James Pilkington* (Cambridge, 1842)

A Plaine and Godlye Treatise Concernynge the Masse (London, 1555), RSTC 17629 and 17629.5

Nicholas Pocock (ed), *A Treatise on the Pretended Divorce between Henry VIII and Catharine of Aragon, by Nicholas Harpsfield DD* (Camden Society, 1878)

Rex H. Pogson, 'Reginald Pole and the Priorities of Government in Mary Tudor's Church', *Historical Journal*, 18, 1975, pp. 3–20

Reginald Pole, *De Concilio Liber Reginaldi Poli Cardinalis* (Rome, 1562)

——, *Reformatio Angliae ex Decretis Reginaldi Poli Cardinalis, Sedis Apostolicae Legati Anno MDLVI* (Rome, 1562)

A. W. Pollard and G. R. Redgrave, *A Short-Title Catalogue of Books Printed in England, Scotland and Ireland and of English Books printed Abroad 1475–1640*, 2nd edn revised and enlarged by N. A. Jackson, F. S. Ferguson and K. F. Pantzer, 3 vols (London, 1986)

J. H. Pollen (ed), 'Dr Nicholas Sanders' report to Cardinal Morone', *Catholic Record Society Miscellanea I* (London, 1905), pp. 1–47

The Primer in Englishe (After the Use of Sarum) Whereunto is Added a Treatise Concerning the Masse (London, 1555), RSTC 16063–5

John Proctor (trans and ed), *The Waie Home to Christ and Truth Leadinge from Antichrist and Errour, Made and Set Furth in the Latine Tongue by That Famous and Great Clarke, Vincent . . . Above XI Hundred Yeres Paste* (London, 1554), RSTC 24754–5

——, *The Historie of Wyates Rebellion* (London, 1554), RSTC 20407–8

Adriano Prosperi, 'Il principe, il cardinale, il papa: Reginald Pole lettore di Machiavelli', in *Cultura e scrittura di Machiavelli: Atti del Convegno di Firenze–Pisa 27–30 ottobre 1997* (Rome, 1998), pp. 241–62

The Prymer in English for Children, After the Use of Salisburye (London, 1556), RSTC 16075 and 16075.5

Angelo Maria Querini (ed), *Epistolarum Reginaldi Poli,* 5 vols (Brescia, 1744–57)

C. Robinson, *Nicolo Ormanetto: A Papal Envoy in the Sixteenth Century* (London, 1920)

Hyder E. Rollins, *Old English Ballads, 1553–1625* (Cambridge, 1920)

William Roper, *The Life of Sir Thomas More,* in Richard S. Sylvester and Davis P. Harding (eds), *Two Early Tudor Lives* (New Haven and London, 1962)

Elizabeth Russell, 'Marian Oxford and the Counter-Reformation', in C. M. Baron and C. Harper Bill (eds), *The Church in Pre-Reformation Society* (Woodbridge, 1998), pp. 212–27

Thomas Sampson, *A Letter to the Trew Professors of Christes Gospell Inhabitinge in the Parishe off Allhallows in Bredstrete in London* (Strasbourg, 1554), RSTC 21683

John Scory, *An Epistle Wrytten by Iohn Scory* (Emden, 1555), RSTC 21854

Alison Shell, *Catholicism, Controversy and the English Literary Imagination, 1558–1660* (Cambridge, 1999)

Paolo Simoncelli, *Il caso Reginald Pole: eresia e santita nelle polemiche religiose del cinquecento* (Rome, 1977)

A Spiritual and Most Precious Perle, Teachynge All Men to Loue [and] Imbrace the Crosse (Wesel?, 1555), RSTC 25256

John Standish, *A Discourse Wherein is Debated Whether the Scripture Should be in English* (London, 1554), RSTC 23207, 2nd edn 23208

——, *The Triall of the Supremacy Wherein is Set Fourth the Unitie of Christes Church* (London, 1556), RSTC 23211

Richard Stewart, 'Thomas Stapleton's Call to Rome', *Clergy Review,* 70, 1985, pp. 311–17

John Strype, *The Life of the Learned Sir John Cheke* (London, 1705)

——, *Ecclesiastical Memorials, Relating Chiefly to Religion, and the Reformation of it, and the Emergencies of the Church of England under King Henry VIII, King Edward VI, and Queen Mary I,* 3 vols (Oxford, 1822)

——, *Annals of the Reformation and Establishment of Religion . . . during . . . Queen Elizabeth's Happy Reign* (Oxford, 1824)

——, *Memorials of Archbishop Cranmer* (Oxford, 1840)

The Temporysour (Wesel?, 1555), RSTC 18312

E. M. Thompson, *The Carthusian Order in England* (London, 1930)

M. A. Tierney (ed), *Dodd's Church History of England,* vol II (London, 1839)

Xenio Toscani, 'I seminari e il clero secolare in Lombardia nei secoli XVI–XIX', in Caprioli et al, *Chiesa e societa,* pp. 215–62

——, 'Recenti studi sui seminari italiani in età moderna', *Annali di Storia depl' Educazione e delle Istituzione Scholastiche,* 7, 2000, pp. 281–307

A Treatise of the Cohabitacyon of the Faithfull with the Vnfaithfull, Whereunto is Added. A Sermon Made of the Confessing of Christe and his Gospell and of the Denyinge of the Same (Strasbourg, 1555), RSTC 24673.5

William Turner, *The Huntyng of the Romyshe Vuolfe, Made by Wylliam Turner Doctour of Phisik* (Emden, 1555?), RSTC 24356

Brett Usher, 'Essex Evangelicals under Edward VI: Richard Lord Rich, Richard Alvey and their Circle', in David Loades (ed), *John Foxe at Home and Abroad* (Aldershot, 2004)

——, 'John Jewel Junked', *Journal of Ecclesiastical History,* 59, 2008, pp. 501–11

T. M. Veech, *Dr Nicholas Sanders and the English Reformation, 1530–1581* (Louvain, 1935)

Vincent of Lerins, *A Boke Written by One Vincentius Leriniensis* (London, 1554), RSTC 24747

Mark S. Weil, 'The Devotion of the Forty Hours and Roman Baroque Illusions', *Journal of the Warburg and Courtauld Institutes,* 37, 1974, pp. 218–48

L. E. Whatmore (ed), *Archdeacon Harpsfield's Visitation Returns 1557* (Catholic Record Society, 1950, 1951)

David Wilkins, *Concilia Magnae Brittaniae et*

Hiberniae, vol IV (London, 1737)

Penry Williams, 'Elizabethan Oxford: State, Church and University' in James McConica (ed), *History of the University of Oxford Vol 3: The Collegiate University*, pp. 397–440

Shafer Williams, 'Geoffrey of Monmouth and Canon Law', *Speculum*, 27, 1952, pp. 184–90

Jane Wilson (ed), *Sermons very Fruitfull, Godly and Learned by Roger Edgeworth* (Cambridge, 1993)

Janet Wilson, 'A Catalogue of the "Unlawful" Books Found in John Stow's Study', *Recusant History*, 1990, pp. 1–30

William Wizeman, *The Theology and Spirituality of Mary Tudor's Church* (Aldershot, 2006)

H. T. Wojtyska, *Cardinal Hosius: Legate to the Council of Trent* (Rome, 1967)

Lucy Wooding, *Rethinking Catholicism in Reformation England* (Oxford, 2000)

Charles Wriothesley, *A Chronicle of England During the Reigns of the Tudors, from A.D. 1485 to 1559*, ed. W. D. Hamilton, 2 vols (London, 1875–7)

W. J. Young (ed), *Letters of St Ignatius of Loyola* (Chicago, 1959)

M. Zell, 'Fisher's Flu and Moore's Probates: Quantifying the Mortality Crisis of 1556–60', *Economic History Review*, 47, 1994, pp. 354–8

Index